STAYING
in
BOUNDS

*In honor of all the pastors
who have helped to shape my life over the years.*

With special gratitude:

*To my pastor, Stephen Tousseau,
for supporting and encouraging me in the writing of this book,
for modeling healthy boundaries
and ministering to me with grace and compassion;*

*And to my children, Elizabeth, Ashley, Emily, and Amanda,
who have cheered me on throughout the process
and willingly gave up time with mom so I could write.*

STAYING *in* BOUNDS

Straight Talk on Boundaries for Effective Ministry

EILEEN SCHMITZ, MA, LPC

CHALICE
PRESS

ST. LOUIS, MISSOURI

Cover and interior design: Hui-Chu Wang

Visit Chalice Press on the World Wide Web at
www.chalicepress.com

10 9 8 7 6 5 4 3 2 1   10   11   12   13   14   15

EPUB: 978-08272-34826   EPDF: 978-08272-34833

Library of Congress Cataloging-in-Publication Data
Schmitz, Eileen.
  Staying in bounds : straight talk on boundaries for effective ministry / Eileen Schmitz. – 1st ed.
     p. cm.
  ISBN 978-0-8272-3481-9 (pbk.)
  1. Pastoral counseling. 2. Pastoral counseling--Moral and ethical aspects. I. Title.
  BV4012.2.S335 2010
  253.5–dc22   2010034906

Printed in the United States of America

Contents

II. BOUNDARY BUILDING BLOCKS

Introduction

Like most others working in ministry, you undoubtedly have heard matter-of-fact admonitions like, "Don't cross the line," "It's not a good idea to get involved with someone in your congregation," and, "You are here to take care of the parishioners, not fulfill your social needs." But when the rubber meets the road, maintaining appropriate boundaries with parishioners and others can be challenging and at times downright perplexing. Yet maintaining boundaries is critical to effective ministry and personal health.

The best way to know "where" the lines are and "how" to respect those lines is to understand "why" boundaries matter. This book fills in the informational gap; it seeks to synthesize the psychological and theological foundations for boundaries and then discusses their application in ministry. Through various stories, vignettes, and examples, boundaries and their role in keeping our parishioners and us healthy and safe will come to life. My desire in writing this book is that ministers become so thoroughly comfortable with the concept of boundaries that their application will become second nature. They will not be viewed as a set of rules, but rather a purposeful way of being that permeates everything we do and every relationship we engage in, so that our mere presence in the lives of those to whom we minister will facilitate spiritual healing and growth.

Know Yourself

Perhaps the most overlooked component of understanding boundaries in our personal and ministry lives is the intentional activity of self-exploration. Inadequate self-knowledge results in inadequate boundaries and hence ineffectual ministry, blunders, damage to self and parishioners, and eventually moral failure. Here I present tools to examine your own relational style, your personal needs and how they affect your vulnerability to blunders that can damage you, your ministry, and your family. We tend to avoid self-exploration for fear of what we may find, what undesirable patterns may be unearthed and what shameful thoughts and behaviors may be exposed to the light. But fearless examination also leads to life—full, satisfying, abundant living. It is the overture to the greatest show on earth: that of God turning brokenness into righteousness, despair into joy, shame into confidence, and fear into courage.

1

Who Should Read This Book

You may have just graduated from seminary and have yet to settle into the rhythm of your first placement. You may have served in a couple of churches and have some cold, hard experience under your belt. You may be a veteran, facing challenge after ministry challenge and still standing. But in any case, you will likely find encouragement, hope, and refreshment in the pages of this book.

If you've not taken the journey of self-awareness, of identifying your needs and vulnerabilities to inadequate boundaries, this book will provide guidance and insight as you pursue intentional self-examination; it may also save you from the untold heartache of running out of bounds.

If you think staying within bounds in ministry can be difficult, you are right, and this book will offer insight and guidance for implementing healthy boundaries, for protecting yourself and your congregation, and for leveraging the practice of healthy boundaries for effective ministry and leadership.

If you think staying within bounds in ministry is unnecessary, remember that you are practicing boundaries now, whether effective, ineffective, or outright damaging. This book will increase your awareness of the dangers of crossing the foul line and of the many benefits of healthy boundaries for an enduring, fruitful ministry.

If you think staying within bounds in ministry is impossible, read on. There is hope for developing a style of ministry that embodies grace and assertiveness, compassion without compromise, servant leadership that does not deplete you but actually promotes maturity and health in both you and your congregation.

As a pastor, you will not escape the confusion, frustration, and heartache of discovering the foul line only as you trip across it. As they say, "it's just a matter of time." You can, however, get back in the game, learn from your mistakes, and stay safe. Appreciation for the dynamics of human relationships, the recognition of your limits, and awareness of what God expects from you will ensure that your efforts in ministry are fruitful, rewarding, and redeeming for you and those whom you serve.

How to Read This Book

Boundaries are learned by trial and error, teaching and modeling. They are not a set of rules. In order to implement good boundaries, we must know the theoretical foundations for boundaries, the basic building requirements for boundaries, and how boundaries operate in the ministerial setting. Thus this book is designed as a "field guide." I address various aspects of boundaries in specific chapters: understanding boundaries within a psychological and theological framework, acquiring the materials necessary for healthy boundaries, putting mechanisms in place to protect against inadequate boundaries and boundary violations, applying boundary concepts in real-life ministry, adjusting boundaries that have not adequately protected the congregation and the pastor, and addressing glaring boundary violations that have already created confusion, harm, and conflict.

Initially, the book may be best read straight through. It is easier to incorporate a principle into our daily lives when we understand the what, why, and how. It is easier to stand by our principles when we recognize the importance of doing so, what the risks are of not doing so, and the contribution of that principle to the broader mission to which we have dedicated ourselves.

If the concept of boundaries in ministry is fairly new to you, this book will provide basic information so that you are able to begin your vocation of ministry with the fundamentals of relational boundaries. It is my prayer that this material will help you avert some of the pain that occurs by the missteps of pastors who are starting fresh in their ministries and have yet to be initiated into the oft-times bewildering relational dynamics of congregation life.

Second, the Contents page will aid you in identifying chapters that address specific issues and can later be referenced when you are confronted with a particular situation. In matters of the heart, faith, and relationships, there are no simple answers to the dilemmas we encounter. So this book does not profess to be the definitive and exhaustive guide to ministerial relationship issues. It can, nevertheless, give you ideas that will help in evaluating and managing those dilemmas.

Finally, as you continue to pursue your ministry of the gospel and grace of our Lord, this book can be reviewed, reread or even used as a devotional. You may find that it facilitates refreshment, self-examination, and contemplation of God's beautiful gift of boundaries that enables us to grow in understanding God's nature, our dependence on God, and the ongoing process of redemption and sanctification.

What This Book Is Not

In this book you will *not* find an exhaustive theological treatise or defense of the concept of boundaries. *Staying in Bounds* is designed to offer real-life, down-to-earth guidance on applying boundaries in ministry. Theological discussions are intended to facilitate the integration of the construct of boundaries to our faith, our understanding of God, and our interactions with creation and humanity. They are presented as discussion points for the purpose of inviting you to reflect on your own heart, faith, knowledge of God, and God's design for human relationships.

I believe that each of us is called to seek God through the Bible, our experiential walk with God, and the stories of those who have gone before us. Isaiah quotes the Lord, "For my thoughts are not your thoughts, neither are your ways my ways" (Is. 55:8). I realize that I will never in this lifetime have a thorough understanding of God and God's mind. Therefore, I hold my interpretations, syntheses, and life applications tentatively, humbly aware that lifelong students of scripture have developed much deeper, more rigorous, and time-tested propositions on the nature of God and God's dealings with people.

This book does not offer a thorough analysis of the psychological theories that have spawned the construct of boundaries. Again, many experts in psychology have already done this, and my attempt to synthesize the various views would result in an indigestible mass of information that would hardly profit a pastor who is faced with a disgruntled parishioner who is feeling misunderstood or misled. A list of recommended reading will be offered at the end of chapter 2, which can be referenced for more in-depth study of psychodynamic theories.

When You Read This Book

The Stories

Chapter 1 tells the stories of people who experienced the tensions of applying boundaries appropriately in ministry. Every story is an amalgam of real-life experiences, not representative of any one specific experience or person. Therefore, names have been changed, details have been modified, and outcomes have been revised to protect confidentiality as well as to illustrate the relevance of boundaries in ministry.

Terminology

The term *boundaries* can connote a range of meanings, both in technical and popular contexts. In this book, *boundaries* refers to the concept of "where I end and you begin." It is not interpreted rigorously from within a particular psychological framework. Furthermore, the term may also be used in either a psychological or a moral sense. For example, *boundaries* may be used to explain why I can't force my husband to change his political views (psychological sense), and it can also be used to explain why I am forbidden from coveting my neighbor's wife (moral sense). Within this book, *boundaries* will encompass both of these senses, because ultimately boundaries prevent us from damaging or hurting those around us, and from bringing pain on ourselves, whether explained in terms of relational dynamics or the violation of God's guidance on appropriate social/moral behavior.

Ministry is a term that is used in this book to refer to the vocation of spiritual care. I recognize that churches from a wide range of denominational traditions use a variety of terms to refer to the vocation of spiritual care: pastoring, ministry, shepherding. Regardless of your denominational heritage, the principles laid out in this book will be applicable to you and your vocation. The term *ministry* or *pastoring* is intended to refer to any activity related to the vocation of spiritual care. It is not intended to distinguish between the type of care, or the setting, whether a local church, parachurch organization, or denominational administrative office. All Christians are called to minister to our neighbors. The concepts in this book are equally applicable to vocational ministers and laity who purposefully minister to their brothers and sisters.

Finally, *pastor, clergy,* and *minister* are used interchangeably in this book, and again, denominational tradition often influences what words are used to describe the spiritual leader of a congregation or other church-related organization. The use of one term over another does not connote the exclusive application to people who are referred to by that specific term. Whether your church calls you "minister," your congregation refers to you as "Pastor Marianne," or you are known in the community as "Brother Scott," the material in this book applies to you.

I.

FOUNDATIONS

CHAPTER 1

The Stories

Robert: The Ornament

Robert remembers well the trouble he never saw coming. Sarah, a widow in his small congregation, had recently experienced several significant losses. Within eight months, her husband died after a long battle with heart disease, her thirty-year-old son was killed in a drunken driving accident, and she found her beloved dog, Princess, dead on her bed one day. Sarah called Robert, asking to come into the church office for a visit. He was grateful for her trust in him and the opportunity to offer his compassion and support.

As she sat in his office, she poured out her grief and her tears. He gave her ample time to talk, listening and empathizing with how she must feel about the losses that had turned her world upside down. After about an hour, he suggested he pray with her, that she call her friend Muriel later that day, and then that they wrap up their time together. He invited her to come back the following week. Sarah looked crestfallen. How could he dismiss her so easily after she had just poured herself out to him? Robert patiently explained that he had another appointment waiting.

Sarah didn't look pleased, but acknowledged that he had other duties to fulfill. The next week, Sarah arrived punctually for her appointment. She began crying again, describing the pain she was in, and how no one really understood what she was going through. Robert did the best he could to assure her that he was interested in understanding her pain. At the end of the session, Sarah presented Robert with a small gift, a handmade Christmas ornament. He accepted her token of appreciation, relieved that she apparently had been helped by their session, and she left.

The next Sunday after the worship service, Sarah pulled Robert aside and again began retelling of her pain and sorrow. Robert was keenly aware that others were waiting to speak with him after the worship service, so he tried to keep his conversation short. Sarah put her hand on his arm and said, "Pastor, I know you are busy, but I really need to talk with someone who understands." Robert reluctantly agreed to a brief pastoral visit in his office after he finished visiting with the parishioners.

In his office, Sarah started fresh with her long story of grief and pain. Robert became aware of the nagging feeling that she wasn't trying to help herself. She just needed to emote. So he let her. After another hour, he reiterated to Sarah his suggestions for actions she could take to help her move through the grieving process more productively. Sarah was appalled. She exclaimed, "I just needed to talk to you! You seem to be in an incredible hurry to get me out of here!" Robert was taken aback. Now what? He really didn't want Sarah to feel dismissed, and he didn't want her to be dissatisfied with his pastoral care. All at once, his thoughts jolted him: Sarah and her late husband had committed to funding the purchase of new hymnals for the church. He backpedaled. He assured her that he would see her again on Wednesday to check on her and her progress in trying some of his suggestions.

On Wednesday Sarah came into the office, walked straight past the receptionist and into Robert's office. She carried with her a plate of Christmas cookies she had "made just for you." He expressed his gratitude, then got down to the business of pastoral counseling. Rather than let Sarah direct the conversation, he took more control of the session and asked her how she had fared in pursuing his suggestions. She mumbled something about her friend being out of town and then began to cry again. Robert interrupted her soliloquy, again asking what she had done to help herself. She became silent, then stood up. "Pastor, I really appreciate your efforts to talk with me. I need to be going, though. I have a lot to do today."

On Friday the president of the congregation called Robert. "I just got a call from Sarah. She said that she decided not to donate the money for the new hymnals. She said something about not feeling appreciated and understood in the church anymore. Do you know anything about this?" Robert was stuck. He couldn't tell the president about the content of his sessions with Sarah, he couldn't discuss Sarah's reactions, and he was worried that the loss of funding for the hymnals would create a stir.

By Sunday the rumors were brewing in the seniors' Sunday school class: Pastor Robert had been negligent in caring for one of their own, and it was a terrible thing the way he had booted her out of his office without so much as a kind word.

Six months later, Sarah had left the church along with five other senior members, the board of deacons had formally reprimanded the pastor, and Robert felt paralyzed in his ability to counsel those who came to him with their problems. He increasingly withdrew from face-to-face interactions with his congregation. The Christmas ornament lay in the back of the top drawer of Robert's desk, and he lacked the courage to take it out from its hiding place.

Beth: Good Neighbors

Few ministers can say they've never had to fight to protect their personal lives and families from the scrutiny of their congregation. Beth thought herself fortunate that her congregation understood the pastor's need for separation of personal and professional life. Early in her calling to this church, the board and she had explicitly laid out the expectations the church had for her availability. The board was very willing to respect her day off, and they were equally willing to understand why her husband, Nate, attended a different church with their two children. They lived in a small town, although the church she pastored was in the next major community down the road. Beth and her husband enjoyed going to breakfast at the small-town diner without running into her parishioners, and she appreciated the freedom from feeling she always had to look "put together."

Beth's neighbors were likeable, with children the same age as hers. It wasn't long after they moved to town that her neighbors and Beth's family became good friends. Her neighbors, John and Cassie, were intrigued that Beth was a minister, and so began long conversations about church, God, and faith. Beth invited them to attend her church, and they readily accepted the invitation. They didn't mind the fifteen-mile drive. Within a couple of months, John and Cassie found their place at Beth's church, becoming active in the ministries and fellowship of the church. The church seemed to be the perfect match for them.

One day, Beth and Nate had words. It wasn't the first time they had experienced disagreements, but in ten years of marriage they had survived them all. They realized the children were in the house and didn't need to hear their disagreement so they moved out to the back porch. A couple of minutes later, Cassie, Beth's neighbor, stepped outside. She stopped and listened, realized that she was overhearing a terse interchange, and pretended to busy herself plucking tomatoes from her vegetable garden. Beth saw Cassie's interest, but decided that it was best if Cassie knew that pastors are human, so she and Nate continued their conversation, albeit loudly.

When Beth and Nate resolved their dispute, they stepped back inside. They ate dinner with the children, then readied them for the next day of school.

On Sunday Beth was in for a surprise. She pulled into the parking lot and was met by her office assistant. The office assistant told Beth that Cassie had called her, asking if she knew that Beth's marriage was in trouble. Beth was stunned. She stammered several words of denial, bustled into the office to prepare for church school and worship services, and saw the blinking light on her phone signaling a message. She retrieved the message; it was her neighbor's husband, John. He told Beth that he was concerned about the fighting that his wife had witnessed between Beth and Nate and was taking steps to make sure the church did not allow the marital discord to interfere with Beth's ministerial duties. He didn't expand, however, on what steps he was taking. John and Cassie were conspicuously absent that Sunday.

After the service, the chairman of the board of elders approached her. He told her, "You probably won't be surprised to know that John called to say that he and Cassie are convinced that you have some serious problems in your family. They said that you and Nate have been fighting a lot lately, and that your kids have told Cassie they are afraid of how angry you get. I've always wondered why Nate and the kids don't attend church with you as a family, and I'm beginning to understand. Beth, we can't have that going on here. I have spoken with the board, and we've decided that, starting today, you need to take a personal leave of absence until you can get help for your marriage and yourselves. I'll call you later to talk about this further, but for now, I think it would be best if step back from your duties for awhile."

Beth was floored. Her heart pounded and her intestines twisted in knots. She sank down in her chair behind her desk. She was generally tough-minded and emotionally reserved, but now her eyes welled up with tears.

Joe: Special Friends

Joe was one of "those" ministers who had enough energy to charge up the entire church staff, leaving everyone to wonder how he found time to do everything he did and still have time for family. He liked his work—he liked the feeling he got from helping people through difficult times, giving spiritual direction and guidance, studying for weekly sermon preparation, chairing various church committees, and managing his six-member pastoral and office staff. Since he had come to Grace Community Church three years ago, things had been going very well indeed. The congregation adored him, the local radio station was broadcasting his sermons, and the church board was very open to his recommendations for change and growth.

Joe's wife, Sarah, and their two teen sons had adjusted well to the move to Grace Community. Joe tried to spend a little time with them, primarily in the late evenings when he didn't have a meeting or a sick call. The weekends were generally filled with church social activities, performing weddings, last-minute sermon preparation, emergency calls from parishioners, and community volunteer work. Sarah had recently begun complaining more to Joe about the very limited time he gave to his family. It was annoying. Joe thought Sarah really didn't have any idea of how much time was involved in running a church of this size. Besides, Sarah and the boys were doing fine. The boys were involved with soccer and track, Sarah led the women's ministry Bible study, and the three of them stayed busy with various school and family activities. Sarah took the boys to Florida for spring break while Joe stayed behind in his ministry. Joe was secretly relieved at how well Sarah managed the arrangements for the trip and kept the boys entertained.

Although Joe wouldn't admit it to even his closest friend, Joe was also secretly relieved that Sarah seemed thoroughly occupied with her family responsibilities. It kept her distracted enough that she didn't seem to notice that Joe was gone for committee meetings on some evenings when no meetings were listed in the weekly church activity calendar.

Joe's lady friend, as he called her, was indeed a special lady. She had visited the church very shortly after Joe began his ministry there, and he was almost immediately struck by her outgoing, friendly way. It started with a warm and enthusiastic handshake, then an invitation for Kat to meet with him to discuss the possibility of her volunteering in children's ministry. The relationship developed quickly from that point. Kat had a way of helping him unwind from the craziness of his ministry work. Their friendship was truly unique—she was the only person who really understood him, that he could completely open up to. They would meet at a small restaurant on the other side of the city. They talked a lot, sharing frustrations and dreams of ministry, jobs, and family. Joe talked about the struggles he faced trying to keep both the church and his wife happy. Kat told him of her dreams to travel, to move up in the corporate world, and of her traumatic childhood. Sometimes they went to her townhouse afterward, making love and dreaming of a life together. Joe appreciated her interest in meeting his sexual needs; things had been pretty bland with Sarah for many years. They tried to make every minute together count before Joe would have to head home for the night.

On one hand, Joe carried some guilt about the affair, and on the other hand, he reasoned he wouldn't be half the pastor that he was if it weren't for his relationship with his Kat. He believed that while he and Sarah had been married for eighteen years, she didn't understand him the way Kat did. At first, Joe's emotions fluctuated between fear of being found out, excitement over the next chance to be with Kat, and guilt over cheating on Sarah. Several times Sarah had asked about a late night at the church, but he had successfully allayed her concerns and the subject didn't come up anymore. Now, a year after their special relationship started, Joe felt much less guilt and perhaps even a sense of "rightness" over the relationship. It was truly meant to be. After all, didn't God send this special friend to the church and to him just when he needed her most?

David: Golf Buddies

David loved golf. He played every chance he could get. He even kept a set of clubs in the church office so that if his schedule opened up, he could head for the greens. The trouble was, he didn't know many people who shared his enthusiasm for the game. So when one of his parishioners, Will, asked about the golf clubs in his office, David was happy to invite him for a round.

Will took to the game quickly, and at last David had found a golfing buddy. When spring came, David and Will made golf a weekly event. Occasionally they talked about church-related topics, but usually, they talked about the stuff of daily life—aging parents, kids who didn't seem to want to grow up, car trouble, and the cost of living. David found opportunities during their play-dates to provide spiritual guidance and mentor Will as well. They developed a fast friendship and even dubbed themselves "The Ball Club."

Once in a while David wondered whether his friendship with Will fell into the category of "dual relationships" that his seminary professors referred to when talking about the roles of pastor and friend in parish life. He decided it would be a good idea to confront the issue head-on with Will, and the conversation went smoothly and easily. Will appreciated David's position as minister and was careful to not pry into areas of David's life that would put David in a difficult position. Will figured if David wanted to talk about something, he would bring it up.

Then one day Will lost his job in a downsizing. He found himself in a sea of fear, loss of self-confidence, and anxiety. David and Will continued to golf together, but much of their conversation revolved around Will's struggle with anxiety and panic. David felt at a loss as to how best to help his friend and parishioner. He knew that Will needed more than a friend, more than a pastor; he needed a counselor. The "dual role" issue now became more real. After some contemplation, David finally spoke with Will. He told Will that while he could love and support his friend, he didn't feel that he could provide the guidance and insight of a counselor at the same time. He gave Will names of several counselors in the area and encouraged Will to speak with one of them more in depth about his now crippling anxiety.

David was greatly relieved when Will told him that he had met with a counselor and was going to continue for a while. The weight of trying to help Will stay above water was being shared now, and David could continue to enjoy his friendship with Will without the pressure to provide counseling support as well.

Two years later the "Ball Club" continued to meet weekly for a round and lunch. Will was doing well in a new job, David's ministry was flourishing, and their friendship was strong.

Maryann: The Power of Prayer

For the third time in as many months, Maryann took a call from Betsy, who was sobbing uncontrollably on the phone while trying to explain to Maryann that Betsy's husband, Alex, was back in the hospital. Maryann did what she could to calm Betsy down, get the relevant details, find out at which hospital Alex was, and reassure Betsy that she would come within the hour to check on them.

Maryann hung up the phone, wrote down the room number, and sighed deeply. Alex was in poor health and continued to fail gradually but steadily. He had been a pillar in the church for decades, her strong supporter, and a blessing to everyone whose lives he touched. She felt a deep sadness as she considered that he would probably not have many more trips to the hospital before he was called to his eternal home. She was also disturbed by Betsy's apparent dependence on her to provide emotional stabilization and spiritual comfort. She certainly understood that Betsy was in turmoil, frightened and worried. But Betsy insisted that Maryann, and only Maryann, visit whenever there was a health crisis. During one of the most recent emergencies, Maryann was out of town and one of the elders had responded to Betsy's call. Betsy was not pleased, declaring that no one was able to pray for healing the way Pastor Maryann could and no one understood Betsy's pain the way Pastor Maryann did.

Now she picked up her coat, drove off to the hospital, and wondered how she could help Betsy to move toward reliance on her own relationship with the Lord. When she arrived, Betsy almost ran to her as Maryann walked down the hallway, then wrapped her arms around Maryann and exclaimed, "I'm so glad you're here! Please come quickly. I want you to pray over Alex. No one can pray like you can." Maryann walked alongside Betsy, Betsy's arm hooked in Maryann's, neither of them speaking.

They walked into the ICU to Alex's bedside. One glance at Alex told Maryann that his condition was very poor indeed. She laid her hand on his forehead and took Betsy's hand with her other hand. She prayed earnestly for Alex's relief from pain, fear, and illness. The ventilator continued to pump air into Alex's lungs, the monitors continued to beep, and the hushed conversations on the other side of the curtain continued to hum. The only thing that changed was Betsy's countenance. When Maryann finished praying, she saw that Betsy was no longer in tears and that her hand had relaxed substantially in Maryann's.

Betsy continued to hold Maryann's hand. "Pastor, I can't tell you how much it means to me that you came so quickly, and that you prayed the way you did for Alex. When you pray, it's like everything in my heart just settles down, like my heart knows everything is going to be OK, because you're here and you care and I just know that God hears you. I don't even try to pray like that anymore." Maryann extracted her hand from Betsy's and shuffled her feet a bit. The compliment felt good. It reaffirmed for Maryann what she believed was one of her gifts: mercy. But she was also concerned. Betsy was not growing spiritually herself, but rather becoming increasingly dependent on Maryann to work out her faith on her behalf. And Maryann was uneasy about feeling like she was being worshiped and put on a pedestal. She knew that Alex's days were numbered by the Lord, not her. She felt anxiety creep into her spirit as she considered that Betsy was placing her faith in Maryann's praying to keep Alex alive, rather than acknowledging God's sovereignty over the outcome of Alex's latest medical crisis.

As Maryann walked back down the hall to the elevators, Betsy followed beside her. "Pastor, I can't thank you enough for coming again. I know that it is such an interruption in your day. I am so honored that you are willing to do this for us, and for me. I feel like you know me so well, like somehow you can read my mind and my feelings. It almost feels like we should be sisters. Please, would you come back later this evening? It would mean so much to me."

Sam: Loose Lips Sink Ships

Sam stared out the window of his pastoral office, pondering his newest dilemma. Since the church had begun incorporating more contemporary music into the worship services, an older man in the congregation, Ronald, had been making noise about how the music was "inappropriate," "left him cold," "lacked theological depth," and was "senselessly repetitive." Most recently, Ronald had unleashed a diatribe during the seniors' Sunday school class, creating quite a stir and polarizing the group into two factions: those who agreed with Ronald and those who felt strongly they should support the leadership's direction toward a "more relevant worship experience." Now the class president came to Sam with his concerns about the tensions that were brewing between class members from the two sides.

It wasn't the first time that Ronald had started something at St. John's. Once he garnered support for a new street sign by encouraging people to call the office and complain that the sign was ratty, not easily visible, unlighted, ugly, or outdated. A couple years later, he succeeded in having the congregational president recalled, ostensibly because the president had been ineffective at maintaining order during congregational business meetings. At the time, Sam believed it was better to let the congregation work these issues through and allow the democratic congregational process to follow its natural course.

This time Sam felt a little differently. Transitioning the church worship style to include more contemporary music was Sam's idea. The incorporation of guitars and drums had played a significant role in attracting several younger families over the past year. Church revitalization was important to Sam, and he was feeling a bit defensive about having his leadership challenged and frustrated that Ronald was trying to derail the initiative. Sam decided that it was time to have a direct conversation with Ronald.

Sam's meeting with Ronald began amicably. Sam quickly brought the conversation around to the topic of Ronald's concerns about the contemporary music. He made an effort to listen to Ronald's issues and find common ground, but there was clearly a gulf between their positions on the role of contemporary music in church worship. Exasperated, Ronald finally said, "Look, it's not just me! My whole Sunday school class is up in arms about this. We don't feel like you care about what us old folks need from a worship service! We're the ones that built this church, and now you're brushing us off like we're irrelevant and feeble-minded and our needs don't count!" Sam's defensiveness ratcheted up several notches. He took a deep breath, then another one… and another one… as Ronald announced that he would be taking an informal survey of congregational members on the subject and then present his "findings" to the church council. In his mind, Sam envisioned the church council rescinding its agreement to experiment with worship styles and his efforts to bring St. John's into the twenty-first century going down the drain.

Something *had* to be done. Sam took the lead in the conversation. He reminded Ronald of his previous efforts to bring about change: the street sign, the church president, and several other incidents. He then confronted Ronald about his habit of stirring up dissension to get his way, his lack of concern for future growth in the church, his pattern of gossiping, and his disregard for church leadership and authority. Except for one cocked eyebrow, Ronald sat emotionless across the desk from Sam. Tension filled the office, and the meeting ended abruptly when Ronald stood up, thanked Sam for listening, shook his hand, and left. Sam hoped that Ronald would consider Sam's admonishment and reconsider his efforts to rid St. John's of the new music style.

To no one's surprise the issue of worship style was raised at the next church council meeting. Copies of Ronald's letter detailing his survey findings were distributed, and the council members began discussing Ronald's concerns. Sam was extremely frustrated. He had all he could do to sit still, much less keep quiet. After more than thirty minutes of discussion, Sam interjected, "We have worked very hard to make St. John's a welcoming place to the younger generations. This feels to me like Satan's attempt to destroy what we've been trying to build. You've got to understand that Ronald is just a bitter old codger with very little in his life except this church—*his* church. But this isn't *his* church!" As in the meeting with Ronald, once Sam stopped talking, everyone was very still and hushed. The agenda item was tabled until the next month.

Sam left with a hollow, sick feeling in his stomach. He wondered whether he had said too much, or not enough. He was angry that the council didn't back him up and that Ronald spent so much energy working against him. He suddenly felt very tired of trying to light a fire in the congregation to be missional, to get involved in the community, to take their faith seriously, to care about thriving rather than dying.

Sam seriously considered taking the next day off so he could work through his frustration, but eventually decided to go into the office and focus on his sermon preparation. About mid-morning, Ronald strode into his office. "You said I was a bitter old codger last night? Satan's agent? And you were preaching at me about creating dissension and not caring about people! You accused me of disrespecting leadership and behind my back you disrespect me? All I can say is it's hard to respect a leader that can't live up to his own standards!"

Katrina: Supervisor or Pastor?

Katrina's church had hired a parishioner, Jonathan, to perform the janitorial duties. The leadership council had decided to "hire from within," thinking that they would be giving Jonathan much-needed work and that a parishioner would do the job better than someone outside the congregation with little personal investment in the church. Katrina was assigned responsibility for overseeing the routine performance of job responsibilities and communicating with Jonathan regarding specific needs as they arose. Jonathan was a diligent worker, apparently happy to do the work and interested in making a positive difference in the physical appearance of the church building. He did not, however, have great organizational skills, and repeatedly failed to stock the bathrooms with necessary paper products. Occasionally Katrina found that the floors had not been adequately cleaned. Once in a while Jonathan would not come to clean on his designated cleaning day.

Katrina's first inclination was to let the small lapses go. She reasoned that everyone can forget a detail. She told herself that as long as the cleaning got done, the day did not matter. It became a problem, however, when a wedding was scheduled for Friday afternoon and Jonathan had not cleaned on Thursday as scheduled. Toilet paper rolls were empty, trashcans were full, the kitchen floor was spotted and sticky, and the sanctuary was still littered with worship programs from Sunday. Realizing that the wedding would not wait for Jonathan's arrival, Katrina did the work. About noon, Jonathan drove up with his cleaning supplies, but Katrina had already cleaned the building.

She was angry. She felt her easygoing nature had been taken advantage of. Jonathan had become accustomed to coming in to clean as he pleased and was increasingly sloppy with his work. "We need to talk, Jonathan," she called from the office as he walked through the doors. Her voice was assertive, but with an underlying tone of irritation. He turned into the office. She asked him to take a seat and began explaining the predicament he had placed her and the church in, told him she had completed the work herself that morning. She enumerated specific performance failures. Jonathan looked downcast. "I'm really sorry," he told her. "I never meant for you to have to do my job for me." He proceeded to explain to her the problems he was having with his teenage son, that he had spent several days this week in the school counselor's office attempting to address his son's behavioral problems. "It's like if no one is on his case, he doesn't do what he's supposed to. If someone is not constantly patrolling him, he finds ways to get in trouble, doesn't come home after school, and now he's trying marijuana."

Katrina's heart went out to Jonathan. She was familiar with the challenges of raising children and the heartache of watching a child obstinately walking down a dangerous path. She wondered if she should stick to addressing the work failures or acknowledge Jonathan's personal challenges and provide pastoral support during his time of crisis. There were definitely two competing issues here. She decided that the best approach was to start by addressing the double challenges. "Jonathan, I am so sorry to hear about what's going on with Jacob. I had no idea. I can see how that might have made it more difficult for you to get the janitorial work done. But I find myself caught between functioning right now as your pastor and as your supervisor. I know you need help dealing with Jacob. And I need to make sure the cleaning gets done. We're going to have to deal with both these problems. Do you have any ideas of how we can tackle both and make sure that you get what you need from me as your pastor and I get the janitorial work done?" She paused for a moment; Jonathan was subdued but thoughtful. "Well, I guess I do need help with both. I don't know what else to do for Jacob, and if you had to do the cleaning, then I am not doing my job well."

He still had not proposed a solution to resolving the conflicting priorities. Katrina waited another half minute, then persisted, "What would you do if you were in my position?" Jonathan was a big, burly man, but now he looked sad, guilty, and scared. "I guess I don't get paid this week." He clearly wasn't capable at this point of offering a solution to his competing priorities of being a parent and church employee. "OK, Jonathan, this is what I suggest. As far as you getting paid, I'll have to think about it and talk it through with the leadership board. I think we should set up some time to talk about how you will get your job done consistently. And then we'll set up another time to talk through what is going on with Jacob and you. Right now I need to run home and get cleaned up before I perform the wedding this afternoon, so we'll have to schedule time next week." Katrina offered Jonathan two appointments, one clearly designated to discuss the job-related issues, the other to support him in his parenting challenges. He stood up and reached across her desk to shake her hand. "Thanks for listening to me and for not firing me," he said with a grimace. "You've been kind."

Then he left. Katrina sat back down and took a deep breath. Things would work out. But she wished she had not waited so long to talk with Jonathan about the problems. She had put off supervisory responsibilities, and in the process, missed that he was hurting and needed her pastoral care as well.

Ann: A Parishioner Tells Her Story

I'm not sure I can even tell my story, because I don't think people will believe me. It happened twenty years ago, so you'd think that I'd be over it. But I'm not. Just in the last couple years I finally got sick enough with anxiety to ask for help. Not until recently did I realize that the affair I had with my pastor was more than an affair and had led to my mental disorder. For twenty years I have lived in fear of others in my church community finding out the awful thing that I did. It has kept me from dating, because I don't want to get into a relationship where I know my husband-to-be will eventually find out or have to know that I was involved with a married pastor. It has kept me from friendship, because I can't deal with the fear of someone figuring out my sordid story.

Now in hindsight, I think that I was the perfect target for what became a two-year affair. I had just moved to the area to start my first job, and I was single and lonely. I found a church and felt welcomed there. They had a young adults group that offered group activities that familiarized me with the area and gave me a social outlet. But I still felt lonely and sad much of the time. The associate pastor took an interest in me. He noticed my sadness and one day asked me if I would consider coming to see him for some counseling. Just that small act of kindness and interest helped me to feel more hopeful and upbeat. My first counseling session was primarily me telling him about myself. He helped me to see that my sadness and loneliness would improve with time as I settled in and found new friends. When we were done meeting, he stood up and asked me, "Would it be OK with you if I give you a hug?" It felt so good that someone was that considerate that they would actually ask me first, and I appreciated the kindness and acceptance he demonstrated with his hug.

I met with him a few more times and at the end of every session, he would say, "So how about my hug?" I liked the predictability, like it was our thing. Then he told me that he thought that I was having trouble making friends because I had trust issues. He pointed out that when I hugged him, I was just a bit tense and tried to keep it short. Now I felt embarrassed. I guess my hugs weren't genuine and trusting enough. After that session, instead of hugging me around my shoulder, he hugged me face-on. I purposely told myself, "relax, hug him like you mean it." So our hug was definitely more intense, more meaningful. He was right, I had been holding back. And a no-holds-barred hug sure felt better than those halfhearted side-by-side hugs that people around our church commonly gave each other.

I was beginning to feel much happier. I looked forward to church activities, if for no other reason than that I could see Brad (my pastor). When he was around I felt understood and accepted. Since I was feeling better, I hadn't rescheduled a counseling appointment with him. One night he came up to me and said, "I noticed you didn't schedule an appointment last week or this week. Is something wrong?" I told him no, that I was just beginning to feel better and didn't want to take up any more of his time. So he explained that just because I was feeling better didn't mean that I didn't have stuff to work through and that he thought it would be good for me to continue counseling for a while, "just to make sure you don't slip backward." I desperately wanted to be a good counselee, a good Christian, and I didn't want my pastor to be disappointed in me. After all, if anyone should know what was good for me, it would be him. So I started meeting with him again.

Hugs at the end of sessions got longer. The sessions themselves got longer; instead of one hour, they stretched into two hours, occasionally three. Brad would encourage me to kneel in front of my chair at the end of each session to pray. It felt awkward, but I thought, "OK, I've got to trust him on this." He would kneel beside me, and that helped me feel more comfortable. One time he put his arm around me, the next time he pulled me over to his side. Pretty soon I was putting my head on his shoulder. On the one hand, I thought, "Boy, this is pretty intimate," and on the other hand I felt that in those moments, I was a different person, one who was safe, growing spiritually, and learning to trust. After one particularly emotional prayer time, he leaned over and kissed my cheek. "You're doing amazingly well. I'm so proud of you!" he said.

I left that session practically floating on air. He's proud of me! Someone is actually proud of me! The next time, Brad told me he wanted to work with me more on learning to trust. I told him I thought I was doing much better. He said, "Well, you're definitely growing, but you still have some work to do." I asked him how he knew that, and he told me, "Well, come sit here in my lap." I hesitated, and I think my face turned a little red. "You see, in a perfectly safe environment, your heart still holds back. In spite of all the counseling we've done together, you still have trouble trusting your own pastor." Now I felt ashamed. Obviously I wasn't as strong and well as I thought I was. And now I was telling my pastor that I didn't trust him.

Things went downhill from there. Well, at the time it didn't feel downhill. It felt wonderful. His attention was everything I needed to feel good. "So this is what it feels like to be loved and accepted unconditionally!" I would say to myself. I began to reach out to other people in the church and get together socially with them. Life was good.

Brad began telling me more about himself too. It was energizing to know that he could trust me too. It was exciting to realize that I was truly learning to trust, and in return, others would trust me. Our sessions became more of a mutual sharing. He told me about some of his frustrations dealing with board members and several congregants who always seemed to challenge the direction he wanted to take the Young Adult Ministry. Occasionally he would tell me about disagreements with his wife. Eventually he began talking to me about how his wife had trust issues too, and how that affected their sex life. I was never sure what to say, but he told me that by just listening, I was being a good friend. "My heaven-sent sister" he would call me. One time he cautioned me about telling others about our conversations because he was afraid that they would get jealous of the level of confidence he placed in me. I reassured him that what we talked about was just between the two of us.

On the one hand, Brad called me his "sister." "This is what the fellowship of believers is all about," he would say. He called me several times a week to talk about whatever issues came up in his world. I felt honored to be there for him. On the other hand, he started telling me, "I love you so much. I don't know what I would do without you; I am falling in love with you." I tried to tell him that, no, I was his sister, but I also found his attraction to me tantalizing, so I didn't get too insistent about the terminology. It wasn't long before he told me that if I asked him to meet him at a motel, he would be there. I didn't know what to say, so I didn't say anything. I guess I didn't really think anything other than, "Is he asking me to ask him? Should I ask him? But that would be wrong." I decided to let his comment go. In hindsight, I realize that by not drawing the line, I was confirming to him that I was open to a sexual relationship, even if I couldn't admit it even to myself.

The actual affair began when Brad's wife left town to visit her parents. He asked me if I'd like to come over and have dinner with him. I'm going to leave out the details. But the upshot was that I ended up having sex with him. He told me how much he loved me, how much he needed me, that even though he was married, I was the one who helped to hold him and his ministry together. I began to swing wildly from horrifying guilt to giddy exhilaration. I knew the sex was wrong; I wanted the connection we had developed to be right.

Our affair lasted about two years. During that time I lived in constant angst and turmoil over my sin, over the possibility of being found out, over not wanting to continue and not wanting to hurt him or disappoint him. He and his wife transferred to a new church out of town, and that pretty much ended our sexual relationship. He continued to call me and talk with me about his life, but I began to pull away. I was beginning to feel used. It dawned on me that our sexual relationship was a convenience for him. When he left town he didn't love me enough to take me with him. When he called, he wanted to talk about himself. Sometimes he never even asked how I was doing.

A couple years more and I began to feel like a stupid fool. I'd been used and discarded. I lived with the crippling guilt of causing a pastor to commit adultery, while he was off to his next ministry assignment. We were never found out. Ultimately, I think living with the silence and secret did more to destroy me than the shame that I would have felt if the affair had become public. Keeping the secret became all-consuming for me. That's how I ended up developing chronic anxiety and isolating myself from everyone around me. And I was angry: I was a wreck, and he was off getting respect and honor as a minister.

After Brad moved away, I felt so guilty and wanted to tell somebody just so I could sleep at night. But I knew that if I told, it would destroy his ministry and his life. I didn't want to hurt him any more than I already had by having the affair with him. I thought about confessing to someone without using his name, but I was afraid that people would figure it out anyway. I also wondered how people would react. Would I be the girl walking around town with a scarlet *A* on my forehead? Would people blame me for leading him astray? Would they believe me at all?

So I never told. And yes, he did it again, this time with a younger girl, seventeen years of age. When I found out, I felt like dying. My silence and cowardice were the reason someone else was abused too.

Counseling has helped me to understand all the damage that has come from the affair, that it was not an affair, but rather clergy sexual abuse. I am learning that I do not carry the full responsibility for what happened. I am learning to forgive myself and place responsibility for the abuse in the right place: with Brad. No doubt I am responsible for my poor choices, but I also realize that he took advantage of me, using his position and his supposedly "special" relationship with God to manipulate me and play on my insecurities and pain. I am grieving the loss of twenty years of my life. Now if I can only get past how angry I feel... Maybe someday I'll be strong enough to speak up.

Time to Reflect

Think back on the stories in this chapter.

1. Was there a victim? Who?
2. What responsibility did the ministers have in creating these difficult situations?
3. What responsibility did the parishioners have?
4. How were each of the parishioners affected by the blurred boundaries?
5. For each story, with whom did you primarily find yourself sympathizing–the minister or the parishioner?

Think about a time when you found yourself "between a rock and a hard place"– stuck in a difficult position–with a parishioner.

6. Did you expect a problem when you first became acquainted with this parishioner?
7. When did you first sense that a conflict or tension was developing?
8. Did the conflict resolve itself, or did you need to address it directly?
9. How long did the tension brew before you took steps to address the problem?
10. What was the final result?
11. In hindsight, what would you have done differently, if anything?

CHAPTER 2

A Psychological Framework for Boundaries

"A good neighbor is a fellow who smiles at you over the back fence, but doesn't climb over it."

ARTHUR BAER

People relate to each other as a matter of course. We were created for relationship–with God, with other people, and with the created universe. The human spirit insists on relationship; without relationships, we would not be human, we would not be aware of our existence. Even in the womb we begin to relate, if only in a most rudimentary manner. It is in relationship that we discover who we are–that we are distinct from the rest of creation and from other people. Relationships mold our personal traits and characteristics, preferences, language, and thought.

We don't necessarily think about the nature of our relationships; we just have them. Often not until we experience conflict around a relationship do we begin to examine its nature, what role we have in the relationship, how we contribute to the conflict, and how the conflict affects us. Think back to a time when your relationship with someone became unexpectedly convoluted or challenging. How did you react initially? As the challenge evolved, did you begin evaluating the factors that contributed to the challenge? In hindsight, were you surprised that the relationship developed difficulties? Were there warning signs? What part did you play in the development of conflict? Was the conflict successfully resolved, and if so, how?

Typically, relational conflict is the result of disappointments or unmet expectations:

- I want you to wash the car. You take a nap.
- You tell me something important. I miss the cues.
- I expect you to know what I am thinking. You're not a mind reader.

23

- I say, "I want a ball for Christmas." You give me a bell.
- You are accustomed to me being a generally upbeat and optimistic person. I get up on the wrong side of the bed.

Roles set the stage for how a relationship will be negotiated and the rules that the relationship will follow. They prescribe the reasonable expectations for a relationship. For example, if my role is that of mother to a young child, it follows that I cannot realistically expect my young child to fill my needs for a friend. If roles are unclear at the inception of a relationship or the roles shift without proper acknowledgement by both sides of the relationship, disappointment and conflict will develop as expectations associated with the roles are challenged or go unfulfilled. The mother who turns to her child to fill the mother's need for companionship will struggle with disappointment and frustration as the child begins to expand his social world, seek privacy, and protest the mother's expectation that his inexorable need for independence be deferred for the sake of her need for companionship.

In the story of Sam (Loose Lips Sink Ships), he was unclear about his role as spiritual leader in his church. He wanted the church to be revitalized, but his goal was to make it happen, rather than encourage the congregation to make it happen. So when Ronald protested the change in worship style, Sam perceived Ronald as blocking Sam from achieving his goal. And when Ronald's needs conflicted with Sam's needs, Sam attacked. Sam did not realize that he was insisting that Ronald meet his need for success with no awareness of Ronald's needs.

Furthermore, roles may be defined and acknowledged, yet expectations within a role may be unclear or unrealistic. Even if the expectation is clear, a person may fail to perform her role according to expectation. I may be acutely aware of my role as mother, understand that within that role I am expected to make sack lunches for the children before they leave for school, and still oversleep one morning, such that they leave the house without lunch. Needless to say, I can anticipate some fairly loud and vocal protest because I did not have sack lunches available for my family, whether I intended to sleep late or not. Failure to meet expectations may occur as a result of inattention, negligence, willful opposition, or an unanticipated deficit of resources, among other reasons.

Sometimes the problem is not that the expectations are unclear, but that they are unrealistic. As a mother, I am responsible for protecting my children from foreseeable dangers. As they mature, I diligently teach them the dangers of using street drugs. I remain aware of the friends they choose and monitor their activities as best I can. However, the older my children get, the more difficult it is to remain apprised of their whereabouts. I cannot realistically expect to prevent them from associating with peers who may exert pressure on them to make ill-advised choices, in spite of my best efforts to educate them and provide them with safe and appropriate venues for socialization.

Sarah, Robert's parishioner (The Ornament), had unrealistic expectations for her pastor. She was hurting and feeling helpless. She wanted to somebody to stop the pain. She viewed the pastor as a potential receptacle for her pain, and by attempting to dump her pain on him, she hoped to ease the discomfort. Since she felt helpless, she was unable to acknowledge her responsibility in alleviating the pain herself, and when Robert also could not do that, she became angry and punitive. Sarah's expectations were clear, but very unrealistic.

The Purpose of Boundaries

How do we discern what roles and expectations are reasonable and healthy? This is the purpose of *boundaries.* Understanding and maintaining our boundaries and respecting the boundaries of those to whom we relate will guide us in determining if roles we accept within a relationship are compatible (for example, mother/friend or pastor/employer) and whether expectations for performance of those roles are reasonable (for example, a mother "with eyes in the back of her head," a teacher who attempts to medically diagnose her student's behavior patterns).

A boundary defines the limits of existence of an object. In the physical world, a boundary is generally easy to observe. Think about all the objects around you in the room. There is no question where the chair ends and the air space begins. The boundary between the chair and air space is a visible and inherent aspect of the physical nature of the chair and air. You can change *where* the boundary lies between the chair and air by moving the chair, but you cannot change the nature of the boundary or the fact that it exists.

Boundaries exist in the interpersonal realm as well, but interpersonal boundaries are not straightforward. In the interpersonal realm, we don't have the benefit of physical senses to detect the boundaries. Personal boundaries relate to our sphere of influence or interactions, not where our skin ends and the fresh air begins. Sphere of influence is, needless to say, not something we see or touch, but is detectable by the behaviors that result from the interaction between two individuals. Unlike a chair, we don't really "see" the boundary—we see the results of the boundary in operation.[1]

Figure 1. Me and You

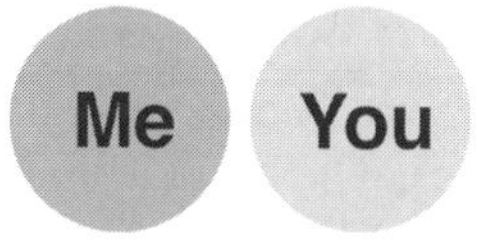

In the diagram above, the boundary between "Me" and "You" is clear because our spheres of influence are not overlapping; that is, there is no interface between us. If we begin to interact–if we move toward each other–the boundary still exists, but it is not as evident. What is evident is the result of the interaction between you and me. In Figure 2, the visible overlap represents the influence of the relationship on each of us.

Figure 2. Overlapping Spheres of Influence

The overlap between the two spheres will be different for each and every relationship. For example:

Table 1. Degrees in Influence

"You" may have more power, more influence, in your relationship with "Me". This can be represented by a larger circle in the diagram, and "You" therefore exert a proportionately greater impact on "Me".	Me You
The closer and more intimate our relationship, the more influence in both "You" and "Me".	Me You
The more similar "You" and "Me" are, the less obvious the overlap is, the more shared and mutual the influence is.	Me You

How Boundaries Develop

According to Margaret Mahler[2], a child does not differentiate between "Me" and "world." A baby's awareness is completely egocentric; that is, the baby has no understanding that "Mommy is separate from me," that "Mommy has a mind of her own," that "the light shines in my eyes because I am looking at it." This is called the *symbiotic phase* of normal child development.[3]

Typically after about five months, the child enters the phase of *separation-individuation*. This phase can be broken into sub-phases: *hatching* (six to nine months), *practicing* (nine to sixteen months) and *rapprochement* (fifteen to twenty-four months). During this time of separation-individuation the baby begins to experience the feeling of separateness from Mommy when Mommy leaves him in the crib whiles she showers. He cries when hungry, and Mommy comes and feeds him; with this he learns that he can cry and make Mommy do something, giving him a primitive sense of control over his world. He begins to experience the reward of a behavior (crying) intended to resolve his discomfort, but eventually also the frustration of repeating the behavior and Mommy not responding (at least immediately). These experiences all contribute to the child's development of a sense of a separate self from Mommy, other people, and things in the world, and eventually leads to his understanding of his ability to effect change in his environment.

In the *hatching phase*, as the child begins to experience separateness from Mommy, his alertness to the outside world increases, which leads to the *practicing phase*. In the practicing phase, the child begins to crawl and then walk, giving him the opportunity to explore his world freely. Mommy remains the primary source of connection and orientation to the world, providing a sense of security to the child as he embarks on the adventure of discovering his world. This gradual movement away from Mommy, perhaps by wandering into another room, spawns wonder and curiosity. And then suddenly the child realizes he has strayed far from Mommy; the physical separateness brings with it increased awareness of psychological separateness. He scurries back to Mommy, or, if he has lost his orientation, falls to the floor and cries, waiting for Mommy to rescue him. This is the *rapprochement phase*, when baby moves back toward Mommy for security. He discovers that Mommy is still there, even though he is gradually developing a sense of self *apart from Mommy*. He also discovers that he can interact with the world on his own terms. The child is learning that he has influence on his surroundings and on those to whom he relates. Upon gaining assurance that he is still safe, that Mommy has not ceased to exist, he gains new ego strength to embark on yet another cycle of exploration/distancing and then returning to Mommy.

Repeated experiences of distancing and reuniting with Mommy also teach the child that Mommy does not cease to exist as a result of his physical or psychological separateness from her. This represents the development of the principle of *object constancy,* the understanding that Mommy is truly separate from the child, but her existence is not annihilated by the development of *his* separateness. The child begins to *internalize* Mommy such that she and all that she represents—safety, rules, empathy—go with the child as he continues to explore and discover his own limits, the edges of his world, and his relationships with other people.

Thus the baby individuates—the process of transforming from an entirely symbiotic and egocentric self ("Mommy and I are one and we are the only thing that is"), to becoming a separate individual with an awareness that he may think and act on his own ("Mommy is Mommy and I am me, but if I need her, she will be there for me"). The following diagram may illustrate the process:

Figure 3. Mahler's Separation-Individuation Model of Child Development

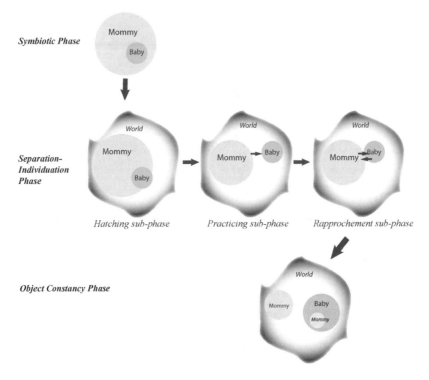

Optimal Individuation Is an Ideal

Mahler's model of a child's ego development is obviously just that—a model. It attempts to describe the process under ideal circumstances, with an optimal outcome. In reality, we do not achieve each phase in its entirety before attempting to master the next phase, and individuation is an ongoing process of maturation that extends throughout our lives.[4]

Ultimately, each person's degree of individuation will determine the ability to exist autonomously, to make decisions, to shape his own opinions, and to experience emotions and feelings independently of others. A person's level of individuation exists on a spectrum between symbiosis (sometimes referred to as *enmeshment* by family systems theorists) and optimal individuation.

Figure 4. The Spectrum from Individuation to Enmeshment

100% individuation   *100% enmeshment*

We may not individuate adequately from Mommy, such that we remain *enmeshed* with Mommy to a lesser or greater extent. Some of the repercussions of inadequate individuation may include

- resistance to exploring the world
- lack of awareness of one's limitations and competencies
- inability to identify or accept the consequences of one's choices
- lack of responsibility for oneself
- resistance to establishing other relationships
- expectations that Mommy (or someone else who represents our child-hood caretaker) will continue to resolve one's discomfort rather than actively pursuing resolution of the discomfort oneself
- beliefs that one can *make* Mommy (or someone else) resolve one's dis-comfort by crying, whining, manipulating
- a belief that if Mommy (or another person on whom one depends) does not resolve one's discomfort, he or she is bad
- limited ego development and low self-esteem, and therefore ongoing and sometimes desperate attempts to seek validation from others or reliance on others to sustain one's ego

Look at the list above. Can you identify behaviors in your own life that reflect one or several of the outcomes? What about other people to whom you relate? Take some time now to consider how you might be displaying behaviors suggestive of incomplete individuation.

Symptom	Example	Sometimes I:
Resistance to exploring the world	David has repeatedly passed up opportunities to attend the denominational annual meeting because he has never flown before and isn't going to start now.	
Lack of awareness of one's limitations and competencies	Jeff has been treasurer for 6 months, but things are falling through the cracks. It seems that everyone sees the problems except Jeff.	
Inability to identify or accept the consequences of one's choices	Margie moved from her parents' home into an apartment. Now her monthly income isn't covering her expenses. She blames her supervisor and she complains to her friends that she can't afford to pay for her own movie ticket because she is overworked and underpaid.	

Symptom	Example	Sometimes I:
Lack of responsibility for oneself	Don's supervisor spoke with him about various performance issues, including his frequent tardiness. Don replied that the traffic is getting worse and he can't possibly predict how long the commute will take each day.	
Resistance to establishing new relationships	Katie's two best friends moved out of town last year. Now she finds herself lonely and isolated but hates the thought of trying to connect with someone new. Besides, everyone at church is too busy with their own lives.	
Expectations that Mommy (or someone else who represents our childhood caretaker) will continue to resolve one's discomfort rather than actively resolving the discomfort oneself	Arlen's brother has suggested Arlen take a do-it-yourself class at the community college so Arlen can make small home repairs himself, but Arlen much prefers to just call his brother when the faucet needs fixing.	
A belief that one can make Mommy (or someone else) resolve one's discomfort by crying, whining, manipulating	Arlen knows that if he casually comments to his brother how unusually busy and stressed he has been at work recently, his brother is more likely to fix Arlen's leaky faucet.	
A belief that if Mommy (or another person on whom one depends) does not resolve one's discomfort, he or she is bad	Marilyn wakes up with a hangover—again. She asks her roommate to call her boss and tell him she is too sick to call herself and won't be in today. Her roommate tells her "no", so Marilyn tells her she's a self-righteous jerk.	
Ongoing and sometimes desperate attempts to seek validation from others or reliance on others to sustain one's ego	Carly loves the attention Steve gives her. Life was never so good before they started dating. Then he tells her he wants to break things off. She sobs, literally clinging to his arm as he tries to walk away. She begs and pleads with him to not leave her, that she will change anything he wants to make the relationship good again.	

Table 2. Symptoms of Inadequate Individuation

Individuation Is a Lifelong Process

Even though a person may achieve an adequate, functional level of individuation during the development process, stressors may precipitate *regression,* in which the individual resorts to more primitive behaviors. A five-year-old child who is tired and hungry will behave increasingly infantile, perhaps curling up into Mommy's lap and resorting to old self-soothing behaviors such as sucking her thumb or stroking her own hair. The same patterns apply to adults. An otherwise competent, confident young lady whose father has just died may find herself sleeping more than usual, being irritable with her children, clinging to her husband by calling him repeatedly during the day, and second-guessing herself at work.

Two of our stories demonstrate the regression that can occur when a parishioner is under unusual stress. Sarah, the widow (Robert: The Ornament), and Betsy (Maryann: The Power of Prayer) both were experiencing stress related to loss and illness. Both may well have functioned fairly well under normal circumstances. Regression was not evident until events exerted pressure that threatened to overwhelm their regular coping mechanisms. Sarah didn't believe she was capable of tolerating the pain of her losses, so she tried to externalize the pain by venting to Robert. Betsy didn't believe her personal faith would sustain her. She told Maryann that she had given up praying; she was unable to internally alleviate her anxiety. She clung to Maryann, literally, in self-preservation. Pastors must be aware of this phenomenon when ministering to parishioners whose means for self-help are being overwhelmed by their circumstances. In these cases, expectations become unrealistic or unreasonable and parishioners may feel abandoned and angry when their expectations cannot be met. The pastor's ministerial boundaries will be sorely challenged and if the pastor is oblivious to the parishioner's regressive patterns, the pastor may fail to clarify the boundaries and be tempted to rescue rather than stabilize the parishioner.

Regression—acting less autonomously than what was previously achieved—is normal human behavior. Recall a time recently when you were unusually tired or overwhelmed. How did your thinking and behavior change? Were you aware at the time that you were less "put together" than usual? What steps did you take to help yourself recover your normal level of functioning? How long did it take? A day, a week, a month, a year? Regressive behavior focuses the resolution of our discomfort or anxiety on

- external others (*e.g.,* blaming others, snapping at those who are close to us, demanding that others make us feel better, unfocused angry feelings)
- self-soothing behaviors (*e.g.,* nail-biting, increased eating, pornography use, masturbation)

- patterns of avoidance (*e.g.,* assuming a position of helplessness, excessive alcohol consumption, increased sleeping, refusing to talk with someone about a conflict)

These behaviors do not necessarily help us to resolve the discomfort. Rather, they allow us to avoid it (temporarily). The infant equivalent of these coping strategies may have been appropriate in infancy, but in adulthood, they prevent us from living fully individuated, autonomous lives.[5]

Whether or not a behavior is appropriate depends on the person's level of development. The behaviors a baby develops, such as thumb sucking, to alleviate his distress are appropriate for its age. The baby cannot feed himself; he is totally dependent on Mommy to resolve his hunger because he is not physically developed enough to be able to go into the kitchen and get some milk from the refrigerator. For the baby, thumb sucking is *adaptive.* It is appropriate and expected behavior for a baby. An adult who sits on the couch and grunts for his partner to bring him a drink and then resorts to thumb sucking (or another regressive behavior such as whining) when "Mommy" does not immediately respond exhibits behavior that is *maladaptive*–inappropriate–because the adult is physically capable of caring for himself in this area of need.

Maturation is in essence the process of learning to resort less and less to regressive behaviors, which ultimately render us incapable of resolving our own discomfort and anxiety. As we mature, we practice maintaining a position of autonomy when stressors impinge on our lives. This does not mean that we ignore our feelings or thoughts, nor does it entail taking on responsibility beyond our reasonable obligations. Autonomy allows us to be comfortable experiencing emotions and thinking for ourselves. It allows us to solve problems in our lives whenever we can, and not demand that others resolve our discomfort for us.

Individuation and Dependence

The natural question regarding individuation is "does individuation mean that I can't depend on anyone else?" Don't we all *need* other people? Of course we need other people. Relationships with others enrich our lives, give us a sense of purpose, and provide us with affirmation and validation. The development of autonomy does not exclude the need for others, but is rather an individual's ability to *internally* maintain a sense of self, regardless of whether or not the *external* affirmation and validation of others is forthcoming. Another way of looking at this is that autonomy without relationships is not autonomy at all. It is isolation, which is life-depleting rather than life-nurturing.

A well-individuated person is able to integrate others' feedback into his self-concept with discretion. Negative feedback is evaluated and the individual has a sufficiently sturdy self-concept to decide how to respond to the feedback: disregard it, file it for future consideration, or modify behavior in response to it. The well-individuated person retains his self-concept regardless of the feedback and does not perceive the feedback as a threat of annihilation or devaluation of his being. Positive feedback is likewise appraised, then either disregarded, retained for future consideration, or used as guidance for modification of behavior. This individual is adept at filtering the relational feedback from a variety of sources and selectively integrating his interpretations of the feedback into his self-concept.

The boundaries of David's friendship with Will (Golf Buddies) were tested when Will lost his job. But because Will was a fairly well-individuated individual, he was able to hear David's recommendations that he see a counselor. Will did not perceive David's boundary clarification as a threat of annihilation or devaluation; Will was able to consider the recommendation and determine its advisability, then pursue the referral for his benefit. Unlike Will, Ann (A Parishioner Tells Her Story) had not achieved adequate individuation at the time she met her associate pastor, Brad. Her behaviors were largely influenced by Brad's feedback to her: that she needed counseling, that she had "trust issues," that she needed more counseling, that she should sit in his lap, that he needed her for emotional support. Her ego soared when he gave her supportive feedback (*e.g.*, "I'm so proud of you!") and plummeted when he was critical (*e.g.*, "you still have trouble trusting your own pastor.") Ann relied on Brad to tell her who she was, what her problems were, and what value she had.

The poorly individuated person cannot maintain a substantive self-concept if he receives negative feedback. Neither can he maintain his self-concept without a continuous external supply of positive validation and affirmation. His self-concept is literally at the mercy of those on whom he depends for a sense of self; he will go to great lengths to secure validation and avoid criticism. An individual who has inadequately individuated may desperately seek affirmation and validation from those on whom he depends, but when he perceives feedback as criticism, he believes that his very essence is threatened and his tenuous self-concept is seriously compromised. Narcissistic personality is the pattern of a self that cannot sustain itself without this massive external buttressing.[6]

So how does one distinguish between healthy and unhealthy dependence on others? We naturally look to others to fill needs that we ourselves cannot fill. If our self-concept is compromised or diminished when a need goes unmet, our dependence is unhealthy, for we are depending on somebody external to us to define us or validate us. If we shift the responsibility for getting our needs met onto others, we will become angry and helpless. We relinquish control over our own selves. Shifting responsibility to others is unhealthy for two reasons: first, we give our right to self-determination away; second, we make demands on others that are impossible for them to fulfill. In colloquial parlance, "I can't *make* you happy; you have to choose to be happy on your own."

A healthy dependence on others is characterized by asking rather than demanding they provide support, help, companionship, or other personal needs. We recognize their autonomy in deciding whether or not they can or want to fill the need, and we do not deprecate them when they are unable to meet our requests. Neither do we "come unglued" when others cannot meet our expressed need. We are able to defer our hope or look elsewhere to have the need met. We do not perceive others' inability or disinterest in accommodating our requests as a reflection of our intrinsic worth. Sam's (Loose Lips Sink Ships) dependence on Ronald's cooperation ultimately rendered him ineffective in moving the congregation forward and damaged his poorly developed sense of worth.

Individuation and Boundaries

As we develop increasing autonomy, we learn effective and appropriate ways of addressing the stressors in our lives and of effecting change to alleviate the discomfort that those stressors exert on us. We learn boundaries. We learn that we can change how we think about an event, but we cannot make someone else think a particular way. We discover that we can work hard when our jobs require it, but we cannot work hard indefinitely. We learn what we are and are not capable of, what influence we have on the world and people around us. We also learn that while we may be able to resort to regressive behaviors to achieve a desired outcome, we are ultimately happier and healthier if we choose more mature, adaptive behaviors that respect the natural boundaries between us and the world and between us and other people.

Our boundaries regulate how we conduct ourselves in relation to the world; boundaries define the nature of our dependence on others. Our competence in maintaining healthy boundaries correlates directly to our level of autonomy. If our boundaries are weak and diffuse, we exist with a greater level of symbiosis/enmeshment. If our boundaries are realistic, well-defined, and sure, we live with greater autonomy. Healthy boundaries are the hallmark of those who have retained responsibility for themselves, are aware of their limits of control over the environment, know their competencies and abilities, and are committed to respecting the autonomy and boundaries of those around them.

Basic Characteristics of Healthy Boundaries

In order to identify and implement healthy boundaries, we need to know what a healthy boundary looks like. Much has been written about boundaries, both in secular and religious circles[7]. Healthy boundaries have three requisite characteristics:

1. They protect us from harm.
2. They prevent us from harming others.
3. They take into account our competencies and limitations.

Whether we are aware of it or not, we have boundaries with the physical world, other people, ourselves, and God. An example of a boundary with the physical world is taking precautions to wrap oneself in a coat when walking in bitter cold. This precaution or boundary protects us from frostbite (harm to self), protects our families from our untimely death (harm to others), and acknowledges that our skin alone does not provide adequate protection from the cold (our limitation).

The distinction between *harm* and *hurt* is crucial for discerning what boundaries are appropriate. *Hurt* hurts, causing pain. *Harm* may hurt, but of more relevance is that *harm* causes damage. Frostbite hurts, and if it progresses too far, it also harms. Injections may hurt, but they don't generally cause harm. Eating too much probably doesn't hurt (unless I get a bellyache), but it will cause harm. Saying "no" to my child may hurt his feelings, but denying his requests judiciously and only when necessary will not cause harm. While excessive permissiveness may not hurt his feelings, it will ultimately harm my child because he will not learn how to handle disappointment (among other things).

Katrina (Supervisor or Pastor?) realized that while she thought she was being patient and accommodating of Jonathan's work ethic, trying not to hurt him, she actually had been disregarding her own boundary—her responsibility to insure the work was being done—and in so doing, harmed Jonathan by permitting him to not take his work seriously. She also missed out on a pastoral opportunity to minister to him when his son was on the road to self-destruction. Think of a boundary you have with a loved one. How does it protect you from harm? How does it protect your loved one from harm you might otherwise inflict on him or her? Does it take into account your competencies and limitations?

Boundaries function at their best when they are flexible if appropriate ("if" is the caveat here). We may choose to adjust them to accommodate changes and growth in ourselves, our relationships, and our environment. It would be ridiculous to wear a heavy winter coat if the temperature was mild and balmy! We may find it appropriate to adjust the extent to which we help someone else if their circumstances have changed or if their ability to help themselves has changed. So while I may not be inclined to get a drink for my husband if he is capable of getting it himself and I am engaged in a phone conversation at the moment, I would more likely stop what I am doing to get that drink if my husband had just sprained his ankle.

In some cases, a boundary is nonnegotiable. Regardless of how hard I wish it, I will not be able to fly if I jump off the roof (at least not without mechanical aid). Gravity is nonnegotiable, it does not change, and no amount of determination or wishing will overcome it. Likewise, no matter how correct I believe my opinion is, I will not be able to force another person to think the way I do on a particular topic.

Unfortunately, healthy boundaries are not always obvious. Identifying the best boundary for a particular situation may require experimentation. The most appropriate boundary will depend on my resources, personality, and health; the personality and health of the other person in the relationship; and the immediate circumstances. I will figure out with time that some phone calls can be answered immediately while others are best left to go to voice mail so that I can focus uninterrupted on my work. As a young adult, I may rely on my parents for support and guidance, but as they age, they will be less available for support and our roles will begin to reverse as I become more caregiver and less care-receiver.

Boundaries Protect Us from Harm

The first of the three requisite characteristics of healthy boundaries is that they protect us from harm. The example of the winter coat is probably fairly obvious. In interpersonal relationships, boundaries protect us from harm as well. Boundaries protect us from

- allowing other people's demands to consume or deplete our resources of time, energy, and health
- engaging in relationships that are toxic—where we are manipulated, shamed, guilted, caught in a double-bind, denigrated, physically and/ or emotionally attacked, negatively influenced
- becoming angry, resentful, or bitter toward others who do not fulfill our expectations of them
- behaving in ways that bring reproach, damage our reputations, are inconsistent with our values and priorities, or that harm us and compromise our future
- accepting responsibility for the choices of others
- attempting to rescue other people from their self-inflicted plights

One of the greatest temptations we face in relationships is that of rescuing other people. If we are highly invested in someone else succeeding—based on our goals for that person—we are far more inclined to jump in and help said person along. Individuals in helping professions are particularly prone to this pattern. This is the crux of the issue: we can offer help to others, but we cannot force them to learn how to prevent the same predicaments in the future. We cannot prevent them from repeating the behaviors that contributed to their original plights.

As an example of how to determine when to allow flexibility in our boundaries, I may offer help to those who have experienced considerable stress, loss, or turmoil in their lives. In one situation, I provided help and over time John regained stability and well being. John clearly valued the help and he has not shown signs of continuing to expect help after his problem was resolved. In another situation, I began to recognize that Joe never seems to rise above the chaos and stress in his life and my help was not being appropriated to improve his life but rather to facilitate his transition to the next crisis. I rethought the wisdom of helping him out. If I continued to help, I would most likely burn out and eventually become resentful because he never improved, while I was "doing all the work." With flexible boundaries, I offer help in both cases, but with Joe, I modify my boundaries to account for his affinity for crisis.

Boundaries Prevent Us from Harming Others

The second characteristic of healthy boundaries is that they prevent us from harming others. Laws prohibiting murder are boundaries that prevent us from harming others. We need boundaries to prevent us from harming others in less obvious ways as well. As a therapist, I need boundaries with my clients that prevent me from using my professional relationship to fill my personal needs—for acceptance, appreciation, admiration. I need boundaries with my children that prevent me from doing for them what they need to learn to do for themselves. I must exercise just enough restraint in caring for them so that they will perceive an unfilled need in their lives and be motivated to resolve it themselves, rather than continuing to rely on me and expecting that I resolve it for them, regardless of their abilities.

Healthy boundaries remind us to respect others—their choices, thoughts, lifestyles, feelings, and preferences. As our level of autonomy increases, we will focus less on imposing our ideas, will, or needs on others, and be more comfortable with allowing others to be self-determining and responsible for themselves. We neither rob others for our benefit nor force our will on them. When we refrain from imposing on others, we assert and affirm their individuality, uniqueness, dignity, and value.

If, on the other hand, we are unclear about the borders of our responsibility, if we disregard boundaries that define where we end and others begin, then we are at risk of assaulting the precious essence of others and of dismissing their right to dignity and honor as God's beloved creation. When we do not respect the individuality of others, we are essentially judging them, communicating that they are inherently unacceptable and incompetent and do not deserve the same freedom of self-determination that we claim for ourselves.

Brad (Ann: A Parishioner Tells Her Story) did not allow Ann the right to self-determination and personal responsibility. In the end, he robbed her of her individuality, her potential for growth, and her self-esteem. David, on the other hand, (Golf Buddies) recognized that he could not help Will with Will's psychological needs and referred Will to a counselor. David's roles with Will as pastor and friend were already complex enough, and attempts to fill the role of counselor would have severely compromised the relationship and prevented Will from taking responsibility for his own well-being.

Boundaries Take into Account Competencies and Limitations

Each individual has his or her own unique set of abilities, competencies, and limitations. The best boundaries account for these differences in people. Our boundaries will reflect our abilities and limitations, as well as those with whom we relate. If I know that my adolescent daughter has not developed adequate discernment with regard to her choice of peers, I will want to meet the new friend she wants to "hang with." If she has demonstrated solid discernment, I will adapt my boundary and give her more latitude in choosing her activities.

Healthy boundaries do not demand more accountability than is needed, but, at the same time, they prudently create hedges where accountability is needed to protect and promote growth. A newly recovering alcoholic will wisely drive out of his way to avoid the bar where he has met his buddies for the past ten years. The same individual, after two years of sobriety, may find that driving by the bar is not a problem, but he knows better than to meet his old friends "just to play a little pool."

Our resources at a given period of time will also impact where our boundaries need to be. We adjust our boundaries in many cases without giving a second thought, depending on the other demands we are experiencing for our time, energy, and physical resources. If I've committed to attend a meeting one evening (and haven't forgotten about my commitment), I will probably say no to a request for my presence at yet another meeting scheduled for the same time.

At times, however, it is more challenging to know exactly where our boundaries should be established. Drain on resources is often incremental and imperceptible, until we suddenly feel overwhelmed, perhaps not even aware of how we got to that point. For this reason, taking stock regularly of our health, resources, obligations, and needs is important. It will reduce our tendency to overcommit, overextend, and then misdirect the blame for our resource deficits onto others. The person that does not adjust her boundaries upon return to work after a bout with the flu will likely relapse or prolong her full recovery.

Growth Requires Humility

Healthy boundaries are easier to implement and maintain if we have had good role models in our lives, if the people we associate with also have relatively healthy boundaries, and if we have successfully achieved at least a modest level of individuation. Most people can point to times in their lives when healthy boundaries were not well modeled or supported. However, poor modeling of boundaries does not necessarily guarantee lack of individuation. The extent to which previous symbiotic or enmeshed interpersonal experiences impede growth and individuation will depend on an individual's level of resistance to

- identifying unhealthy relational patterns
- accurately assessing one's response to the environment and relationships
- personal change

Growth requires that we become comfortable with saying to ourselves and others, "If I change, I might be able to do this better," or, "What I am doing now isn't working so well." It also requires a willingness to perform self-appraisal and accept feedback from others who have our best interests in mind. The following chapters will challenge you to consider how you can improve your boundaries in life and ministry. You may find the ideas, concepts, and information presented here to be interesting, but ultimately the information is only as valuable as the extent to which you interact with it, engage in reflection, and commit yourself to growth.

Ultimately, poorly maintained boundaries result in us losing our autonomy and feeling as if we do not have ownership of ourselves. When I overcommit or take on more responsibility than is reasonable, I will begin to feel pulled, torn, no longer in control of myself or my life. I will feel more like a cue ball than a cue stick! As a cue ball, I get smacked around, shot at, and scratched. On the other hand, if I protect my autonomy, I am the cue stick. I get to call the shots of my own life.[8]

Take a moment to consider: what percentage of your life do you spend as a cue ball, and what percentage do you spend as a cue stick?

Time to Reflect

1. Who in your life has exemplified healthy boundaries? How were their healthy boundaries beneficial to you?
2. Who in your life has exemplified poor, weak or diffuse boundaries? How have your relationships with them been affected by their poor boundaries? How have you been personally affected?
3. Review your responses in Table 2, Symptoms of Inadequate Individuation. Do you notice patterns in your behaviors? In what circles are you more apt to exhibit regressive behaviors: family, friends, acquaintances, professional peers, parishioners? Are there particular circumstances, events, or stressors that make you more vulnerable to these regressive behaviors?
4. Make a list of people on whom you depend for something: love, friendship, fixing something, making meals, backing you up at a committee meeting. Can you think of times that they did not come

through in meeting your expectations? How did that feel? What were your primary reactions? How did you deal with those reactions? What did you do to get the need met in a different way?

5. In what area of your life do you currently have the most difficulty maintaining healthy boundaries and maintaining your autonomy?

6. What steps might you take to enhance your individuation in this area?

CHAPTER 3

A Theological Basis for Boundaries

"Because of the LORD's great love we are not consumed,
for his compassions never fail.
They are new every morning;
great is your faithfulness."

LAMENTATIONS 3:22–23

No single field of study can exhaustively describe a phenomenon or concept, but only the conceptualization of one facet of that phenomenon. So it is with the concept of boundaries. Psychology attempts to explain how our spirits work; theology attempts to explain how our souls work. The term "boundaries" was initially coined within the discipline of psychology, but its operation is no less relevant to our understanding of God and our relationship to God. As ministers, pastors, and soul shepherds, we do well to bear in mind how human nature expresses itself with God and others, for it is in those relationships that our souls and our spirituality find expression.

People relate to God in the same ways that they relate to each other. One's level of individuation will significantly inform the quality of relationship with God as well as the depth of understanding and experience of God. Not surprisingly, those parishioners in our care who struggle to "be," apart from their parent figures and significant others in their lives, will also struggle spiritually. In contrast, those who develop a strong sense of self, those who have individuated adequately,[1] will be more spiritually mature and will relate to God at a more autonomous level. With greater individuation comes greater self-awareness (which itself is the complement of other-awareness). As the discussion in this chapter demonstrates, the quality of our relationship with God depends on our ability to view God as "other," another being, with an existence distinct from our own and not reduced to an extension of ourselves, of our demands, and of our human finiteness.

The purpose of our examination of the theological basis of boundaries is to integrate the concept of boundaries within the framework of faith and spirituality and to examine the role that boundaries play in the exercise of our faith, our congregational life, and our ministerial vocations. Examination of the boundaries between God and humankind obviously entails some level of confidence that God is knowable and that our understanding of various intrinsic traits of God reflects at least moderately the truth of God. A discussion of the heuristics of theology is outside the scope of this book, and, as such, I will not present arguments in support of the traits of God that are examined. However, what we know, how we know what we know, and how accurate our knowledge are all factors in our search for and our connection to God.

The concepts presented in this chapter may feel like a review for you. You may have become intimately familiar with them as a result of seminary training and years of ministry, preaching, and studying. However, familiarity may dull appreciation and so I present them again, with the hope that you might experience a renewed appreciation for the beauty of God's nature and the divine design for human relationships.

"What Is Truth?"–Pilate

I do not profess to know God perfectly or fully. Foundational to our discussion here is my belief that "Truth" is qualitatively distinct from "knowing" or "understanding." Truth is. Truth is real, it is true, it is complete, and it is absolute. We often casually toss around the terms "true" and "truth" as a way of emphasizing the high level of confidence that we have in the veracity of our knowledge of something. "Are you telling me the truth?" "No, that is not true." Used in this sense, "truth" refers to the fervor of our conviction about something we profess to know. "Are you absolutely sure?" "Yes, I am telling you the truth!" To distinguish between fervor of conviction (what we know) from what is, I have opted to capitalize the term when referring to the absolute ("Truth"), while employing standard lower case ("truth") to denote its familiar and common usage.

Truth stands apart from the inquisitiveness of our minds and our ambitions to understand it. What we understand is not the same as what is Truth. What we profess to understand or know is the synthesis of several elements:

1. our present interaction with Truth
2. prior related experiences
3. how we gather information
4. how we mentally organize information
5. and the philosophical filters through which we interpret events

To illustrate, assume that I have an abrupt interaction with Truth when I decide to jump off the rooftop of my house (#1). I know that I have jumped off a diving board before, headfirst no less, and that went smoothly (#2). In Myers-Briggs typology, I am predominantly an "intuiter" rather than "senser," and I "just have a feeling this is going to work" (#3). I tend to focus on details more than big picture (#4). I've also been told throughout my childhood that I can do anything I set my mind to (#5).

This is undeniably an outrageous example, but it illustrates hyperbolically why Truth and what I know are not the same thing. So, I jump off my rooftop. I land hard on the grass below. My ankle twists and I crumple to the ground. I lie there wondering, "What just happened? I was so sure this was going to work." As I catch my breath, I ponder the meaning of my most recent interaction with Truth. In keeping with the ridiculous nature of my illustration, I synthesize a newer, more refined understanding of Truth from this incident: clearly, I had not committed myself adequately to the endeavor and was lacking sufficient determination to make this rooftop jump a success (see #5). Fortunately, I am not much worse for the wear, I limp back into my house and decide that I will do a better job of "setting my mind to it" for my next attempt.

You have surely made better sense of your experiences with gravity than I did in the example above! While my interaction with Truth and my conclusions are absurd, we nonetheless make sense out of our experiences in this manner all the time. Our children may conclude that "Mommy is mean" when she says no to their requests. They may lack sufficient experience to understand that Mommy is keeping them safe, preventing an injury, or making allowances for other constraints unknown to the children. We may pray that God alleviate our suffering, yet receive no resulting change in our condition, and therefore conclude: God doesn't care about us, we are not his children, he is busy, or that we have fallen out of favor with him. Accordingly, what we know about God is not necessarily the Truth. What we know may reflect inaccurately, inadequately, or only approximately who and what God really is–the Truth about God.

In our spiritual journeys, we seek earnestly for a broader, more thorough, and more accurate knowledge of God, which in turn allows us to engage in a healthier and more realistic relationship with God. So we must continually examine, evaluate, and adjust how we arrive at conclusions that make up our understanding of who God is. And we must hold our understanding–our knowledge–tentatively, always aware that it may require adjusting as we grow in faith and experience. This is the beauty of our relationship with God. It is dynamic, challenging, and always drawing us toward God. Out of a yearning to know God better, we engage with God, and, in that relationship, God is able to reveal Godself to us ever more deeply and intimately. "But if from there you seek the LORD your God, you will find him if you look for him with all your heart and with all your soul" (Deut. 4:29).

Acknowledgment of our lack of absolute certainty in understanding God combined with cautious conclusions regarding God's nature is one of the most important boundaries that we must exercise in our walk of faith.

First, it protects us from reducing our understanding of God to human characteristics and limitations and therefore missing the experience of awe that comes with being personally touched by the Most High God personally. Second, it prevents us from professing to fully know the mind of God. "As the heavens are higher than the earth, so are my ways higher than your ways and my thoughts than your thoughts" (Isa. 55:9)[2]. The tendency is strong to attempt to read the minds (albeit inaccurately) of other people we relate to. How much more tempting it is to believe we fully know the mind of God, and how much more erroneous!

Third, it protects us from believing that we as ministers have a greater knowledge of God than our parishioners and that they must therefore rely on us for understanding and insight. Such a belief robs others of the opportunity to search for God in their own lives and develop their own intimate, dynamic, and personal relationship with God. Fourth, this boundary recognizes our own human limitations, frailties, erroneous syntheses, and constraints of time and space. It acknowledges that God is God and I am not. If God is Other than me, then my spirit will be prompted to search for God and I will acknowledge my need for God.

In the Beginning

The most compelling argument for the separateness of God from humankind is found at the very beginning of the Bible. "In the beginning God created the heavens and the earth" (Gen. 1:1). This simple statement invites considerable reflection, deliberation, and meditation. For our purposes, suffice it to say that if God created us, then we are *not* God, nor are we *equal to* God. However, this does not mean that we are without honor in our position as created: "You made him a little lower than the heavenly beings and crowned him with glory and honor. You made him ruler over the works of your hands; you put everything under his feet" (Ps. 8:5–6).

God created us in his image, male and female. "So God created man in his own image, in the image of God he created him; male and female he created them" (Gen. 1:27). One of the attributes of God is that the three persons of the Trinity exist in relationship with each other. God's nature is relational. Made in God's image, people will also seek relationship, with God and with other people.

Almost immediately in the Genesis narrative, Adam and Eve are tempted with the thought of doing something to make themselves like God. "And the LORD God commanded the man, 'You are free to eat from any tree in the garden; but you must not eat from the tree of the knowledge of good and evil, for when you eat of it you will surely die'" (Gen. 2:16–17). With God's creation of Adam and Eve (and all humankind) came an intrinsic boundary represented for them by the command to not eat of the tree of the knowledge of good and evil. With this boundary, God was reminding Adam and Eve that "I am God and you are not." The temptation to challenge the intrinsic boundary between God and human came in the form of the voice of a crafty serpent: "'You will not surely die,' the serpent said to the woman. 'For God knows that when you eat of it your eyes will be opened, and you will be like God, knowing good and evil'" (Gen. 3:4–5). One can only wonder what the attraction was for becoming like God. Did they believe that being like God would increase their closeness to God? Did they perceive themselves as subordinate because they were created rather than Creator and therefore thought they were inferior in the order of creation? Were they thinking at all? Regardless, so began the protracted saga of sin, sickness, and war with God.

Justice and Mercy

As long as Adam and Eve respected the boundary, they were immune from the results of violating that boundary. Despite one's preference for a more literal or more figurative interpretation of the story of the creation and fall from grace, protection from the consequences of challenging God's intrinsic boundary is discernible in the portrayal of the garden of Eden. Even today, a reference to Eden connotes an ideal, utopic, and blissful existence in a perfect place with an absence of strife, struggle, sweat, sickness, and sorrow. Adam and Eve's consequence for violating the boundary was separation from God, both physically and spiritually.

Theologically, one might debate whether the consequence of removal from the garden and loss of eternal life was a curse or a blessing, punishment or kindness, law or grace. Consider this: "The wages of sin is death" (Rom. 6:23a), but "because of the LORD's great love we are not consumed, for his compassions never fail" (Lam. 3:22). He is not *all* mercy and *no* justice, or *all* justice and *no* mercy. This is an elegant demonstration of how the perfect fusion of the attributes of God exceed our ability to fully comprehend and reconcile. Typically, we consider these traits to be juxtaposed, even antithetical. Thus arise questions such as "How can a loving God condemn people?" and "If God cares about justice, why does God allow oppression?" These are very profound questions, difficult to ponder and not easily answered. They represent the themes of many a Sunday school curriculum and Bible study.

Had God not removed Adam and Eve from the garden of Eden and from the possibility of eating more of the fruit from the tree of life, they would have experienced the most extreme and final of curses–eternal separation from God with no possibility of reconciliation. So, while eviction from the garden and the injunction of toil and labor[3] was a curse that continues to afflict humanity to this day, it was also an expression of the profound kindness of God. By way of the curse, God set the stage for the possibility of forgiveness, reconciliation, and restoration. Justice begat mercy. Later in history, his mercy required justice, through the incarnation of the Second (last) Adam and the expiation of sin. "For since death came through a man, the resurrection of the dead comes also through a man. For as in Adam all die, so in Christ all will be made alive… 'The first man Adam became a living being'; the last Adam, a life-giving spirit" (1 Cor. 15:21–22, 45). The realization of the depth of God's love for God's creation, to the extent that God would not only create a physical world but a perfect natural order that was consistent with God's infinitely faceted and unfathomable essence, led the apostle John to exclaim, "How great is the love the Father has lavished on us, that we should be called children of God! And that is what we are!" (1 Jn. 3:1a).

Natural Law

When we disregard the intrinsic boundary between God and ourselves our psychological and spiritual health deteriorates, the result of alienation, estrangement, and conflict. Not surprisingly, people have the same inclination to violate the intrinsic boundary of "me/not me" in their relationships with other people. Children are notorious for trying to act as the parent with their younger siblings; they try to become like the parent they idolize by assuming the parent's responsibilities, with no regard for the inalienable relational structure of the family. As was discussed in chapter 2, ego development entails the internalization of the parent while working through the process of symbiosis-separation-rapprochement-individuation. And, throughout life, we work out the delicate balance of admiring and attempting to integrate another's desirable traits, all the while establishing our own unique individuality. The process of maturation is fraught with boundary violations as we learn how relationships work. We also come to a deeper understanding of who God is from our firsthand experience, just as personal relationships with other people allow us to know them better.

Violation of intrinsic boundaries always has consequences. The alienation that ensued in the garden of Eden between God and those God created is the same alienation we experience today when we challenge the intrinsic boundary between God and ourselves. This can be described as *natural law*–the consequences of disregarding intrinsic boundaries are built into creation. The consequences of violating intrinsic boundaries are integral to the boundaries themselves.

Think back on the example in which I jump off the roof of my house with naïve disregard for the fundamental boundary of gravity. One could say, "Naturally, you're going to hit the ground." Hitting the ground–hard–is the natural consequence of my disregard for the immutable force of gravity. So it is with our persistent challenge of the intrinsic boundary between God and us. If we try to be God, or try to act like God, we're going to hit the ground–hard. We will fail, and we will get hurt–not because God doesn't care about us, but because we don't respect God and God's boundaries.

To extend this analogy, let's assume that having jumped off the roof, I now walk with a limp. My ankle will never be the same. While I can still walk, I am affected by the consequences of my action and become a faded resemblance of my original glory. I am a curious mix of attributes reflective of God's image and the effects of having challenged natural law. If I am unusually obtuse, I may try to jump again and again. One of two things may happen. The pain may increase each time I challenge the boundary of gravity, until I finally get it: don't mess with gravity. In this case, natural law has had the desired effect of self-correction. Or, I may continue jumping, breaking bones, hitting my head, suffering slow brain hemorrhaging, to the point that I become desensitized to the pain and oblivious to the insanity of my attempted defiance of the boundary of gravity. In this case, I become hardened—maybe even senseless—and can no longer benefit from the consequences of natural law.

Theologically, the same thing happens when we transgress the boundary between God and us. There are consequences. We can respond to the consequences in one of two ways. We may learn from the consequences, adjust our understanding of God's ways and being, and modify our behavior to align with a more accurate understanding of the relationship between God and us. "Yet now I am happy, not because you were made sorry, but because your sorrow led you to repentance" (2 Cor. 7:9). Or, we may become obstinate and calloused, and lose sensitivity to the call of God for repentance. This is spoken of as the "hardening of our hearts": "They are darkened in their understanding and separated from the life of God because of the ignorance that is in them due to the hardening of their hearts" (Eph. 4:18).[4]

This is the human state: our unrelenting challenge of the intrinsic boundary between God and ourselves and the alienation that comes from trying to *be* God rather than seeking to *commune* with God. In theological terms, this is the sinful nature that the apostle Paul refers to when he laments, "...I have the desire to do what is good, but I cannot carry it out. For what I do is not the good I want to do; no, the evil I do not want to do—this I keep on doing. Now if I do what I do not want to do, it is no longer I who do it, but it is sin living in me that does it" (Rom. 7:18b–20).

The Advent of the Covenant of Law

If we stop reading here, the picture of our struggle against God is bleak. But this is only a fraction of the story that has been revealed of the interplay between the justice and mercy of God. It is truly glorious to have the assurance that God was not remiss in executing a plan of creation and redemption! We will return to discuss the fulfillment of God's plan for redemption, but for now we will continue to review the development of boundaries through biblical history.

Your ministry training will hopefully have supported your exploration of the question: If God knew we would attempt to become like God, why give us free will? Wouldn't it have been easier on everybody if we didn't have to *choose* to respect the boundary? The free will of man is the design of a perfect, complete, and self-sustaining God who wanted—not needed—a creation that could share in loving relationship. God's creation, God's people, would not be able to love God if they did not have a choice, since love must be freely given in order for it to be love. And, in order for God's people to love freely, they also must have the option of *not* loving, *not* respecting God their creator. Once again, I am humbled by the wisdom of God as manifested in God's design!

Old Testament history chronicles the difficulties that humankind encountered in their journey with God and in choosing the way of love. Thus the need for Law summarized in the Ten Commandments to Moses. People needed more guidance in knowing where the intrinsic boundary between God and themselves lay, so God provided rules that pointed people toward God: ceremonial and religious rules, social rules, rules of safety and hygiene. These boundaries were imposed, and not fundamental to the original and natural order of creation. They reflected people's need for regulation in a now fallen world, where strife against God was overt and pernicious. Some of the rules carried with them mandates for punishment or consequences to be enforced by the religious leaders. Other laws carried with them warnings of God's withholding of blessing if they went unheeded, while natural consequences were embedded in yet other laws (especially those related to hygiene and diet).

> These are the commands, decrees and laws the LORD your God directed me to teach you to observe in the land that you are crossing the Jordan to possess, so that you, your children and their children after them may fear the LORD your God as long as you live by keeping all his decrees and commands that I give you, and so that you may enjoy long life. Hear, O Israel, and be careful to obey so that it may go well with you and that you may increase greatly in a land flowing with milk and honey, just as the LORD, the God of your fathers, promised you. (Deut. 6:1–3)

At that time in history, observing the *imposed* boundaries of the law of Moses was the way in which God's people could demonstrate their respect for the *intrinsic* boundary between them and God. In the book of Jeremiah, the prophet quotes the LORD God, "For when I brought your forefathers out of Egypt and spoke to them, I did not just give them commands about burnt offerings and sacrifices, but I gave them this command: Obey me, and I will be your God and you will be my people. Walk in all the ways I command you, that it may go well with you" (Jer. 7:22–23). As early as Genesis 4, we see the progressive development of the idea that the observance of God's boundaries leads to relationship and intimacy with God, while disrespecting God leads to alienation, suffering, and loss.

The Second Adam–The Covenant of Grace

Because God is God, limitless and perfect, God is neither a God exclusively of justice, nor a God exclusively of mercy. God is the God of justice *and* mercy. Justice and mercy are two facets of the same attribute–unfailing love. Definitions of "love" abound, perhaps because the construct of love is at once profound and immense. One succinct definition of love is "always seeking the highest good for another." Theologically, this has been God's focus for humanity from creation onward. At times, God's search for the highest good for God's people required the application of justice–at other times, the application of mercy. But with God, there is no mercy without justice and no justice without mercy.[5]

The covenant of Law demonstrated God's love to a fallen race primarily through the application of justice. This was God's invitation to God's people to seek and know God. God's people had the prerogative of honoring the boundaries, demonstrating their love and respect for God, and were also given the opportunity to cooperate with God in God's pursuit of their highest good. At the appointed time, God chose to intervene in creation's history in a new way: through the application of mercy. Enter the second Adam into God's dealings with humankind. A new covenant was established, not of *law,* but of *grace,* whereby God demonstrated God's love to God's people primarily through the application of mercy, rather than justice. "For just as through the disobedience of the one man the many were made sinners, so also through the obedience of the one man the many will be made righteous" (Rom. 5:19). However, the apostle Paul was quick to add, "Now wait a minute–just because God has shown you mercy doesn't mean you can blow off his boundaries!" (author's very loose paraphrase of Rom. 6:15–16).

Consider this very elegant passage from Romans describing the symmetry and congruence of God's justice and mercy:

> But now a righteousness from God, apart from law, has been made known, to which the Law and the Prophets testify. This righteousness from God comes through faith in Jesus Christ to all who believe. There is no difference, for all have sinned and fall short of the glory of God, and are justified freely by his grace through the redemption that came by Christ Jesus. God presented him as a sacrifice of atonement, through faith in his blood. He did this to demonstrate his justice, because in his forbearance he had left the sins committed beforehand unpunished–he did it to demonstrate his justice at the present time, so as to be just and the one who justifies those who have faith in Jesus. (Rom. 3:21–26)

Indulge my momentary impulse to preach for one paragraph. Brothers and sisters, think about this: God, in all God's wisdom, richness, and power, created a universe in which every event, every living being, every interaction between God and God's creation carries God's watermark: justice and mercy. Who among us could ever come up with such a majestic, profound, and all-encompassing order for life? As we look back on the steady progression of God's revelation to people–from the benevolent creation of Adam and Eve and the world that would harbor them, to the gracious provision of a path to reconciliation with God–the intricacies of God's being and essence are mind-staggering. Even a brief meditation on this Truth sends chills down my spine!

Boundaries in God's Image

We've laid a foundation of the operation of boundaries from a spiritual standpoint: how God reveals Godself to God's creation, and how people respond to God. How does this inform our behavior and walk of faith? The apostle Paul wrote to protégé Timothy, "All Scripture is God-breathed and is useful for teaching, rebuking, correcting and training in righteousness" (2 Tim. 3:16). We can learn much in our search of Truth from God's design of the universe and the relational order that was integrated into the creation of human beings. Because we were made in God's image, understanding God's attributes and how God relates to us will guide us in achieving wholesomeness in our dealings with each other.

So, what wisdom can be mined from the discussion thus far? I will summarize a few thoughts here and then elaborate on each point.

- Boundaries are God's idea.
- Some boundaries are intrinsic, while other boundaries are imposed. Both types of boundaries are important.
- The Truth that we are not God relieves us of enormous pressure to manage divine responsibilities.
- God has good boundaries, so our whining, tantrums, and accusations do not manipulate God.
- It is easier to get our boundaries right with other people when we have our boundaries right with God.
- Boundaries are essential to love.

Boundaries Are God's Idea

The term "boundaries" was coined by the community of psychological professionals to describe the construct that defines how one separates oneself from others. It is an attempt to approximate our understanding of Truth and is certainly not Truth itself. (We employ here the boundary that Truth and our understanding of Truth are not the same.) While God did not call it "boundaries," God did incorporate a principle into God's creation that can be described as boundary. If the principle of boundaries is intrinsic to the nature of creation, then it is wise to heed this principle, just as it is wise to heed the boundary of gravity. Disregarding intrinsic and imposed boundaries does not nullify them; it brings pain, first in our relationship with God and second in our relationships with others.

Intrinsic and Imposed Boundaries

Let's go back to my rooftop experience one more time. The boundary I am challenging is that of gravity. Regardless of how I attempt to spin my beliefs about my understanding of gravity and myself, whether consciously or subconsciously, the intrinsic boundary of gravity will not change. No matter how many times I jump off my roof, I will continue to hit the ground hard, until either I come to my senses or I am knocked senseless.

Now suppose that because I don't appear to be coming to my senses, my neighbors become increasingly concerned for my welfare and a new city ordinance is passed that requires that all rooftops be fitted with a sign that states: "WARNING! Jumping from or falling off this roof may cause serious injury or death. Use extreme caution when climbing on this roof. Willful jumping from this roof is a violation of city ordinance 154.08 and will be prosecuted."

The new rooftop signs and the city ordinance that mandates their installation are boundaries, but not intrinsic to the order of creation. These are imposed boundaries. They are intended to help me consider my folly in challenging the intrinsic boundary of gravity, motivate me to stop my behavior, and hopefully forestall my untimely demise. The imposed boundary denoted by the rooftop sign is intended to heighten my awareness of the intrinsic boundary of gravity, to guide my behavior such that I don't naïvely ignore the boundary of gravity and explicitly delineate the consequences of ignoring gravity and the city ordinance.

Joe's (Special Friends) relationship with Kat is also an example of the effect of disregarding the intrinsic boundary (parishioners are not to be used for personal gain) and imposed boundaries (such as not engaging in sexual behavior with parishioners). In ignoring the intrinsic boundary–apparently believing that he deserved to have his sexual and emotional needs met, one way or another–he also chose to ignore the imposed boundaries proscribing appropriate clergy behavior. By the end of the story, his conscience had been knocked senseless. He no longer felt guilty for his behavior. He became his own god, taking for himself whatever he wanted, and he brought untold pain and harm to his family, his church, his parishioner, and himself.

The intrinsic boundary is: "God is God and I am not." God's intention for the law of Moses was to help people reconsider their obstinacy in challenging the intrinsic boundary, motivate them to stop their transgressing behavior, and prevent their self-induced destruction. While observance of the Law prevented harm and alienation, it did not offer reconciliation to God when the intrinsic boundary was violated. Reconciliation after a boundary trespass requires three things: confession, repentance, and reparation. Confession is the acknowledgment by the transgressor of the violation; repentance is the transgressor's agreement to not transgress the boundary again; reparation is the act of repairing the damage caused by the violation in order to restore the relationship to its original state.

Because the Law did not have a provision for reconciliation–only prevention and protection from the consequences of violating the intrinsic boundary between God and humankind–God offered a means of reconciliation (Christ's atonement), which was the ultimate fulfillment of the Law. Jesus Christ did not abolish the Law (Mt. 5:17), although he did introduce a new interpretation of it (see Mt. 5:17–48).

We can use this same model of intrinsic and imposed boundaries in our relationships with other people. Intrinsically, you are you and I am not you. This boundary is immutable. However, we have difficulty remembering this at times, and even more difficulty observing the boundary. For this reason, imposed boundaries are indispensable for helping us to know the operational parameters of the intrinsic boundary. Later in this book we elaborate on how imposed boundaries protect those of us who work in vocations of soul care from violating intrinsic boundaries between us and God and between us and our parishioners, as well as how boundaries factor into interpersonal reconciliation.

We Don't Need to Take on God's Responsibilities

Attempting to take over God's business is one of the most curious behaviors that people exhibit. There are at least two reasons we do this: (1) we may not be clear on what is our responsibility; (2) we may think God is not doing it right or doing enough, so we choose to help him out. (However, who among us would actually admit to this attitude?)

The first reason seems less willful. Think of times when you have recently wondered, "Is this something I should step into? Should I be doing something here?" Think of times when in hindsight you realize that you were unwittingly drawn into a situation because the lines of responsibility were unclear. Truly, knowing the limits of our responsibility takes experience, a willingness to learn and adjust, and a lot of determination to constantly weigh our resources against the demands. It is difficult to know where the limits of our responsibility end with respect to any particular situation. Apparently, Sam (Loose Lips Sink Ships) was unclear about his responsibility in revitalizing the church. He took it upon himself to make it happen and not only was he unsuccessful, he also disregarded both God's and the congregation's role in determining the future of the church. We can rest assured that, because God is God, and God is the creator, sovereign, omnipotent, and omniscient, God is able to take care of what God has created. We do not need to worry that, if we are unable to take care of a need, or if we are mistaken about the parameters of our responsibilities, God will be unable to manage the situation. This principle may seem self-evident, but so easy to forget![6]

Second, the more we doubt that God is the Creator, compassionate and wise, the more difficult it is to live by the principle that God can take care of creation and therefore the more difficult it will be for us to remain clear on our boundaries of responsibility in a situation. Generally, while we will not readily admit that we question God's wisdom in dealing with humanity, an earnest soul-search will usually reveal dark recesses of our spirits where we have sat in judgment of God's wisdom and actions. Periodic soul checkups are therefore critical for the shepherds of God's church. "Be shepherds of God's flock that is under your care, serving as overseers—not because you must, but because you are willing, as God wants you to be" (1 Pet. 5:2a).

The most significant benefit of a clear grasp of our limits is the relief from the pressure of the weighty responsibilities that are God's to manage. We can minimize stress when we concern ourselves only with situations for which we carry some responsibility. So our psychological health is benefited when we are clear on our responsibilities and our abilities and are proactive in our responses. If the situation is out of our control but we are unclear about our responsibilities and abilities to respond, we will be overrun and paralyzed by worry and anxiety. The anxiety of feeling incapable, ineffective, helpless, and hopeless is crippling. But if we resist the urge to assume responsibility for situations that we do not have the resources to manage, and consciously turn over those situations to the one who *can* manage, we will maintain our sanity and our boundary with God.

Psychology tells us that to manage stress and reduce anxiety, we must take appropriate action in situations in which we carry responsibility and let go of situations that we have no control over. Faith tells us that even better than just letting go of situations that we have no control over is actually giving them back to God! Releasing to God our concerns about everything from the trivial to the catastrophic can be a rewarding spiritual exercise. In doing so, we acknowledge our human limitations, exercise humility, and tame the temptation of pride, honoring God by acknowledging God's beneficence and role as creator and assert our trust in God to work everything for the good (Rom. 8:28).

In the narratives of chapter 1, none of the pastors is described as having consciously relinquished to God circumstances beyond his or her control. Obviously, their relinquishment would have been merely an act of recognition, since God is sovereign and already in charge! We also won't assume that these pastors never prayed or sought the Lord's guidance in the challenges of their ministries. One must wonder, however, if, in the intensity of the moment, any of these pastors thought to call on God's wisdom as a means of discerning his or her responsibility and the appropriate boundaries.

God Has Good Boundaries

After all, God is the author of natural order and boundaries!

From a psychological perspective, we know that children have a better opportunity to develop a strong self-concept and healthy relational patterns if they are provided clear expectations and a safe "holding environment," both of which are necessary components of the boundary between parent and child. At one level, providing comprehensible expectations to children reduces anxiety. Clear and consistent expectations prevent a child's unsettling and disconcerting fears that the child may at any time be capriciously punished for an unknown transgression.

Beyond this, a child needs to feel safe and secure in order to flourish. The "holding environment" provides this security that allows a child to feel confident in exploring and testing abilities and limitations. The concept of "holding environment" refers to more than a parent wrapping his arms around the child or cradling the infant. In the first years, the holding environment is largely physical, but even as early as the first year, the holding environment also has an psychological element. Emotionally, the child needs to know that her behavior will not cause the parent's holding environment to disintegrate. A child who throws a tantrum is testing what affect her behavior will have on her boundaries. If the parent becomes distraught, reacts with anger, or retaliates, the child learns that the holding environment—the safety of the parent-child relationship—cannot be trusted.

The same concept holds true for our relationship with God. God's boundaries provide clear expectations of how to conduct ourselves in such a way that we will neither harm ourselves nor others, and we can rest in the peace of knowing God is not capricious, mercurial, or temperamental. (Deut. 6:1–3). Obviously, if we insist and persist in challenging God's boundaries, our relationship with God will be impacted, just as it will if we violate boundaries with people to whom we relate. But while we may experience distancing in the relationship, the nature of God will not change.

God also provides us with a safe holding environment. "I the LORD do not change. So you, O descendants of Jacob, are not destroyed" (Mal. 3:6). Similar to a parent that is not swayed by whining, thrashing about, and declarations of "I hate you," God will not be manipulated; neither is God's essence diminished by our human testing of the divine boundaries. At a very primitive level, we may interpret this as an indication that God is harsh and calloused, but from the perspective of a parent, God's holding environment provides us with the safety and freedom of being able to test God's love—and discover that it is unconditional.

David described this experience of holding beautifully in Psalm 18. In verse 2, David sings, "The LORD is my rock, my fortress and my deliverer; my God is my rock, in whom I take refuge. He is my shield and the horn of my salvation, my stronghold." Rocks and fortresses do not move; in fact, they are generally emotionless from the standpoint of typical human emotional experience. However, David did call out to God in a panic (having found himself in a perilous tangle with Saul), and he experienced God's response, aid, and rescue (v. 3ff). God is *the* Rock that responds, not *a* rock that crumbles. Because of David's experience of God's help, David declared, "I love you, O LORD, my strength" (v. 1). This is a biblical example of how God's holding environment stimulates our spiritual and relational maturation.

Attempts to manipulate are essentially born of a human fantasy of omnipotence–that people can be made to act or think by another's behavior. In this respect, manipulation is the result of arrogance and pride ("I am stronger than you so I have the right to impose my will on you"). Notice I used the term "fantasy," because we are not omnipotent and we do not have the right to impose our will on others.

Likewise, attempts to manipulate God are indicative of a belief that we are at least as strong as, if not stronger than, God, and that we have a right to impose our will on God. This is spiritual pride. And it does not work. Childish demands ("I *want* a candy bar, *I have to have it!*"), attempts to negotiate ("I'll only take out the trash if you give me..."), attempts to extort ("I'll tell my teacher you hit me if you don't do...for me"), are all met with the rock-like steadiness of God's ultimate holding environment. And, as a result, we receive the blessing of experiencing the steady, unfailing, unconditional love of the ultimate heavenly parent.

The Importance of Right Boundaries with God

Treating other people well, exercising appropriate boundaries with others, and living a socially responsible life all begin with having a healthy relationship with God. When asked what the most important law was, Jesus said, "The most important one...is this: 'Hear, O Israel, the Lord our God, the Lord is one. Love the Lord your God with all your heart and with all your soul and with all your mind and with all your strength.'" He then added, "The second is this: 'Love your neighbor as yourself.' There is no commandment greater than these" (Mk. 12:29–31). Jesus specified an order of importance for a reason.

If we have a strong, vibrant, and passionate relationship with God, we will pursue God's heart, and from passages such as Micah 6:8, we know what God wants from us: "He has showed you, O man, what is good. And what does the LORD require of you? To act justly and to love mercy and to walk humbly with your God." Jesus elaborated on the idea of not just following a formula, but rather pursuing the heart of God's law: "Woe to you, teachers of the law and Pharisees, you hypocrites! You give a tenth of your spices–mint, dill and cummin. But you have neglected the more important matters of the law–justice, mercy and faithfulness. You should have practiced the latter, without neglecting the former" (Mt. 23:23).

Later in this book, we will discuss in greater depth the pursuit of God's heart, the practice of spiritual disciplines that nurture our relationship with God, and the protection this affords us in serving our congregations with justice, mercy, and faithfulness without just going through the motions.

Boundaries Are Essential to Love

Chapters 2 and 3 have presented the concept of boundaries from a psychological and theological perspective. All the discussion can be distilled into this one statement: If love is the pursuit of another's highest good, then loving well requires healthy boundaries.

The parent who truly loves a child implements boundaries with the child that allow the child to develop as a whole person, not shackled by demands that the child become an extension of the parent or fill the parent's unmet needs for validation and self-esteem. In a similar fashion, God did not create human beings as objects to be possessed, but rather beings to love and relate to, demonstrating the utmost respect and "unconditional positive regard"[7] by affording free will.

Occasionally, an individual may protest, "Your boundaries are mean; they are hurting me!" Boundaries may indeed be implemented in a mean-spirited manner or be misguided. But the boundaries may also be protective and intended for good. A poorly individuated person is unaccustomed to healthy boundaries. When confronted with another's well-defined self that is not easily manipulated, the poorly individuated person may become agitated, frustrated, and angry. This person is unable to acknowledge the wisdom of the appropriate and healthy boundary, its intent to protect, and its conveyance of respect for that person's ability to develop and mature. The person with a compromised self-concept may perceive the boundary as "mean," but that in itself is not evidence that the well-individuated person is mean-spirited.

Sarah (Robert: The Ornament) perceived Robert's attempts to maintain his pastoral boundaries as mean-spirited. When she was unable to solicit the level of care she believed she needed with gifts and affirmation, she resorted to punitive behavior by withdrawing her financial support and attacking her pastor's reputation. Jonathan (Katrina: Supervisor or Pastor?), however, did not interpret his pastor's efforts to maintain and clarify boundaries the same way. Sarah's and Jonathan's distinct personalities probably impacted their reactions to the boundaries, but their pastors also handled the relational challenges differently. Sarah's pastor, Robert, struggled to articulate his boundaries and limitations, while Jonathan's pastor, Katrina, realized that confronting the boundary challenges head-on would more likely result in a positive outcome.

The purpose of healthy boundaries is to further another's highest good, and, as such, is the essence of love. Every healthy boundary is premised on the original creational boundary: that God is God and I am not. With that in mind, our effectiveness in ministry, our personal fulfillment in life, and the quality of our walk of faith with the Lord all hinge on a permeating acceptance of the intrinsic boundary between God and us.

Time to Reflect

1. How have you experienced God's grace in your life? How have those experiences intersected with your experience of God's boundaries with you?
2. How have parental figures in your life impacted your understanding of God and God's desire for your spiritual maturity?
3. How has your understanding of God and God's ways changed over time, through life experience, observing the lives of others, and through Bible study?
4. How well do you think you model healthy boundaries with your parishioners, family members, and others?
5. What spiritual disciplines can you practice to improve your discernment of where your responsibility lies between you and your family members, between you and your congregation, and between you and the needs of your wider community?

CHAPTER 4

Boundaries in the Body of Christ

"Now the body is not made up of one part but of many. If the foot should say, 'Because I am not a hand, I do not belong to the body,' it would not for that reason cease to be part of the body. And if the ear should say, 'Because I am not an eye, I do not belong to the body,' it would not for that reason cease to be part of the body."

1 CORINTHIANS 12:14–16

Up to this point, our discussion has been primarily theoretical, laying the foundation for the practical application of boundaries in ministry. Attempting to describe and understand, even imperfectly and incompletely, the nature and work of God is formidable, albeit exhilarating. My prayer is that if the material in the previous chapters is able to evoke only one response, it would be an awestruck appreciation for the wisdom and goodness of God. So now we begin the transition into an exploration of these principles applied in everyday life and ministry.

Whether from the perspective of a local congregation, a religious denomination, the Church universal, or our personal and particular web of relationships, we know that we belong to the body of Christ and have gifts, skills, and abilities that uniquely qualify each of us for our specific roles within that body.

The body is a unit, though it is made up of many parts; and though all its parts are many, they form one body. So it is with Christ. For we were all baptized by one Spirit into one body—whether Jews or Greeks, slave or free—and we were all given the one Spirit to drink... Now you are the body of Christ, and each one of you is a part of it. (1 Cor. 12:12–13, 27)

This is an exquisite picture of God's design for relationship among his children—to belong, to have worth and purpose, to work toward unity, and to experience the cohesion brought about by the baptism of the Holy

Spirit. For our purposes, we will focus our attention on the operation of the body of Christ from the standpoint of the local congregation, with the understanding that the principles presented here are equally applicable to the body of Christ on a broader scale, as well as at the personal level.

Life Can Be Painful

Every person who takes part in the life of a local congregation experiences the effects of a fallen creation and brings with him or her into the life of the church his or her heartache and pain. A discussion of the functioning of a local church begins with an understanding of the characteristics of the people who make up a local body of believers, and the most ubiquitous of all characteristics is the experience of pain. Pain essentially results from one of three causes, or, more likely, some combination of all of three: my brokenness; others' brokenness; a broken creation.[1]

Some pain is brought about by our own willful violation of boundaries, be they boundaries with God or with other people. Over and over again in the Old Testament, the children of Israel turned away from God's law and encountered natural consequences that resulted in pain and suffering, along with God's promise that "if my people, who are called by my name, will humble themselves and pray and seek my face and turn from their wicked ways, then will I hear from heaven and will forgive their sin and will heal their land" (2 Chr. 7:14). Lest we acquire an attitude of arrogance by thinking that the children of Israel had a unusual disposition for obstinacy and defiance, Paul also reminds us, "You, therefore, have no excuse, you who pass judgment on someone else, for at whatever point you judge the other, you are condemning yourself, because you who pass judgment do the same things" (Rom. 2:1).

The law of Moses commands, "You shall not commit adultery" (Ex. 20:14). If I disregard this boundary, I will bring pain upon myself (and many others as well). Willful disregard for God's rules results in pain.[2] And lest I think that my married neighbor is sinful because of his adultery, while minimizing my own wayward lustful thoughts, Jesus reminds me, "You have heard that it was said, 'Do not commit adultery.' But I tell you that anyone who looks at a woman lustfully has already committed adultery with her in his heart" (Mt. 5:27–28). "Don't commit adultery" is the manifest boundary, but disregard for the underlying boundary—"don't even entertain the idea"—also leads to pain, heartache, and suffering. It is tempting to sit in judgment of Joe (Special Friends), reckoning his behavior to be outrageous and grossly out of bounds. But Joe didn't start out thinking that he would engage in a sexual relationship with his parishioner. He undoubtedly entertained the thought in his mind, which eventually led to his inability to discern the manifest boundary.

Likewise, Moses' law commands, "You shall not murder" (Ex. 20:13). Most of us feel fairly confident, to the point of smugness, that we are not murderers, and have never nor ever will kill someone. After all, we are not criminals and we know right from wrong. Murder is what people in prison have done—but not us. Yet we are far more cavalier about observing the spirit of this law: "[A]nyone who is angry with his brother will be subject to judgment... [A]nyone who says, 'You fool!' will be in danger of the fire of hell" (Mt. 5:22). How many of us cross this boundary regularly? How frequently does our disdain for another person culminate in our pain, to say nothing of the pain it inflicts on the other person?

Our brokenness also clouds our judgment with respect to our relationships and our assessment of our capabilities and ourselves. In this case, we may experience pain, not because we intentionally choose to violate a boundary, but because our judgment is impaired. A man tries to beat the rain on his way home, but the road is slick and he slides off the road, down an embankment and as a result, is injured and totals his car. An excessively trusting young lady accepts a ride home from the school library with an acquaintance only to realize that he never intended to take her home, ultimately leaving her for dead on the side of a rural road. Unfortunately, we are not exempt from consequences, even from just clouded judgment, ignorance, or inexperience.

Ann (A Parishioner Tells Her Story) knows firsthand how her brokenness contributed to her vulnerability and eventual abuse at the hands of her associate pastor. Ironically, she took responsibility for his violation but remained unaware of how her brokenness clouded her judgment and prevented her from fleeing the abuse.

Sometimes pain is the result of other people's brokenness. The family of a mother who is killed by a drunk driver experiences the loss and grief inflicted on them by the drunk driver's actions. Seniors living on dividends generated by financial instruments managed by an unscrupulous investor suffer great loss when the dividend income disappears along with the investor they trusted. Although Ann's vulnerability prevented her from fleeing her abuser, her abuse was directly the result of her pastor's brokenness.

Much pain is the end product of a broken creation. Physical and mental illness, death, catastrophic weather events, and geological disasters fall in this category. The intrinsic natural order of creation has been sentenced to disarray and turmoil—not the way it is supposed to be[3], and the apostle Paul says, "The creation was subjected to frustration, not by its own choice, but by the will of the one who subjected it, in hope that the creation itself will be liberated from its bondage to decay and brought into the glorious freedom of the children of God" (Rom. 8:20–21).

That's a lot of pain. And all this pain, brought about by brokenness, comes to church with us. Because we are so disposed to trespassing the boundaries that God set up for our benefit, we suffer, others suffer, and our relationships suffer. How can anything good come out of such a mess?

The answer is relationships. They are challenging. Sometimes they bring pain. But they also afford growth.

Relationships Make Us Human

Even though our brokenness and the brokenness of others play a large role in producing the pain that we experience, we cannot avoid relationships. We are not truly human, nor are we vibrantly alive, without relationship, since we were created *for* relationship with God and others. This is not to say that *some* relationships aren't best avoided, practically speaking. But without experiencing the discomfort and pain of relationships, we would not also be able to experience the joy and pleasure of relationships.[4] Neither would we be challenged to grow and mature.

Relationship is the environment that causes us to grow. At times, relationships are "warm and cozy"—a greenhouse to protect us from the extremes of stress and temptation, where others nurture and support us in the process of maturation and sanctification.[5] But on other occasions, relationships serve as a chisel that hews away the raw and rough stone that obscures the veiled beauty of our sculpted God-image. They act as the grinding stone that files off burrs and sharp edges that would otherwise interfere with our ability to show kindness, understanding, and grace. They are the iron that sharpens iron (Prov. 27:17), so that we become perceptive and discerning, tempered and conditioned to confront difficult situations. And, sometimes, relationships are the crucible of testing, to reveal our substance and true character. Relationships can create friction, heat, and pain.

Have you noticed how you just don't like some people? Think for a moment about why that is. Perhaps you feel uncomfortable around them, or you feel slightly threatened by them, or you don't agree with their choices. If we get close enough to certain people to know we don't like them, then we have a relationship with them, whether we want to or not. In these difficult relationships, we have a golden opportunity to grow. First, we must clarify why we don't like them. Usually, our dislike is the result of one of two causes: we either feel uneasy with them, or we don't like their actions. Typically, we feel uneasy around someone if that person's behaviors trigger a fear of being threatened—for example, the possibility of being pushed around, coerced, or manipulated, or a threat to our reputation or self-esteem. On the other hand, sometimes a person's behavior does not impact us directly, but we observe its impact on others and feel a certain level of disapproval or aversion to the damage and pain that person is causing others.

Having clarified within ourselves why we do not like someone, we can make informed decisions about the nature of the relationship and extent of interaction we want to have with that person. If we are uneasy around the offending person, is it because our boundaries are inadequate to address the possible incursions that person may attempt upon our sense of self? What can we do to shore up our boundaries and make them more explicit? What level of relationship is appropriate with someone we sense may attempt to violate our boundaries? If we disapprove of an offending person's behavior but it has had no direct impact on us to date, are we in a position as soul shepherds to address this behavior? What kind of relationship is necessary for the person to be receptive to our feedback, exhortation, or correction? Have we earned the right, regardless of our formal role, to offer guidance?

Ministers should rigorously pursue this exercise of examining our feelings, our boundaries, our awareness of the impact of others on ourselves. In future chapters, we will elaborate on the importance and process of doing this. For now, suffice it to say that we will experience growth and maturity when we exercise discernment and self-evaluation in the context of relationships within the church. We may enjoy and need comfortable relationships; they give us rest, peace, nurture, solace. But our spiritual and psychological muscles are developed through challenge—the difficult relationships.

The human spirit is designed to pursue growth and development. Perhaps this is why we commonly find ourselves wrestling with difficult relationships—our spirits seek out challenge even when we know intellectually that challenge means work. People unconsciously tend to repeatedly engage in challenging situations and relationships of a similar nature as a way of affording themselves another opportunity "to get it right." So we are bound to grow, to refine our humanity, as we relate to others. Growth happens!

Finding God in Our Brokenness

Desperation, suffering, and pain have a singular ability to propel us toward God and to sensitize our hearts to spiritual matters. Those who are in the throes of chaos, grief, pain, loss, or desperation are highly receptive to spiritual guidance and care, often seeking relief from their trouble, needing compassion, and searching for meaning to their affliction. It is no wonder that many people are drawn to a local congregation while in the midst of crisis; churches are filled with people who believe that spirituality, relationship with God, or a faith community will provide them with direction, meaning, purpose, hope, and comfort.

Jesus saw better than anyone the suffering, heartache and longing of the people he encountered (Mt. 14:14; 23:37; Mk. 6:34; 8:2; Lk. 19:41; Jn. 11:35). Jesus experienced loss, betrayal, abandonment, loneliness, and unspeakable suffering, and, having done so, he is perfectly able to comfort us (2 Cor. 1:4; Heb. 2:14–18). Jesus' compassion for the people motivated this invitation: "Come to me, all you who are weary and burdened, and I will give you rest. Take my yoke upon you and learn from me, for I am gentle and humble in heart, and you will find rest for your souls. For my yoke is easy and my burden is light" (Mt. 11:28–30). Because the Father of compassion comforts us as the sufferings of Christ flow into our lives, the comfort we receive can then overflow into the lives of others who encounter trouble. To parishioners, pastors are "Jesus with skin on"; we embody Jesus' ministry of healing and reconciliation to God.

People who join in the life of a local congregation fall on every point of the spectrums of psychological and spiritual development. Each person is unique in gifts, maturity, suffering, and history, and so plays a unique role in the congregation. The interplay between all these elements becomes the life and ministry of the church. It is fascinating that God is able to bind together a group of people with their God-images and brokenness and use those to breathe life and healing into a church body of God-seekers and God-followers. This phenomenon provides a glimpse into God's blueprint to redeem and resurrect the broken. It is reflective of the power of God that resurrected Jesus Christ bodily after Jesus took on the entirety of creation's brokenness at the crucifixion. And just as he did at the resurrection, God now has the power to breathe life into the body of Christ in its manifestation as the Church.

Relationship challenges stimulate growth. A church board meeting is the vehicle by which we may address staffing issues, decide on programming, budget for ministry activity and building repairs, or divide ministry work among the elders or other leaders. Yes, the board meeting is a mechanism for "doing church," and so it is vital to the overall function of the church. But underlying the obvious business of a board meeting is a more subtle operation: that of human beings engaging in relationship; working together for a common goal; learning to listen, discuss, cooperate; learning to disagree; learning to agree; and learning to balance conviction with consensus. A comfort ministry for those who are ill, grieving, or hurting is a great ministry indeed.

Had Sam (Loose Lips Sink Ships) recognized that he was not single-handedly responsible for revitalizing the church and that Ronald's concerns were representative of the work the entire congregation was faced with, Sam might have been able to spare himself and Ronald the barbed words, name-calling, and exhibits of dishonorable behavior. Sam was so focused on his conviction that he was unable to see the need for consensus. He was so focused on fulfilling his need for significance that he was robbing the congregation of the work they needed to do in order to more forward.

The local church is the place where people gather to work out their salvation (Phil. 2:12), find fellowship with likeminded believers (Acts 2:42), to be edified (Rom. 14:9), and to be equipped (Eph. 4:16). With the gathering of believers comes not only the presence of the Holy Spirit, but also the amalgamation of their pain, hurt, suffering, and struggles. All the programming in the world cannot replace the benefit received by those who work together. Ultimately, the *process* of working together, and working out our salvation together, is as much the mission of the church as the more obvious ministry *activity*. So "doing church" is a challenge; shepherding a flock of hurting people requires extreme patience, compassion, sensitivity, and grit. It is even more challenging because the shepherds are human too!

Staying Healthy in a Ministry of Healing

The Church is called to extend Jesus' earthly ministry into all time (Mt. 16:18; 28:19). Thus it is exposed to the most desperate needs, the sickest of the soul-sick, and the most demanding of relationships. Indeed, the local church is not truly alive unless it actively reaches out to anyone who is in search of the healing power of a ministry of grace. Is the banquet table at your church set only for the healthy, wealthy, and highly respected people in your community? What about those of lowly means and those who are unmistakably broken, out of the mainstream or considered just plain odd? Are they viewed primarily as validation of your church's token ministry to the disadvantaged? Are they a precious few? Or is your church filled with hungry, needy, and broken souls?

Observations of human behavior demonstrate that people tend to converge toward the average level of functioning of their social groups.[6] So how does one participate in the activity and ministry of a local church while maintaining one's own health? As in a hospital, health care providers must take precautions not to contract the diseases of those patients they are treating. They are well advised to pursue healthy routines of exercise, rest, good nutrition, and stress management, to fortify their bodies and spirits for optimal performance in their duties. They must also preserve a barrier between themselves and the germs that surround them as they are providing care to their patients. Sick doctors are not very effective healers. The same principle applies to pastors and other soul shepherds. The key to maintaining health in the midst of brokenness and the rigors of ministry is good boundaries and good self-care.

Pastors face a unique challenge in staying healthy while exercising their call of shepherding and ministry. First of all, pastoring does not typically come with a clear delineation between work life and personal life. From a social standpoint, church participation is generally considered to be part of one's personal life. Because the pastor is involved daily in the performance of church-related activities, the line between personal and professional obligation is hazy, sometimes imperceptible. Furthermore, the primary asset employed in ministry is a pastor's humanity and his relational self, so a pastor brings his or her personal self into his or her professional role in a way that few other professions require. Unlike with other professions, it is very difficult, if not impossible, to adopt a professional persona that protects the pastor's personal self from vocational scrutiny and role-related demands.

Ministry is about sharing oneself. In other professions, people perform duties, usually not dependent or contingent on their personhood. In ministry, the calling *is* to share one's personhood. The apostle Paul set this precedent:

> As apostles of Christ we could have been a burden to you, but we were gentle among you, like a mother caring for her little children. We loved you so much that we were delighted to share with you not only the gospel of God but our lives as well, because you had become so dear to us. Surely you remember, brothers, our toil and hardship; we worked night and day in order not to be a burden to anyone while we preached the gospel of God to you. (1 Thess. 2:7–9)

Sharing oneself personally within the context of ministry without losing oneself, becoming depleted, or ending up destroyed is probably the most consequential challenge that any pastor faces. Jay Kessler, in his book *Being Holy, Being Human,* states, "There are so many needy people out there who want to be with you. They need a friend; they need counsel; they need someone to just give them a little attention... After a while, you can begin to feel as though you're being nibbled to death by minnows."[7] One of the most basic protections that a pastor has from being personally consumed and from deteriorating to the average level of functioning of those being ministered to is to exercise clear and firm boundaries.

Second, ministerial demands place a strain on the pastor's pursuit of self-care and personal growth. Performance of ministry is not constrained to a clearly defined workweek, during discreet work hours, with definitive job duties. With very little more than a desire to serve those in need, pastors can find themselves drowning in ministerial activity, shackled to unrealistic to-do lists, and having lost the freedom to block out time for themselves and their personal relationships.

The majority of pastors are natural caregivers and nurturers. Although some may focus more on administrative aspects of ministry, the majority is attracted to ministry at least partially because of their desire to serve and care for others. The temptation is high to sacrifice self-care for other-care. Physical exercise is sacrificed for a committee meeting or hospital call. Devotional time is sacrificed for sermon preparation. Dinner with family is sacrificed for dinner with the new visitors at church. Little sacrifices don't seem like much, and do not necessarily signify gross self-neglect if they are balanced by adequate self-care. But like the proverbial frog in the slowly heating pot of water, the pastor is unaware of how high the heat has gotten until he has been cooked. An accumulation of little sacrifices for the sake of parishioners and ministry without a commensurate commitment to cultivate one's own health add up to one shattered pastor.

One Body, Many Parts

Here is one of those instances in which Bible teaching and psychology do a beautiful job of describing the same principle of natural order from a different point of view. Psychology says, "If I am me, I can't also be you; everyone is different." Scripture says, "I may be a foot in the body of Christ, and someone else may be an eye; everyone is a different part of that body" (1 Cor. 12:14–16).

You probably don't need me to tell you that you can't do it all in your church. You probably remind yourself of that periodically just as you are approaching burnout and exhaustion. Ministers find it tempting, however, to jump in and do whatever needs doing whenever they see a need. The concept of the body of Christ provides permission for ministers to *not* do it all, not try to be all things to all people all the time[8]. Pastors are human too, so they are only one part of the body of Christ, just as is every other saint in a local church. Pastors do not need to be–neither should they be–hands and feet and eyes and ears and mouth and skin and stomach.

Occasional jumping in and doing whatever needs doing is a good model of cooperation and teamwork for parishioners who are inclined to sit on the sidelines (the 80 percent who only do 20 percent of the work). But when pastors jump into everything, they do not leave enough needs unmet to inspire others to find their strengths and gifts, derive self-esteem, and gain confidence by contributing and participating in the life of the body of Christ. Thus, we have a good example of how a good boundary is good for both sides. In this case, pastors will be healthier if they do not attempt to do it all. In maintaining this boundary, the parishioners also benefit because they are given an opportunity to grow psychologically and spiritually, extend themselves, take responsibility, and use their skills and abilities in the body of Christ.

Getting "nibbled to death" is the result of poorly defined boundaries in the minister's role in the church as an organization and in relationships with parishioners as individuals. The minister that tries to be both hand and foot and thumb and ears will eventually be eaten up. It's just a matter of time. Diffuse, lax, or unrealistic boundaries occur when the pastor

1. may believe that he or she can do more than is realistic
2. feels pressure from the church to do more than is realistic
3. carries guilt for not performing to others' expectations
4. has a distorted view of sacrifice

Sometimes poor boundaries are a combination of these. In any case, both sides are affected negatively–both the pastor and the parishioners. On the other hand, when the boundaries are clear and well maintained, the pastor is free to be the part of the body the pastor was designed to be, and the parishioners are able to function as the parts of the body they were designed to be.

Sacrifice or Bad Stewardship?

A toxic and insidious philosophy within some Christian subcultures asserts that in order to be "faithful Christians" we must sacrifice, and our work is not sacrifice unless it hurts and we suffer as a result of our sacrifice. We may intellectually denounce this belief, but it may nonetheless have found its way into our subconscious thinking patterns. If we grew up in Christian circles in which holiness was measured by the degree of sacrifice and suffering, or if we struggle with a sense of unworthiness and are seeking validation of the quality of our faith, or if we have learned to enjoy the attention and admiration from others who take note of our self-sacrificing lifestyles, we may be more vulnerable to this distortion. Sometimes sacrifice becomes the means by which we seek status and by which we achieve a self-perceived "higher level of spirituality." In this case, sacrificial behavior equates with spiritual pride. At other times, what we call "sacrifice" may really be our attempt to control a situation or someone else's behavior.

In Romans 12:1, Paul exhorts us to be "living sacrifices." He did not say "dead sacrifices." Except under the most extreme and rare circumstances, sacrifice does not require our very lives. If we sacrifice ourselves to death, we're not ministers; we're dead. And if we are not quite dead yet, we are at least very unhealthy.

For an action to be truly sacrificial:

1. the action must be the only way that the need can be met
2. the action must be something we are capable of doing or providing
3. the action must be performed with no other motive than to meet the need and because of love for God or another person
4. the action must cost us something

In order to give sacrificially, we must have something to give. Our resources for sharing can be viewed as a bank account. If we spend wisely the resources God has given us, we are wise stewards; if we spend frivolously or carelessly, we are poor stewards. There is no wisdom in using up the resources of our health, our sanity, and our families to meet needs that can be met in other less depleting ways. That is overspending that will eventually lead to debt (burnout, psychologically speaking).

Staying healthy in a ministry of brokenness entails having clear discernment of when sacrifice is called for. It also entails keeping a balance in our bank account of resources so that when a true need arises, we can respond, withdrawing from our account to meet the need. It is not nearly as easy to know when sacrifice is necessary as it is to write about it. Knowing when sacrifice is necessary requires careful thought, prayerfulness, and good self-awareness in order to discern the motives of our hearts and wisdom to discern the real need (as opposed to the perceived need) of the individual who is seeking help. But when we practice these disciplines, we insure that our choices are truly sacrificial and redemptive rather than self-serving and growth-inhibiting.

Good for the Goose, Good for the Gander

Again, a good boundary promotes health for the individuals on both sides of the boundary. Pastors that practice good boundaries–knowing what part of the body of Christ they are, knowing when to sacrifice, knowing how to use their resources to the maximum benefit of all involved–protect themselves from being nibbled to death, going into debt unnecessarily, and practicing ministry for self-serving reasons. They also model the practice of healthy spirituality and healthy relationships to their parishioners.

Much brokenness comes from unhealthy and enmeshed relationships. Many parishioners come into a local congregation with all the baggage of past and present personal dysfunction and dysfunctional relationships. They are often unaware of how boundary incursions–theirs and others–have shaped distorted beliefs about themselves, their expectations of others, and their understanding of God. All the ministerial activity in the world cannot replace a healthy pastor engaging in healthy relationships with the parishioners. This may be the most important work a minister can perform and is the embodiment of the ministry of presence. Pastors who have cared for themselves, who do not seek relationships in the congregation for their own fulfillment, and who maintain wholesome boundaries are in many cases a parishioner's first experience with mature, healthy relationship.

This is the crux of effective ministry. The pastor *must* model health–physical, mental, emotional, and spiritual. "Actions speak louder than words." The flock will follow, either upward toward health and growth, or downward into sickness and stagnation. The stakes are high.

Time to Reflect

1. What are some of the most significant relationships in your life, both personal and professional? Which relationships function (at least some of the time) as a nurturing greenhouse for you? How have they nurtured you? Which relationships have served to sharpen, chisel, or polish you? Which relationships have provided both greenhouse and chiseling functions?

2. What have you learned about yourself and God through your relationships? How has your character changed because of your relationships?

3. Consider what "part" you are in your local congregation. What strengths do you bring to the operation of your church body? What aspects of church function are better left to someone else?

4. How have you grown spiritually and emotionally as a result of engaging in relationship with others in your congregation?

5. Do you know the warning signs in your life that you are beginning to over-function in your ministry? What are they? How well do you heed those signs?
6. What is the distinction between receiving personal satisfaction from your vocation and engaging in ministry for self-serving purposes?

II.

BOUNDARY BUILDING BLOCKS

CHAPTER 5

Know Yourself

"The heart is deceitful above all things and beyond cure. Who can understand it?"

JEREMIAH 17:9

Relationships are not an exact science; they cannot be measured with a ruler and they are not static. As if relationships were not uncertain enough, there is another, even bigger challenge when attempting to set appropriate and healthy boundaries: the human heart. Perhaps you can remember a time when you said something and later ruminated, "Why on earth would I have said that?" Or you reacted to a situation and then later told yourself, "That was dumb! Whatever possessed me?" Or you still cringe when you think back on something you did or said twenty years ago.

Our behavior and thinking is largely determined by a "rulebook" unique to each individual, which is created over time. This rulebook dictates how we respond to frustration and blessing, how we perceive others and ourselves, our preferences, the level to which we can experience feeling, and much more. It typically remains buried in our spirits, shrouded by our unconscious. Most often, the rulebook is something of a "hidden agenda." Rules develop over time, from infancy on, and with very little or no conscious determination on our parts. They are influenced by early relational experiences, our genetics, our characteristic responses to external events and other people, and what we have learned about our effectiveness in controlling our environment (a combination of "nature" and "nurture"). As we saw in chapter 2, having experienced healthy parenting will greatly improve the chances that the rules of our personalities will be relatively healthy and that we will enjoy mature, autonomous lives. In chapter 3 we saw that healthy respect for and dependence on God also greatly improves the chances that we will enjoy mature and autonomous lives.

If our personality rulebooks are largely hidden from consciousness, how are we to know what makes us tick? To complicate the matter, "The heart is deceitful above all things and beyond cure. Who can understand it?" (Jer. 17:9). So, not only are our motives buried in our unconscious, but also our hearts will literally lie to us about what our motives really are. Relationships can be convoluted, complex, and challenging. But the biggest reason we struggle with relationships and boundaries is not because of the nature of the relationship, but because we are unaware of the true motives of our own hearts—our rulebooks. Thus, in order to maintain a healthy and morally principled ministry, we must respect the intrinsic boundary between God and ourselves, and then we must *know ourselves.*

What drives us informs everything we do, say, think, and feel. The rulebook also determines the filters we use when we assess the relative health of other people and the risk of association with them. How does a pastor discern if it is wiser to visit with a parishioner in the church office or at a coffee shop unless the pastor is aware both of the relational dynamics and the internal rulebook that governs how said pastor pursues fulfillment of personal needs? If Maryann (The Power of Prayer) were aware of her need for affirmation of her value as a minister, she would be more careful to not foster Betsy's unhealthy dependency in order to feel valued and needed, to the detriment of Betsy's spiritual development.

"Know yourself" sounds like a simple mantra. But those who have grappled with knowing the Truth about themselves acknowledge that "know yourself" is a lifelong quest, not a catchy slogan. For those who work in ministry, keen self-awareness and understanding of the motives of the heart are key to successful ministry.

The Challenge of Knowing Yourself

My experience with clergy suggests that ministers have developed somewhat greater skill for self-reflection than the general public, ostensibly because clergy are drawn to the pursuit of spiritual formation and its attendant introspective disciplines such as prayer, meditation, fasting, study, and solitude. Chances are you have pursued some introspective practices as you examined your call to ministry, sought guidance in decisions regarding vocational placement, or participated in seminary coursework in pastoral theology and counseling. You may have lain awake at night contemplating the nature and reasons for a recent conflict with your spouse. You have probably caught yourself lost in thought while driving, reflecting on your apparent inability to motivate a parishioner toward greater spiritual maturity. All of these experiences have led you to a greater understanding of your inner self, personality, values, thinking patterns, and behaviors.

However, much of our introspective searching is driven by the urgency of the present. We tend to wait until there is a problem, a conflict, an assignment—or until things are not going as planned—before we look for possible explanations. And even then our initial reaction is not to look at ourselves, but to focus outwardly on how others are behaving or on the circumstances that have precipitated our difficulty.

Waiting until there is a problem with a parishioner or with our vocational ministry before engaging in self-assessment is tantamount to waiting until it rains to get the roof fixed. The roof may get replaced, but not before the leak causes damage. Staying healthy in ministry and maintaining an effective ministry requires regular preventive maintenance: a commitment to the process of self-discovery, even when there is no urgency for self-examination.

The distinction must be made between the process of self-examination and the attainment of full self-knowledge. Remember our discussion about Truth in chapter 3. The same principles apply when seeking to know our own hearts. At best, our understanding of the depths of our souls will only approximate the Truth of ourselves. We are dynamic living beings; we continuously grow and change, and who we are today is different than who we were yesterday. So our insights must be revised with the changing landscapes of our spirits. We are complicated and multidimensional beings; we exist in dual realms: physical and spiritual. We are perfectly and wholly amalgamated creations of body, mind, and spirit.[1] The essence of our beings is a grand mystery and has been the life's work of many philosophers, theologians, and psychologists, none of whom have described it conclusively and with authoritative finality.

In addition, as psychoanalytic theory asserts, the spirit (or technically, psyche) exists across multiple levels of consciousness. The unconscious is out of reach of conscious awareness, and so we are, by definition, unaware of the forces of our unconscious. Because defense mechanisms—those strategies we use to preserve our self-esteem and defend against anxiety—emanate from the unconscious, we lack conscious awareness of their influence on our behavior and thinking patterns. This makes getting at the Truth of ourselves all the more difficult.

Another reason getting at the Truth of ourselves is difficult is that our fallen nature has led to a universal experience of shame. Shame is the belief that I am defective, bad, a failure, and unlovable; shame makes me want to curl up in a ball and hide under a rock. The first human experience of shame came in the garden of Eden, when Adam and Eve made coverings for themselves and cowered from God's presence. They were more worried about being naked (or vulnerable) than having crossed *the* boundary and sinned. When God asked them what they had done, they became defensive in their shame and started passing the blame. So ashamed were they that they tried to explain away their transgression rather than confess it (Gen. 3). The man blamed the woman, and the woman blamed the serpent. Here we see the significant distinction between guilt and shame. Guilt is what we feel when we have done something that is contrary to our moral standards; we believe we have done something "bad." Shame transforms "I did something bad" into "I am bad." The shame about shame is that it obstructs our ability to confess to the transgression ("I did something bad"). Instead we are preoccupied with defending ourselves against the belief that our transgressions betray our intrinsic worthlessness ("I'm no good"). Shame prevents us from directly confronting unhealthy behavior.

Shame also motivates us to construct a façade that we believe is more desirable, more lovable, more acceptable to others than what is at our core. Having built this elaborate façade, we nonetheless fear that, someday, someone is going to find out something about us that will expose the defectiveness, deficiencies, and weakness, the unsightliness of our true selves that cower behind the façade. We will be found out, so we expend enormous emotional energy maintaining and fortifying the façade, leaving little energy for sincere self-evaluation. We are loathe to look inwardly because we fear the discrepancy between what we project and what we think we will find inside. Ann (A Parishioner Tells Her Story) expended enormous energy trying to defend against the shame she felt. She withdrew from her social network, lived in isolation out of fear of being found out, and, although she functioned well in her profession, she spent all her emotional resources maintaining the façade that allowed her to work. So much energy was spent protecting herself from shame that it took her twenty years to gather the courage to ask for help.

The more shame we feel, the less capable we are of candid introspection and the more defensive we are against evaluation by others. If we accept Christ's propitiation for our sinfulness, we can cognitively reject the shame that binds, but, at a deeper affective level, shame persists. It is one of the curses of living in a broken creation, an effect of living between the "already" of the first advent of Christ and the "not yet" of the second coming. Awareness of how shame pervades our spirits and drives us into hiding rather than toward the light of accurate self-evaluation is a first step toward knowing ourselves well. And learning to live as freed people (Rom. 8:2), redeemed (Gal. 3:13–14) and loved (1 Jn. 3:1), will disarm the grip of shame and enable us to search our spirits without fear.

"See, I lay a stone in Zion, a chosen and precious cornerstone, and the one who trusts in him will never be put to shame" (1 Pet. 2:6). The passage that Peter quotes from Isaiah 28:16 is variously translated using the words *dismayed* (NIV), *disturbed* (NASB), *disappointed* (NCV), and *in haste* (ESV)[2]. Dismay connotes being disconcerted, shocked, horrified, unnerved, taken aback. In other words, trusting God for our salvation and redemption from brokenness will allow us to examine our spirits without being so dismayed, disturbed, and disappointed that we are compelled to run away from ourselves.

The Danger of Hiding from Yourself

What happens when people either buy into the lie of their façades, or have not worked toward penetrating self-knowledge? Let's review a couple of the stories from chapter 1. While we cannot know all the circumstances and thought processes surrounding their stories, we will look at some potential contributors to challenge and conflict in ministry.

Robert: The Christmas Ornament. From the narrative, we may assume that Robert was a hard-working pastor, committed to the welfare of his church and parishioners. Sarah was in crisis, and Robert found himself in the compelling role of comforter. Her early demands were met with Robert's appreciation for her trust in him. He was aware that the trust she expressed felt rewarding and affirming for him. Perhaps he was at a point in his ministry where he wondered about his relevance to the flock and its mission. At any rate, he was affected by the depth of her heartbreak, she having suffered multiple losses in a brief period of time. Perhaps her losses resonated with him, especially if he had not sufficiently grieved losses of his own.

Remembering his training and previous experiences where he had set boundaries with parishioners who had turned to him with overwhelming need, he attempted to do the same with Sarah. She resisted. She was perceptive enough to know that he feared being accused of callousness. She was manipulative enough to know that she could keep Robert engaged by alternately throwing him tidbits of affirmation or praise, while reprimanding him (with words or body language) when he did not meet her demands for attention. His attempts to communicate with her the limits of what he could do for her were ineffective. Possibly this was the result of him relenting of his better sense to refer her out for professional counseling, or because he had multiple competing goals:

- keep Sarah happy because she had expressed her intention to donate money for new hymnals;
- maintain his image as a caring pastor;
- gain reassurance that he was effective in pastoral care;
- provide pastoral care for Sarah that would motivate her to grow psychologically and spiritual.

In the end, none of his goals were achieved. At times, even a pastor with the best boundaries will not experience a favorable outcome. When competing interests vie for priority, the probability of an adverse outcome is high. Furthermore, when the pastor is *unaware* that some of his own personal interests (unconscious) are co-mingling with his professional obligations, the probability of an adverse outcome is exceedingly high. In this situation, Robert lost the gamble.

David: Golf Buddies. Like Robert, David found himself grappling with competing interests. Will was a parishioner, a golf buddy, and personal friend. As their friendship developed, David confronted head-on the potential conflicts, both with himself and with Will. Although we do not know what enabled David to candidly discuss the potential conflicts of interest with Will, we might presume that David was well aware of his need for social companionship. He was aware of his obligation to maintain the confidences of his parishioners and church leadership, so that he would not discuss ministry-related issues with Will. He knew he could not provide professional psychological care since this was outside his realm of expertise. And, equally important, he did not relinquish his commitment to function as Will's pastor for the sake of the friendship.

This is a story with a happy ending. Why? Possible contributors may have been:

- David did not carry submerged shame for being unable to meet all of Will's needs;
- David was clear about his roles and their relative priorities;
- David had gauged well Will's ability to respect his boundaries;
- David did not assume that role and boundary issues would work themselves out;
- David insured that his need for friendship did not obstruct his ability to fulfill his pastoral obligations.

In David's case, the outcome was positive. He handled the boundary issues prudently and used his self-awareness to his advantage.

Nevertheless, even with all of David's precautions and self-awareness, the story could have ended very differently. David could have misgauged Will's ability to respect boundaries. Because of the stress of losing his job, Will could have regressed so severely that he would have been unable to respect those boundaries. Other parishioners could have become resentful of David and Will's friendship (even if neither purposefully publicized it) and ignited congregational discord and conflict.

These two vignettes underscore a significant reality: ministry is inherently risky. Even with precautions, sound self-awareness, and observance of "the rules," things can go wrong. Relationships can go wrong. People are complicated, relationships are complicated, and ministry is complicated. We can *reduce* the risk of ministry failure due to inadequate boundaries, but we cannot entirely eliminate the risk. Ministry risk comes in degrees, but the risk is never zero.

The most effective tool that pastors have for reducing the degree of risk in ministry is honest and penetrating self-awareness. It is one aspect of ministry that pastors have control over. They are not able to control who walks through the doors of the church, what those people's needs are, or how they respond to disappointment or unmet needs. Neither can pastors control organizational dynamics that have evolved over the course of the church's history. However, they can control themselves.

The Quest to Know Yourself

Each person has his or her own unique personality rulebook. Each one is as different as the individuals' fingerprints. However, as with fingerprints, when comparing rulebooks, there are observable similarities or patterns. Psychology describes these similarities in terms of personality structures or styles. A framework of personality style can be very useful when we work to understand ourselves better and uncover some of the unconscious patterns we find ourselves repeating, either for better or for worse. Similarities and patterns aside, personality is complex. One might imagine that personality is comprised of components, dimensions, interactions between dimensions, levels of development, and so forth.

A single construct that fully describes personality in all its complexity has yet to be developed. But as the discipline of psychology has matured, various paradigms for understanding personality have been postulated, which have in turn become the foundation for several helpful taxonomies. Two of the most common paradigms employed to describe personality (our behavioral "rulebooks") are psychodynamic theory and character type theory. Some understanding of these paradigms and taxonomies will provide us with vocabulary, concepts, and frameworks to map our discoveries as we attempt to plumb the depths of our hearts and make sense of our personalities and behavior patterns.

The concept of defense mechanisms has its roots in Freudian psychoanalytic tradition and was expanded by the psychodynamic paradigms of object relations theory and self psychology. Defense mechanisms are unconscious thought and behavioral patterns that we develop to protect ourselves from anxiety, maintain self-image, and cope with reality. Our preferred defense mechanisms become the basis for describing our *personality organization*. The MMPI (Minnesota Multiphasic Personality Inventory)[3] is sometimes used to identify personality patterns and organization, defense strategies and the individual's level of defensiveness toward self-discovery. Note that personality organization does not imply mental disorder. Only if an individual's defense mechanisms are maladaptive or inflexible and impinge on the individual's ability to adequately function in life is that individual said to have a *personality disorder*.

There are a multitude of taxonomies based on character type inventories; one of the better known among the general public is the Myers-Briggs Type Indicator (MBTI)[4]. Several others are commonly used as well, such as Robert Cloninger's Temperament and Character Inventory (TCI), which, as its name suggests, focuses on temperament; and the DISC, a four-quadrant model often used in professional and teamwork environments that describes interrelational patterns.

These frameworks for describing personality can be useful as tools for self-exploration. None of them will definitively describe you. But they can help you begin to assess your personality, behavioral patterns, temperament type, and character traits. It's a place to start.

Personality Organization

Psychodynamic theory postulates that people develop defense mechanisms, or strategies for protecting the self from anxiety, to cope with the world and maintain self-esteem. The preferred defense mechanisms that each person employs determine the general personality organization.[5] Personality organization is a theoretical construct intended to help us conceptualize an abstract, intangible reality. In real life, people do not fit neatly into mutually exclusive categories. The defense mechanisms that are characteristic of a particular personality organization also tend to overlap with other organizations. As a result, the list of discreet personality organizations has been a point of discussion among theorists and will vary. Nonetheless, a typical list will likely include some of the following organizations: dissociative, histrionic, obsessive-compulsive, dependent, depressive, manic, paranoid, schizoid, avoidant, psychopathic (antisocial), borderline[6], narcissistic, and self-defeating (masochistic).

Perhaps some of these categories are familiar to you. It is beyond the scope of this book to discuss the dominant operating defenses for each category. My purpose for enumerating these personality organizations here is to invite you to consider the richness of descriptors, become more aware of these categories from a professional standpoint, and pique your curiosity toward further education and self-awareness.[7]

It is also humbling to come to the realization that all of us—every one of us—can be characterized by our defense mechanisms and personality organization or combinations thereof, by the very patterns that we would like to shield from external scrutiny. The experience of undergoing psychotherapy or psychological testing is enlightening for a couple reasons. First, pastors are challenged to learn about themselves and to come to terms with the patterns that foster unhealthy behaviors and thinking. Second, pastors learn empathy for those individuals coming to them seeking guidance for the concerns of life. Every counselee will experience pangs of shame or embarrassment when presented with unfavorable feedback, fear of vulnerability when the therapist begins to rummage around in the dark recesses of the counselee's spirit, and defensive anger when the therapist's insights are unnervingly astute, profound, and accurate. Pastors are not exempt from the disquieting feelings experienced in psychotherapy.

Pastors' experiences in psychotherapy foster a more empathetic, more compassionate, humbler, and gentler attitude when working with parishioners who themselves seek counseling and guidance from pastors.

Psychotherapy—particularly psychoanalytic psychotherapy—has its drawbacks. It can be experienced as unsettling, intrusive, and judgmental. It is best undertaken when an individual has adequate ego strength to tolerate the uneasiness of feeling vulnerable and analyzed. A good psychotherapist is able to facilitate self-examination at a pace that is comfortably tolerated by the patient, but the insights gleaned in the process will nonetheless generate at least occasional discomfort, contemplative self-examination, self-reproach, and a sense of intense vulnerability.

Character and Temperament

Another approach to understanding personality comes in the form of examining character and temperament. Many have had the experience of completing a character or temperament inventory as part of a team-building project, evaluation for employment, in pre-marital counseling, or other situations in which the focus is on learning how individuals relate to each other. Temperament/character inventories have the advantage that results are generally not perceived as negative or critical. The temperaments are presented simply as "ways of being" with no diagnostic indicators with respect to health and mental distress. Education is available to increase the participants' awareness of their relational styles with people of other temperaments, and how participants might modify behaviors to relate more effectively with others. Most people tolerate this approach well and even welcome the opportunity to participate.

One of the most accessible, understandable temperament frameworks is David Keirsey's and Marilyn Bates' work, *Please Understand Me: Character and Temperament Types.*[8] Drawing from the more elaborate and intricate Myers-Briggs Temperament Inventory (MBTI), the Keirsey Temperament Sorter systematizes temperament across four axes:

- *I*ntroversion–*E*xtraversion (where people derive their energy, either from interaction from others or from their internal world of ideas and reflection)
- I*N*tuitive/*S*ensing (the perceiving functions; how people gather information about the world)
- *T*hinking/*F*eeling (the judging functions; how people make decisions)
- *J*udging/*P*erceiving (whether people prefer the perceiving or judging functions when relating to their world)

Assessing preferences along the four axes then identifies temperament. Using these four axes, a total of sixteen discreet temperament styles can be identified. The sixteen temperaments are coded using the highlighted letters for the polarities of each axis (shown above). For example, individuals who derive energy from interaction with other people (*E*xtraversion), prefer the *S*ensing function over the intuitive function, prefer the *T*hinking function over the feeling function, and prefer to engage the *P*erceiving functions when relating to their world have a temperament which is coded ESTP.

INTP	INFP	ENFP	ENTP
INTJ	INFJ	ENFJ	ENTJ
ISTJ	ISFJ	ESFJ	ESTJ
ISTP	ISFP	ESFP	ESTP

Table 1. Myers-Briggs/Keirsey Temperament Types

One of the benefits of this construct is that the behavioral patterns and preferences for each temperament type have been well-researched and validated. The cognitive (thinking) and affective (emotional, feeling) patterns for each temperament type have been described, and relational styles between temperament types are quite predictable. In their book, Keirsey and Bates have done a good job of depicting the behavioral patterns, relational styles, the areas of potential difficulty, and relational challenges for each temperament type.

Facing God, Facing Ourselves

Ministry is hard work, entails sacrifice, comes with risks, and requires honesty and authenticity. As with all people, ministers will give an account to God for themselves: "So then, each of us will give an account of himself to God" (Rom. 14:12). In Hebrews, we are further reminded that while we may hide from others and ourselves, we cannot hide from God. "Nothing in all creation is hidden from God's sight. Everything is uncovered and laid bare before the eyes of him to whom we must give account" (Heb. 4:13). While we may not want to be aware of the less becoming parts of our spirits, we can rest assured that anything we find lurking in the shadows is already known by God. Our standing with God is not diminished or demoted and thus God has provided for us the perfect model of unconditional acceptance. God beckons us to follow suit, practicing compassion and mercy toward those for whom we care and ourselves.

Not only will we give an account to God for our own selves, but Hebrews 13:17 suggests that ministers will also be held accountable for the care they provide to their flocks. The prophets Isaiah (*e.g.*, chap. 56), Jeremiah (*e.g.*, chap. 23) and Ezekiel (*e.g.*, chap. 34) prophesied against the shepherds who mismanaged the care of their flocks. So, ministry is not a vocation or calling to be undertaken lightly, given that we will be giving account for the quality of our ministry.

Ministry is primarily a function of presence. It is the use and sharing of the self for the comfort, healing, affirmation, and exhortation of others. The most powerful and efficacious presence is one infused with integrity, authenticity, and empathy. The more mature and developed the traits of integrity, authenticity, and empathy, the more compelling is our presence. The more compelling our presence as ministers, the more we have to offer those we serve and the more our presence can benefit them. However, none of these traits—integrity, authenticity, or empathy—can exist apart from a penetrating and accurate self-knowledge.

Integrity is the quality of behaving consistently and congruently with stated moral and ethical standards. It has been said that integrity is "doing the right thing even when no one else is watching." It is also doing the right thing even when it is inconvenient. It is doing the right thing because it is the right thing, not because we want people to think more highly of us. We cannot act according to our values and moral standards when our behavior is being influenced or driven by baser, more archaic psychological needs that remain submerged in our unconscious and that compete with the loftier virtues that require conscious choice, empathy, and sacrifice. Parishioners who detect a lack of integrity in the pastor will eventually disregard and distrust the pastor's leadership, guidance, and presence.

When what we project on the outside is congruent with what we are on the inside, we exhibit the quality of *authenticity*. Incongruence between the outward presentation (our "presence") and inner existence is readily detected by others and leads to mistrust and relational distance. An effective ministry of presence depends on others' recognition of our authenticity. If we are controlled by shame and driven by the need to project a censored and sanitized façade, we are not authentic.

When we are able to identify with others' feelings, struggles, and pain, we are using *empathy* as a way of expressing presence. Just as God is our rock—our steadfast "holding environment"—we can provide a safe, steadfast, and nonjudgmental environment for parishioners who need to feel understood and supported by exercising empathy. Empathy is "joining with," not "doing for." Unless we are sufficiently individuated to identify with others' feelings without being overcome by those feelings or feeling compelled to rescue, we cannot practice empathy effectively. Without clarity on where the boundaries of responsibility lie, we will sink into the morass of others' struggles and our presence becomes impotent.

Solid, healthy, and effective ministry depends on the development of integrity, authenticity, and empathy, which in turn rely on accurate and penetrating self-knowledge. Without these traits, ministry will be ineffective and potentially damaging. The best way to face God as we give an account of our ministry is to face ourselves first.

Time to Reflect

1. Can you remember a time when you shocked yourself by something you did or said? What did you learn about yourself as a result?
2. If you have completed a temperament or character inventory, what did you think of the results? What did you learn about your relational style?
3. How have you been able to extend what you have learned to your present relationships and ministry?
4. List a few things about yourself that you would prefer no one know about. Take a moment to scan your body for physical sensations that are aroused by completing this exercise.
5. How can you continue to remind yourself of your status as a "free man" or "free woman," i.e., freed from law of sin and death (Rom. 8:2). How might you use your status to confront feelings of shame when they crop up?

CHAPTER 6

In Pursuit of Truth

"Then you will know the truth, and the truth will set you free."

JOHN 8:32

Effective ministry depends on accurate self-knowledge. But how do we go about seeking the Truth of ourselves? You are familiar with Jesus' words, "I am the way and the truth and the life" (Jn. 14:6a). Jesus was referring to the path by which people can approach God: "No one comes to the Father except through me" (v. 6b). However, in chapter 8, John also connected knowing the Son of God with freedom from slavery to sin:

> To the Jews who had believed him, Jesus said, "If you hold to my teaching, you are really my disciples. Then you will know the truth, and the truth will set you free."
>
> They answered him, "We are Abraham's descendants and have never been slaves of anyone. How can you say that we shall be set free?"
>
> Jesus replied, "I tell you the truth, everyone who sins is a slave to sin. Now a slave has no permanent place in the family, but a son belongs to it forever. So if the Son sets you free, you will be free indeed. (Jn. 8:31–36)

If you have ever found yourself failing miserably at changing an undesirable habit or pattern, or have wondered why it is so easy to spew angry words at those you love the most, or told an off-color joke and cringed later, then Paul's words will resonate with you:

> I do not understand what I do. For what I want to do I do not do, but what I hate I do... As it is, it is no longer I myself who do it, but it is sin living in me... For what I do is not the good I want to do; no, the evil I do not want to do–this I keep on doing. (Rom. 7:15, 17, 19)

While the psychological concept of a personality rulebook (which carries no moral connotations), and the "sin nature" that Paul speaks of (which does have moral connotations) are not exact parallels, I do believe that our rulebooks are permeated with the effects of our sinful nature. Using the working definition of sin as violation of the boundary between God and ourselves–trying to *be* God or be *like* God (Gen. 3:5)–then "sin nature" is the propensity to behave in ways that violate that boundary. The unconscious defenses that we develop in response to psychological injuries are our attempts to be God. They are attempts to imbue ourselves with value, to bestow significance on ourselves, to make ourselves "a little lower than the angels," and to crown ourselves with honor. All those things are God's prerogative, God's business:

> What is man that you are mindful of him,
> the son of man that you care for him?
> You made him a little lower than the heavenly beings
> and crowned him with glory and honor.
> You made him ruler over the works of your hands;
> you put everything under his feet. (Ps. 8:4–6)

We are driven to find significance in our activity and success, rather than in relationship with God (Am. 5). To feel acceptable, we try to please others rather than please God (Mic. 6:6–8 and Acts 5:29). We attempt to calm our existential fears with a host of behaviors, relationships, and addictions rather than accepting the peace made for us through Christ (Eph. 2:13–14). In other words, our spirits yearn for peace, security, acceptability, value, and significance that only God is capable of filling.[1] Yet we attempt to fill those needs ourselves with behaviors, relationships, and beliefs. We usurp God's rightful place in our lives as Creator. Violation of this boundary with God produces a ripple effect with increasing amplitude in the concentric rings of our world, resonating in everything we do until our entire lives are permeated with the results of the most cardinal of sins.

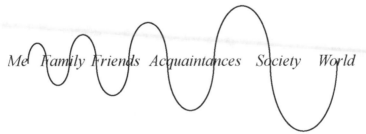

Me Family Friends Acquaintances Society World

Figure 1. Effect of boundary violations are amplified as they reverberate throughout creation

Is It Hopeless?

Go back and read the last couple paragraphs again. What are your reactions? Even in writing this, I find myself thinking: "My goodness, am I really that bad? Is humankind really that reprehensible? Ugh!" Adam and Eve were unable to face God and the significance of their transgression. I do not suppose that it will be any easier for us, especially given that as a race we have had thousands of years experience hiding from God and ourselves.

Our condition would indeed be desperate were it not for the gift of reconciliation–thanks be to God! But let us not skim too hastily over the reality of our brokenness. There is no healing, no growth, and no redemption without confession. Even though we may be reconciled to God by the work of the Last Adam, we are not free from the bondage to decay (Rom. 8:21) of this present world or of the sin shackles of our nature. After all, we still have to live in this world, and it is still a mess. "Ugh!" is indeed an appropriate reaction. We echo Paul's thoughts: "We know that the whole creation has been groaning as in the pains of childbirth right up to the present time. Not only so, but we ourselves, who have the firstfruits of the Spirit, groan inwardly as we wait eagerly for our adoption as sons, the redemption of our bodies" (Rom. 8:22–23). So even though we have the gift of reconciliation to God (2 Cor. 5:18), we continue to wait for the redemption of our bodies.

This tension between the "already" and "not yet," of having been reconciled yet waiting for redemption, presents an interesting challenge. Shall we live as free men, or slaves to sin and shame? Freedom is ours, but we must be willing to walk away from the shackles. The shackles, having been broken by Christ's resurrection, no longer bind us in the dungeon of death. However, we often forget that we are not bound; we forget that we are free to walk out. Sometimes, we walk out into the light of the gospel, only to return to the rancid stench of shame. It is understandable. Shame is our most familiar emotional state, we having been born into sin (Ps. 51:5).

The propensity to return to a familiar albeit miserable state of existence is well documented in the field of psychology. People tend to resist change, even for the better, if change entails living in a less familiar environment. If one family member begins to exert change toward a more healthy and individuated–less enmeshed–dynamic, other family members will redouble their efforts to return the family dynamics to their original state, regardless of how chaotic and damaging the original state was. Physically or emotionally abused individuals repeatedly return to their abusive mates after they initially walk away from the shackles and begin to heal from their physical or psychological wounds, even though there is no consistent indication that the abusive partner's behavior has changed. The abused person often will comment, "I miss my spouse," "I just can't live without him/her," "I don't know how to survive on my own," "He/she is not really *that* abusive," "Maybe if I come back, he/she will see that I want things to be better," "Maybe this time things will be different."

As demonstrated in chapter 5, it is human nature (beginning with Adam and Eve) to act on our shame instead of our guilt when confronted with shortcomings, our boundary violations, and our transgressions. Living in the freedom of God's grace entails confronting the reality of our shame-shackled natures, confessing our short-comings, and seeking the Truth about our hearts, so that we can choose a better path and pursue the freedom we have been granted. It is work, it takes courage, it requires patience. But it is not hopeless.

Confronting Shame, Confronting Sin

Shame is experienced differently depending on personality. Some personality types favor repression of shame while other types are organized around an acute, conscious sense of shame. Two very different experiences of shame are illustrated in the stories of Ann (A Parishioner Tells Her Story) and Joe (Special Friends). Ann experienced crippling shame for years after her pastor abused her, while Joe exhibited little if any shame for his behavior, even though he was responsible for the abuse he perpetrated on his parishioner Kat. An absence of awareness of shame does not signal that shame does not exist in an individual's spirit, or that it does not influence behavior and thinking. The influence and potency of shame may vary from person to person, but, at some level, shame affects all of us, with one exception.

A small group of individuals live without any awareness of shame whatsoever. Within the behavioral health professions, these people are diagnosed as having a psychopathic or sociopathic personality organization. They do not report much by way of feelings or affect at all, except possibly pleasure from highly stimulating, jolting experiences and blind rage. These individuals lie at one extreme of the scale of experienced shame. Their lives illustrate the tragedy of shame's absence: no shame, no guilt, no conscience, no ability to empathize and therefore a total inability to relate to others.

More toward the middle of the shame scale, some people have buried their sense of shame deeply in their unconscious. It is barely accessible, but is experienced occasionally. The awareness of shame surfaces when a behavior is met with external disapproval or is perceived internally as being objectionable. In these situations, shame is experienced as embarrassment, a hot face, a strong urge to curl up and hide, dread, slumping head and shoulders, or avoidance of eye contact. When confronted with their behavior, or when experiencing shame feelings, their primary reactions are defensiveness ("Look, I was just trying to…"), deflection ("I'm not the only one who loses her temper when…"), minimization ("I didn't *mean* to!" or "At least I didn't…"), justification ("You don't know the whole story!" or, "You would have done the same thing if you were in my shoes."), self-contempt ("I'm a real screw-up"), self-berating ("What was I thinking?"), and so on.

Moving further to the opposite pole, shame increases its grip and influence. The daily lives of these individuals are permeated with an all-too-vivid sense of shame. Every breath is wretched. They struggle desperately to escape from humiliation and a sense of defectiveness and emptiness. Shame may be experienced as a crushing weight on the chest, feelings of panic, despair, and frantic efforts to gain validation. Shame this dominant and powerful is usually accompanied by excessive guilt, hopelessness, and worthlessness. It cripples, immobilizes, incapacitates.

Shame is not always a bad thing. Shame that is legitimate and proportionate to the "crime" can provoke us to reconsider our behavior and commit to change. However, remember the difference between shame and guilt: guilt is the feeling that I did something wrong; shame morphs the guilt of doing something wrong into self-contempt: "I am bad." Shame is generally outward-focused; guilt is an internal experience. We feel shameful because of how others—either God or people—judge us or because of our fear of how others *might* judge us. On the other hand, we feel guilty because our conscience condemns us (Rom. 2:15).

For shame to be useful, it must be confronted. It must be acknowledged as a symptom rather than a judgment of self-worth. It can be a symptom of illegitimate contempt or legitimate guilt for wrongdoing, boundary violation, or trespass. Sometimes shame is related to specific behaviors and choices we have made, while at other times shame is related to cognitive patterns—distorted beliefs about ourselves. Once we recognize the feeling of shame and identify the precipitant (why am I feeling shameful?), we can do something about it. Do I need to confess something to God or to another person? Do I need to make amends? Do I need to change the attitude of my heart? Is my thinking distorted? Am I doubting my worth to God? Do I believe my life is insignificant? Am I worried that others think I am loathsome, disfigured, or undesirable?

Most importantly, having addressed what prompted the feelings of shame, it is time to denounce the shame. "I found error in my ways; I am changing that. I have asked for mercy and God has granted me forgiveness. I have no reason to hide anymore." King David did just that:

> Have mercy on me, O God,
>   according to your unfailing love;
> according to your great compassion
>   blot out my transgressions.
> Wash away all my iniquity
>   and cleanse me from my sin.
> For I know my transgressions,
>   and my sin is always before me...
> Restore to me the joy of your salvation
>   and grant me a willing spirit, to sustain me. (Ps. 51:1–3, 12)

David goes on to say that after being forgiven, he will teach others, declare God's praise, and sing of the Lord's righteousness. That is hardly the spirit of a man who is paralyzed by shame!

The Deception of Half-Truths

Some shame results from distorted beliefs, rather than from specific failures, trespasses, or boundary violations. It might be argued that a distorted belief is the equivalent of telling oneself a lie, which, of course, is sin (Lev. 19:11). However, distorted beliefs about ourselves are particularly pernicious.

- They sound so believable.
- They make self-examination all the more daunting.
- They activate defensiveness, minimization, deflection, excuse-making.
- They distract us from the Truth about God.
- They cripple our spirits by breeding fear.
- They usually have some measure of Truth, but it is clouded by the suffocating fear of being found worthless.

Let's do an autopsy on a distorted belief. John, having been married fifteen years, engages in an affair with a young supervisee at his workplace. After the affair crumbles and ends badly, the young lady presses charges against John for sexual harassment. He is terminated after investigation and, with the history of the affair made public, his wife divorces him. John loses his job, his financial security, and his family. Shame pervades his spirit and he isolates himself socially, becomes clinically depressed and unproductive. Three years later, tenuous attempts at a job search yield an offer, although for a position that is well below his level of education and experience. John begins the tortured process of trying to decide whether he should take the job.

John must decide within five days whether or not he will take the new position. The recurring theme in his thinking is, "I've really made a mess of my life. It's never going to get any better." At the deadline, he still has not made up his mind. He does not call the manager back with his decision; eventually the position is offered to another applicant. Having failed to act decisively on the offer, John believes that the loss of this opportunity is further confirmation that his life will never get any better.

A belief like this is rarely conscious. Rather, the individual is just never quite able to redeem the opportunities; he sabotages his future by indecision and psychological paralysis. In our case study, John cannot even acknowledge his self-defeatist attitude. This illustrates the unconscious influence that shame exerts on our choices and actions (or lack thereof).

If John should at some point consciously voice his distorted belief, those around him may validate his belief. John's ex-wife is quick to remind him, "Yeah, you've sure done some stupid things. You made your bed—you sleep in it." There is some truth to the distorted belief; he *has* destroyed his marriage and lost his job because of sexual misconduct. Now John extends his beliefs: "I'm the one who messed things up. I really can't expect God to bail me out. I'm an embarrassment to him, I'm sure." He has now subtly shifted the focus away from his responsibility to move forward and onto why he can't expect God to help him.

John is stuck in a rut, he believes, not because he made unwise choices and is hiding in shame, but because God isn't going to bail him out. John believes that, having messed up his life, he is unqualified for redemption and that the locus of control to improve his situation lies outside of himself, that he is a passive bystander in the narrative of his own life.

The shame underlying the distorted belief is crippling him. It creates fear of rejection and judgment and prevents him from examining his true guilt (similar to what Adam and Eve did). And so, his life never gets any better. The story should not have to end this way. John made the mistake of extending "I made a mess of my life" to "It will never get any better," The first half was true. The second half was a lie (until he turned it into a self-fulfilling prophecy). Identifying and correcting our distorted beliefs is challenging. But it is critical to having healthy boundaries and a healthy ministry. Truth goes hand in hand with vibrant life.

Getting at the Truth

We have seen how important it is to identify and confront shame and its effects on our spirits. That is a good place to start, but it is not the total solution. We confront the shame in order to break through our defensiveness, so that we can explore the "real" Truth: the unique and preferred style that each one of us has developed for interfacing with our world, protecting ourselves from anxiety, fulfilling our needs, and challenging God's rightful role in our lives. Learning about ourselves is a lifelong process and we will not learn much if we are not intentional about it.

Numerous practices, disciplines, and activities can help pastors discover what lies beneath their professional persona and conscious awareness. All of these will be much more effective when the detrimental effects of shame are being arrested as discussed earlier in this chapter. I will divide the practices by sphere: spiritual, personal, and relational.

Spiritual Practices

Spiritual mentoring. This can take the form of discipleship, spiritual direction, spiritual guidance, and other one-on-one mentoring relationships that focus on the mentee's spiritual development. Self-awareness is not necessarily the goal for all topics of exploration and guidance. However, inasmuch as increased spiritual understanding serves as a mirror that reflects our inner selves, spiritual mentoring is a powerful mechanism for self-discovery.

Selection of a spiritual mentor need not be an arduous process. We all have had unstructured conversations with people who shed light on a current personal concern or situation and we then recognize the wisdom and value of their insights. We can find mentors among the elderly, children, spiritual leaders from within and without our denomination or religious tradition, friends who have walked similar paths, and those whose paths challenge our comprehension. Several keys to an effective mentoring relationship are the mentor's ability to listen for what remains unspoken, to ask the questions that we resist answering, and to communicate insights with clarity. Qualities of an effective mentor aside, we as mentees are responsible for whatever benefit we receive from a mentoring relationship. We do not benefit from the relationship by virtue of having arranged it, but by being transparent and open to divergent ideas and insights that arouse contemplation.

Private worship. Worship is the act of giving due reverence to the object of adoration–in this case, God Almighty. What reverence and homage is due the Creator of the universe? *All* reverence. No one, nothing else deserves our reverence. We must know something of the nature of the One we worship, if only the stark disparity between God's infiniteness and our finiteness. Worship is an act, but it is also an attitude. It is an attitude of humility stemming from a continuous awareness of the presence of God in our daily lives, in our every step, and within ourselves. Cultivating within ourselves an attitude of worship allows us to experience the awe of God's transcendence and otherness juxtaposed to God's imminence and desire for relationship. This begets a posture of humility in our spirits, which enables us to pursue accurate self-knowledge and appreciate God's perspective of our humanity–glory, brokenness, and all.

Because clergy prepare and lead public worship as part of their profession, private worship is sometimes neglected. Unfortunately, leading public worship requires a heightened level of cognitive awareness. It is hard to worship with all of our heart and soul when our minds are juggling the order of worship! Our private worship requires no stage presence, no mental reminders, no vestments, no awareness of anyone else except the Lord. For pastors, private worship may be one of the few periods of spiritual rest.[2]

Private study and meditation. Beyond the act of worship, private study and meditation on the Word of God enhance our understanding of God's nature, our nature, and our relationship with God. Study allows us to learn; meditation allows Truth to penetrate our spirits and take root in our minds. "The word of God is living and active. Sharper than any double-edged sword, it penetrates even to dividing soul and spirit, joints and marrow; it judges the thoughts and attitudes of the heart" (Heb. 4:12). What better way to test the attitudes and motives of our hearts than to submit to the penetrating discernment of God's Word. As a tandem benefit, we also enjoy the blessings, promises, and overtures of love that God has conveyed to us through scripture!

Most people prefer sensate cognition over spiritual insightfulness. Some of the "higher order" defense mechanisms involve the overuse of cognition (*e.g.,* rationalization, intellectualization, moralization) to the exclusion of other forms of awareness. Ministers are highly susceptible to the temptation to *think* their way through life. Seminary training emphasizes the acquisition of knowledge; sermon preparation is all about literary and historical criticism, exegesis, word analysis, thesis formation, and so on; the demands of day-to-day ministry require a certain level of emotional detachment to protect oneself from empathy overload and burnout. So our goals may include meditating on scripture, quieting our minds and cognitive chatter, increasing body awareness, emotional attunement, or spiritual consciousness.

To support a healthy balance between sound mind and tender heart, meditation offers an unparalleled benefit. It exercises the spirit, quiets the mind, and reduces the clattering of nonessential external stimuli. Spiritually, it allows the Truth of God to percolate through our spirits without cognitive distortion. And it strengthens our spiritual stamina as we embark on the unsettling quest for the Truth about ourselves.[3]

Prayer. Prayer is more than the act of dumping our wishes on God. It is communion with God and an affirmation of our openness to God's communication with us. In prayer we can echo David's plea: "Search me, O God, and know my heart; test me and know my anxious thoughts. See if there is any offensive way in me, and lead me in the way everlasting" (Ps. 139:23–24).

Psalm 139 is an excellent prayer-psalm, a starting point for conversation with God. David begins by acknowledging that the Lord knows everything about him, and yet that he is safe and protected by God's presence and cannot do anything or go anywhere that God will not be to guide and protect him. David recognizes that God created him by God's design, for God's purpose, and that he was wonderfully made. He then exclaims that God's thoughts for him are precious and vast, that even when he is asleep, God's attention is still on him as he awakens. For a moment, David's focus turns toward God's greater purposes. He pleads with God to address those who rise up against God and expresses his allegiance. Quickly he returns to his personal concerns–anxious thoughts and motives of his heart. He invites God's examination of his spirit and guidance toward a fulfilling and enduring (everlasting) life.

Because we know that God will not be overwhelmed by our heartfelt cries and that our neediness will not undo the Lord, there is security in running to God when we are contending with any situation common to the human condition. It also helps us to quiet our spirits, to listen for insights and understanding that may arise from deep within our spirits and from the Holy Spirit.

Personal Practices

Personal time. Probably more than any other professionals, pastors experience the incessant and urgent demands on their time, emotional availability, and empathy. Because pastors minister with their presence and it is difficult to separate personal and professional spheres, personal space is easily eroded. Maintaining a healthy and balanced amount of personal time is paramount. Scheduling personal time into each week affords pastors the downtime needed to relax, rest, reflect, recreate, and rejuvenate. Self-awareness and examination cannot be effectively pursued without this downtime, when the spirit is quiet and undisturbed by external demands.

Personal time is *not* time to catch up on work, take care of personal business, tend to friendships, help a child with homework, or take an ailing parent to the doctor. It is time to tend to the needs of self. Each of us has needs specific to our physical and psychological makeup. We may have greater or lesser need for time alone, casual social interaction, affirmation and validation from others, tangible personal industriousness, learning and mental stimulation, creative activity, physical exercise and challenge, affection and love, entertainment, and reflection. Often an unmet need or a need that is out of conscious awareness becomes a driving force behind ministry failure and boundary violations within ministry. We must first *know* what we need and then be intentional about filling our personal needs in healthy and productive ways. Joe's story is a good example of what happens when we do not guard personal time. Joe was very industrious in his ministry but completely out of touch with his spirit, eventually to the point of not even recognizing the gross violation of sexual misconduct.

Retreat. Even the best self-care cannot substitute for occasional retreat. Retreat allows us to separate ourselves from the routines, roles, goals, and expectations that govern our daily lives. Routine and roles give us direction; goals and expectations give us drive. But excessive direction and drive eventually desensitizes our spirits and blinds us to new possibilities and insight. It dries up our creativity and squelches our awareness of the Holy Spirit's direction.

Most of us think, "Ah, retreat sounds so good; I would *love* a time of retreat!" Then we turn our attention to the activities for today. Occasionally, we get burned out enough that we seriously contemplate our need for a retreat. It just never happens. But retreat is vital to our well-being and pursuit of self-knowledge. The purpose of retreat is *nothing*. In retreat, we experience the sense of *being* rather than doing. It provides the time and space to give expression to our essence as *human beings* rather than human doings. Any activity during retreat is born out of who I am, not from what I do.[4]

Solitude. Solitude may be practiced as part of retreat. However, it can also be practiced within the confines of our daily routines. Among the spiritual disciplines, solitude is highly regarded because of its ability to reduce the noise and chatter of the physical world and allow the spirit to attune itself to God's presence. Its focus is on the removal or blocking of externally fed stimulation–TV, radio, street noise, conversation and small talk, ringing phones and pagers, e-mail, texting, social networking via Internet, and so on. In contrast, the focus of retreat is the experience of being apart from the roles that drive daily life. The practice of solitude is intentional, for a predetermined period of time. It should not be confused with isolation or withdrawal, which are unconscious reactions to emotional pain or overload.

It may not be possible to eliminate all sources of external stimulation, but the more the better. The chaotic, shrill, accelerating, and incessant pounding of today's electronic age has become an addiction in its own right. People tend to rely on this stimulation as a distraction from emotional, cognitive, and spiritual tension or dissonance. Do you automatically turn on the radio, listen to music, or pick up voice mail when you drive off in your vehicle? Do you leave the television on so there is some background noise in your home? Do you get lonely easily if you do not have frequent or constant interaction with other people? Do you check and respond to e-mail all day and well into the night as a way to stay connected? These may be signs of an overreliance on or addiction to external distraction.

People who are naturally introverted may find the practice of solitude less difficult to implement. However, whether introverted or extraverted, we all benefit from designated times of quiet, when our spirits must search for peace and comfort from within and learn to sustain our self-concept without immediate availability of affirmation and validation from outside sources. We must acclimate to being alone without becoming lonely. Ideas for the practice of solitude include

- a walk alone through a park
- thirty minutes in a hot tub/sauna
- a day with no technology–no phones, no e-mail, no Internet, no TV, no radio, no CD player, etc.
- a day of silence
- a weekend, week, or 30-day stay at a silent retreat
- sitting in an easy chair while cuddling a sleeping baby
- driving to work with no radio or CD playing, no phone calls, no passengers–simply listening to silence

Psychotherapy. Counseling or psychotherapy provide the opportunity to explore recesses of the spirit that are out of reach to normal conscious awareness, including the personality "rulebook," memories that have receded from consciousness due to "selective inattention,"[5] and aspects of ourselves that we have disowned (or split off, in psychological parlance). In psychotherapy, we enlist the aid of a trained outside observer to read between the lines of our story and to interpret back to us the patterns that we repeat unaware. It provides an environment in which we can safely, without fear of judgment, sift through less-than-attractive aspects of our selves–broken dreams, repudiated anger and disillusionment, unacknowledged grief, shame and guilt, patterns of addiction, resistance to personal responsibility, intolerance toward change, and ambivalence.

Generally, the biggest disadvantage of psychotherapy is its cost. Medical insurance may subsidize mental health services if a mental health disorder can be diagnosed. When we are experiencing extreme emotional turmoil, as with a major depressive episode, our immediate focus is on resolving the symptoms to regain a baseline level of functioning. Psychotherapy is indispensable to recovery from mental disorders such as anxiety, depression, and bipolar disorder.

However, we do not need to experience a psychological crisis in order to seek counseling. Nor do we need to wait for tragedy or emotional upheaval before we implement change. There is something to be said for pursuing self-discovery when our lives are *not* in tumult. Psychotherapists– especially those with analytic or psychodynamic training–are able to work with the client toward greater self-awareness within the context of the client's ordinary experience.

Emotional recovery and Twelve-Step groups. Another avenue for self-examination is what has been dubbed "emotional recovery," often in the form of Twelve-Step groups. The principles of the Twelve Steps originated with Alcoholics Anonymous, but have been extended to other forms of emotional recovery–from addictions to food, shopping, sex, gambling, mood swings, codependence[6], etc. For our purposes, the Twelve Steps provide a framework for identifying behavior patterns that are intended to manage our emotional pain or unmet needs. The Twelve Steps acknowledge our difficulty in controlling our unconsciously driven and addictive behaviors, our need for redemption from slavery to those behaviors by a "Higher Power"–God–and the lifelong process of learning to live free of the shackles created by addiction and shame.[7]

As with most social movements, debate has stewed and brewed between supporters and detractors of "the program." There has been debate over whether the Twelve Steps are truly "Christian," whether those of religious traditions other than Christianity can call on a "Higher Power," whether the steps should be worked through in the context of a group or individually, whether they are equally applicable to areas of emotional recovery besides the abuse of chemical substances, and so on. Nevertheless, thousands upon thousands of people have been greatly helped by working through the Twelve Steps and, ultimately, their success is owed to their commitment to working through the steps and to recovery in general, not the validity of various pundits' opinions.

Most important, whether or not we openly struggle with unwanted behavior or addiction, the Twelve Steps provide a framework for examining ourselves, pondering the possibility that our behavior has been or is detrimental to others. It can be a very productive undertaking for self-assessment and examination.

Relational Practices

Personal and family relationships. Pastors often find themselves so consumed with the relational demands of ministry that little energy remains for cultivating and nurturing personal relationships. The relational drain is high. Once pastors "leave the office" for the day, they may have no interest in relating to anyone at all the rest of the day (or night). Yet pastors need personal relationships, relationships that have nothing to do with vocational ministry, relationships that nurture pastors as persons[8] and that sustain pastors' personhood independent of their ministry. Gary Harbaugh states, "[T]he whole person is always a person in relationship... [T]he biblical perspective on individuality always includes participation with the community."[9]

Relationships are the mirrors that allow us to see ourselves. Relationships confirm to us that we exist. However, if we study our image carefully in the mirror of relationships, we learn about our features—what we look like on the outside, how we are perceived by others, how our actions are interpreted by others. And while we cannot rely exclusively on the feedback of others[10], their responses to us are nonetheless a significant source of affirmation of our worth, significance, and agency.

Furthermore, personal relationships serve as the testing ground and workout gym for a pastor's integrity and faith. Parish relationships tend to have a role-based quality that protects both pastor and parishioner from inappropriately transparent transactions. The professional boundaries of vocational ministry require this. However, if we never allow greater transparency to select others within our personal relational spheres, we forfeit the blessings of experiencing unconditional acceptance and love, allowing light to reveal the inconsistencies between our inner self and the outward persona we project.

Accountability partnerships. In an accountability partnership, a commitment is made between two people to be unusually transparent and open about personal difficulties and challenges, formally take responsibility for necessary personal change, and answer to the accountability partner for progress toward stated goals. Accountability as a driving force for change is most effective when change is measurable; however, personal growth is very difficult to measure.

Some of the best accountability relationships already exist in our lives: our spouses, our children, our friends. The people who are best suited to hold us accountable are those with whom we share life and who are most directly impacted by our behavior patterns. If I extol the virtues of patience and compassion but lose my temper with my spouse, my spouse is in the best position to call me to account for the behavior and expose the discrepancy between my behavior and the virtues that I claim to value. If I profess to be highly considerate of others but I am habitually late for appointments with a friend, that friend is in a unique position to challenge my lackadaisical time management and inconsiderate behavior.

The effectiveness of accountability partnerships with people outside our daily routines is contingent on the truthfulness and completeness of self-disclosure. The chief disadvantage of accountability partnerships is that because we do such a good job lying to ourselves about the motives of our hearts, we are not very good self-reporters. We begin to believe that the accountability partnership itself is inherent proof of our willingness to submit to evaluation, regardless of our willingness to self-disclose and receive undiluted feedback. The accountability partnership has the potential for becoming another means of constructing a façade that masks the conflicts, guilt, and shame of our inner selves.

Disadvantages aside, accountability partnerships can be an excellent method for self-discovery[11] when both partners are equally committed to disclosure and when the level of transparency is approximately the same for both partners. Pastors who resist self-disclosure in accountability relationships ultimately fool no one but themselves. No matter how diligently we protect our inner selves from discovery, God still knows us completely and, in the end, we are accountable to God for our character work and for those under our care.

Ministerial fellowship groups. Generally speaking, professionals can benefit from exposure and social interaction with others in similar positions from a variety of organizations. Ministers and other clergy typically find support among colleagues for common ministerial challenges, as well as professional advice, personal feedback, and spiritual edification. Camaraderie is precious to those who might otherwise feel isolated because of their leadership positions. In ministerial fellowship groups (sometimes also called ministerial or clergy alliances), pastors can find reassurance for their mutual challenges, wisdom from those who have gone before, and the support to examine underlying personal issues that impact congregational dynamics and the ability to minister effectively. Self-evaluation seems less daunting when shared with others who have experienced or are experiencing similar challenges. Transparency, humility, and admission of personal weakness are less daunting endeavors when we do not feel alone in the pursuit of Truth about ourselves.

Time to Reflect

1. Describe a behavior pattern that you struggle with. Each time you catch yourself doing it, what do you feel inside? Have you felt embarrassed or ashamed of your behavior?

2. What typical signs and symptoms do you experience when feeling embarrassment or shame? How might you protect yourself from the shame? For example, do you: get busy and stay busy? pass the blame? justify your actions? apologize and move on?

3. Are there any themes of shame in your life? For example, if you remember being called "Tinker Bell" in the eighth grade, has that bred shame or embarrassment about being slight and emotionally sensitive?

4. Thinking back on the situation you identified in question 3, how has the shame from that situation influenced your behavioral patterns today?

5. Think back on a time when you made a serious blunder. You trespassed and you knew it. How did you deal with your trespass? Did shame take a foothold? Did it take a while before you could bring yourself to confess? Were you able to release the shame? If you are still struggling with shame and guilt, take steps now to speak with a trusted friend, a spiritual leader, or counselor.

6. When was the last time you assessed your specific personal needs? What are they? Do you care for yourself with the same compassion and attention as you do for those in your congregation?

7. What practices have you pursued to maintain your health and increase your self-awareness? How have these practices benefited you?

8. Are there areas that you have neglected or would like to develop? Choose one now to focus on. What can you do *right now* to begin implementing a new practice in your life for the purpose of strengthening your ministry effectiveness?

CHAPTER 7

The Measure of Our Character

Step 4: "Made a searching and fearless moral inventory of ourselves."

ALCOHOLICS ANONYMOUS BIG BOOK

"If I take care of my character, my reputation will take care of itself."

D. L. MOODY (1837–1899)

Having laid a foundation for self-discovery, we press on to face what we uncover in the closets of our spirits. What do we keep, what do we want to remove? By what yardstick do we measure the motives of the heart?

Making a "searching and fearless moral inventory of ourselves" requires effort, courage, wisdom, and, most importantly, compassion. Self-examination may be conducted as an intentional exercise to survey an accumulation of patterns and defenses, but it is ultimately most effective as a progressive lifelong habit. Why did I do that? Did I do it to prove something? Was I acting in my own interests to the exclusion of the interests of those around me? Did I act harshly or with grace? The goal of examining our motives, urges, and defenses; the thoughts behind our actions; and the emotions that accompany our responses to the world is not to second-guess everything we do. The goal is to become familiar with the contents of our personality "rulebooks."

Gary McIntosh and Samuel Rima, in their book *Overcoming the Dark Side of Leadership,* propose that everyone has a "dark side," which is as natural to human beings as shadows are in a world bathed in sunlight. Pastors need to become aware of their dark side—the inner urges, compulsions, and dysfunctions—and then redeem it; that is, manage it: redirect those potentially "dark side" patterns and compensate for them.[1]

The dark side of our personalities is not something to be feared but rather reckoned with. My tendency to manipulate other people's behavior can be redeemed by redirecting my sensitivity to others' reactions for consensus building. My compulsion to avoid conflict can be refocused into assertive peacemaking. I can transform my efforts to portray an air of confidence into a realistic assessment of my abilities and exude confidence in pursuing what I do best. My impatience with others' lack of progress toward team goals may be reworked into valuable project management skills.

Jesus Loves Me, This I Know

Without a balanced appreciation of the magnificence of our God-image offset by our penchant for trying to replace our need for God with other things, a moral inventory may lead to dejection or even despair. But we are not lost causes. The bedrock of Christian faith tells us so: "For God so loved the world that he gave his one and only Son, that whoever believes in him shall not perish but have eternal life" (Jn. 3:16). No matter the state of our hearts, no matter the guilt that we carry for past wrongs, no matter the shame that disfigures us, we are loved with an everlasting love that sees beyond our childish ways and beckons us toward maturity and reconciliation to God.

Does this sound elementary and timeworn? Did you read the previous paragraph and wonder why I would take the time to reassert the basics of our faith? The daily busyness of ministry has a way of obscuring its basis: God's love for us through the gospel of grace. We preach it, teach it, and represent it, but the Truth of God's love still becomes stale and impotent in our own lives unless we purposefully and regularly contemplate its significance and impact at a personal level, apart from our roles as ministers.

Consider this: "Very rarely will anyone die for a righteous man, though for a good man someone might possibly dare to die" (Rom. 5:7). Do you know of anyone who would be willing to die a horrifying, excruciating death for you? Neither do I. "But God demonstrates his own love for us in this: While we were still sinners, Christ died for us" (v. 8). Christ died for us because of God's profound, enduring, and desperate love for us. Christ's actions had nothing to do with our achievements or our righteousness (which cannot be compared to the righteousness of God–Isa. 64:6). Like children "who only a mother could love," we are lovable to the One who made us.

Is the significance of this Truth sinking in? Take some time to meditate on the glorious gift of God's love for you, personally and individually. What emotions are you experiencing as you contemplate God's love for you? Relief? Peace? Confusion? Awe? Shock? Serenity? Joy? Contentedness? Inspiration? Vulnerability? Appreciation? When you put this book down and move on with your day, what will you do differently in your life because of your renewed appreciation of your salvation and the high regard that God has for you?

Taking into account God's inestimable love for you, how do you think God conceives of you? Scripture describes God's thoughts regarding us in many ways. A few descriptors include: precious, God's children, justified, loved, wanted, cherished, protected. As you undertake the process of self-examination, remember to keep God's passion for you at the forefront of your consciousness. Doing so will counteract the temptation to despair or devalue yourself. The purpose of inventorying the motives of our hearts is not to unearth evidence of how broken we are. It is to allow us to function more effectively as ministers and present to God the most valuable offering of thanksgiving that we have—lives marked by integrity, authenticity, and compassion.

Why Do I Do That?

Usually behavior is not the product of a single motive, whether altruistic or self-serving, conscious or unconscious. It is motivated by complex interrelated forces, including personality organization, immediate circumstances, present needs, current emotional state, and reactions to prior events leading up to the behavior. Our actions may also be morally upright, but done for the wrong motives: "All a man's ways seem right to him, but the LORD weighs the heart" (Prov. 21:2). Unacknowledged and unattended motives wreak havoc on our pursuit of healthy and productive lives; those are the motives that must be uncovered and evaluated.

The activity of self-examination may focus on one of several goals: to identify moral failures, to assess competencies, to evaluate the level of autonomy and development of self-esteem, etc. For the purposes of our discussion, we will focus on self-examination of motivations to determine vulnerabilities to boundary violations, and specifically boundary violations in ministry. The practices discussed in chapter 5 facilitate this quest. Even so, earnest soul-searching can easily transform into confusing and mired introspection with no particular conclusion other than bewilderment. It is therefore helpful to have an organized and systematic method for examining our behaviors and the underlying forces in our "rulebooks." Table 1 delineates an assessment process that focuses on the behavior, motives, and possible resulting damage.[2]

Behaviors are listed in *column 1*. The gist of this exercise is not to judge behavior, but to examine the motives behind it. List any behavior, whether you consider the behavior or the motives "right" or "wrong." Be as descriptively accurate as possible: "told Dan off about not getting the report to me" vs. "discussed performance issues with Dan." The list of behaviors can also include "unbehaviors" or inactions; for example, "procrastinated writing Sue a thank you note."

In *column 2*, list your motives for the behavior. Notice the plural form; assume that any behavior is driven by more than one motive. Sift through your thought processes and your heart's recesses to identify as many motives as possible. It may be helpful to list the most apparent (usually the most altruistic) motive first and then work your way down to the more subliminal and self-serving motives.

In identifying motives, it may be helpful to consider Abraham Maslow's hierarchy of needs[3]. Maslow proposed that motivation is driven by innate needs, which exist in a hierarchy, the most basic of which must be fulfilled before higher order needs can be addressed. They are, beginning with the most basic:

1. *physiological:* breathing, food, water, excretion, sleep, sex, homeostasis
2. *safety:* physical/bodily safety, security of employment, family, property, health, moral code, other resources
3. *love and belonging:* family, intimacy, friendship
4. *esteem:* confidence, respect by others, respect for others and self, confidence, achievement, competence
5. *self-actualization:* creativity, morality, problem-solving, lack of prejudice, spontaneity, and acceptance

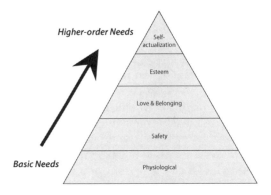

Figure 1. Maslow's Hierarchy of Needs

Another way to identify motives for behavior is to ask this series of questions:

- What is the behavior? (*e.g.,* I remind my spouse every morning to take the kitchen trash out.)
- If I don't act in this way, what do I think will happen? (If I don't remind/nag my spouse to take out the trash every day, my spouse may forget.)
- Why does it matter? (If my spouse forgets to take out the trash, the house will stink and people will think I'm a poor housekeeper; I like an orderly home.)
- What need(s) or desires am I filling? (I want people to view me as a tidy and orderly housekeeper; I need order in my life; I want to know my spouse cares about my feelings.)

Write down what needs and wants you are meeting with this behavior in *column 3*. Then in *column 4* write down the people that you are relying on to fill them. In my example of reminding my spouse to empty the kitchen trash, I am using my spouse to achieve order and feel like I am in control of achieving that level of order. I am using others who enter my home to affirm my appearance as a neat housekeeper.

"Using" other people generally has negative connotations, but this is not necessarily so. How damaging our use of another person is depends on a number of issues:

- Has the other person agreed to be used in this way? (Has my spouse agreed to empty the trash daily? Has my spouse agreed to be reminded daily?)
- Is the expectation that my need be fulfilled by someone else realistic? (Can my spouse realistically empty the trash every morning? Does my spouse realistically require a daily reminder?)
- Is this a need I can reasonably fulfill for myself? (Can I take out the trash too?)
- Am I taking something away from others by my expectation that they fulfill my need? (Am I robbing my spouse of self-esteem by constant nagging?)
- Is the fulfillment of my need the responsibility of another person? (Is it up to my spouse to make me feel organized and competent as a housekeeper?)

Determining what motivates our behavior and who we expect to meet our needs is seldom straightforward. It requires a commitment to honest self-evaluation, time, a hearty dose of sleuthing, and the security of knowing that our worth is not diminished by the discovery.

The Results of What I Do

These questions help us to examine the extent to which we use, misuse, or abuse others. The appropriateness of demands is determined by the distinction between use, misuse, and abuse. Abuse refers to using other people in a manner that injures those people or robs them of something that is rightfully theirs. Abuse is *always* a boundary violation, regardless of the nature of the behavior, because abuse is the abject disrespect for the intrinsic worth of other people. Misuse is defined as using others in a manner outside their intended roles. While misuse may not cause immediate or apparent injury, it often results in relational conflict and can easily transform into abuse.

If I send my spouse to do the grocery shopping, I am using my spouse to get the grocery shopping done. The result is positive; the family has the necessary groceries, I am free to get something else done, and my spouse has contributed to the family's welfare. If I call my spouse three times to remind him to do the grocery shopping so that I can feel comfortably in control of the outcome, I am misusing him. My spouse may dismiss my meddling with "that's just the way she is" and is able to retain self-esteem in spite of my nagging. But upon arrival at home, he may tell me that he did not need three reminder calls and is perfectly capable of planning his own day. With that, I launch into a protest that nothing gets done around the house unless I nag. He turns on the TV to block out my lecturing and the result is relational distance.

No harm is done if I encourage my daughter to study for a test because I want her to achieve academically to the best of her ability. But if I exert pressure on my daughter to study because I want her academic achievement to validate that I am a good parent, I am misusing her. It is not the responsibility of our children to prove our competence as parents. (It *is*, however, her responsibility to learn what she needs to become a self-supporting adult.) And if I harangue her, tell her she is lazy, and denigrate her, I am being abusive because I am robbing her of her self-worth, her confidence, and my respect.

In *column 5,* write down whether you think you are using, misusing, or abusing the person on whom you are relying to meet the need you listed in column 4. A couple examples have been provided on the chart, derived from the vignette of Sam (Loose Lips Sink Ships) from chapter 1. Notice that in this example, Sam's role with Ronald began to change from one of ministry to using Ronald, then misusing, and eventually abusing Ronald because of Sam's ongoing subconscious struggle to feel relevant, effective, and respected.

The purpose of the exercise is to examine actions and motives and to increase awareness of how behavior affects other people. It is not so important that you discern accurately between motive and need—or use, misuse, and abuse—as it is that you give the questions some thought. This is not an exercise that can be completed in a day, or even a week. Optimally, it is an exercise that is best undertaken on a regular basis. Get in the habit of asking yourself, "Why am I doing this?" Even if you do not examine every behavior (it is not possible), over time you will begin to notice patterns in how you fill your needs, which relationships carry the brunt of providing affirmation and self-esteem, and whether your expectations of others are realistic or unreasonable.

Turning Ourselves Around

Having made a "searching and fearless inventory" of ourselves, the logical next question is: What should I do about my hurtful behavior? All of us find areas of our lives that require work, but understand this: the act of identifying areas in our lives where we have violated boundaries does not change who we are. None of our discoveries are news to God. God's view of us, love for us, desires for us have not changed just because we have come face to face with our inadequacies and failures. We have several

Behavior	Motives	What need or desire am I trying to fill?	Who is meeting my need?	Use, misuse or abuse?
Talk to Ronald about stirring up dissension in church	1. want Ronald to learn healthier ways of spearheading movements for change 2. don't want factions in church 3. want contemporary worship style to continue 4. frustrated that Ronald is working against me	1. want to fulfill role of spiritual shepherd in church 2. want church unity 3. want to make a difference at St. John's 4. want to feel respected as pastor and leader	1. Ronald 2. Ronald, church council 3. congregation 4. Ronald	1. use 2. use 3. use 4. misuse
Scold Ronald for taking informal survey of parishioners	1. feel like Ronald is usurping leadership 2. Ronald didn't listen to me the first time I confronted him 3. I am angry with Ronald 4. fear major church conflict	1. need to feel in control 2. need to feel respected 3. need to vent 4. feel competent as pastor	1. Ronald 2. Ronald 3. Ronald 4. Ronald	1. misuse 2. misuse 3. abuse 4. misuse
Tell church council that Ronald is "bitter old codger"	1. convince council that Ronald's views are not valid 2. dispute Ronald's sincerity and good will 3. frustrated by lack of growth in congregation 4. let council know how frustrated I am	1. need to protect my project 2. need to protect my image as good leader 3. need to blame someone for lack of growth 4. be understood and validated by church council	1. Ronald 2. Ronald 3. Ronald 4. council	1. misuse 2. abuse 3. abuse 4. use/misuse?

Table 1. Assessment of behaviors, needs and motives

Behavior	Motives	What need or desire am I trying to fill?	Who is meeting my need?	Use, misuse or abuse?

Table 2. Assess your behaviors, needs and motives

options after making a discovery about our character and what motivates our behavior.

- We can drop our heads in defeat, lose heart, and reject the opportunity to grow.
- We can vow to change, move on, and hope it does not happen again.

- We can purposefully work to change our motives, identifying healthy and appropriate ways to meet our needs without continuing to hurt, misuse, or abuse others.

While the first option may seem obviously counterproductive, it is the position that many people opt for when confronted with their humanity. Defeat requires no responsibility, courage, or action. It is the easiest of the paths and guarantees failure. The second option guarantees stagnation. We acknowledge our responsibility for our behavior (confession), but stop short of whole-heartedly pursuing change (repentance). With no intentional strategy to change what is deficient, we will not grow. We are bound to repeat history.

The third option embodies the process of sanctification: we confess, we repent, we claim the blood of Christ to cleanse us of our unholy motives, and we embrace the power of the Holy Spirit to bring about change. That is, we work out our salvation. The third option is also represented by the fifth through ninth steps of the Twelve Step recovery program.[4] It is of utmost importance, however, to understand that stopping a behavior is fruitless unless we replace it with a different mechanism for attending to our needs. Jesus tells this story to illustrate:

> When an evil [unclean] spirit comes out of a man, it goes through arid places seeking rest and does not find it. Then it says, "I will return to the house I left." When it arrives, it finds the house swept clean and put in order. Then it goes and takes seven other spirits more wicked than itself, and they go in and live there. And the final condition of that man is worse than the first. (Lk. 11:24–26)

It is not enough to denounce the old way. We must take responsibility for own our neediness and redirect our pursuits toward healthier and more honorable means of meeting our needs. We commit to seek fulfillment through appropriate relational channels. Unless we replace the unhealthy behavior with a healthy one, we will succumb again to the destructiveness of our old ways. Furthermore, efforts to change behavior will be unsuccessful without addressing what lies beneath–the motives and values of our hearts. Our sights must be set on what is right, healthy, and honorable. Motives that do not reflect the heart of God breed behavior that is misaligned with God's design for God's people.

We turn ourselves around with the same tenacity and humility required for fearless self-examination. The practices described in chapter 6 serve equally well here. Contemplate the qualities, the virtues, and traits that God desires for you. What do you want to be known for when you die? Paul asserted that he considered all his worldly success rubbish in comparison to gaining the righteousness of Christ, knowing him in the power of his resurrection and sharing in his sufferings (Phil. 3:7–11). "He has showed you, O man, what is good. And what does the LORD require of you? To act justly and to love mercy and to walk humbly with your God" (Mic. 6:8). This is a far cry from the image of success that permeates society today. Even though we proclaim God's standards for success to those under our care, the temptation to surrender to the social standards of success is no less powerful for ministers.

The more we meditate on the measures of success by God's standards, the more they will saturate our spirits and reshape the motives of our hearts: "Delight yourself in the LORD and he will give you the desires of your heart. Commit your way to the LORD; trust in him and he will do this: He will make your righteousness shine like the dawn, the justice of your cause like the noonday sun" (Ps. 37:4–6). If I delight in the Lord, God's desires will become my desires, and success by God's standards will follow: I will *want* to act justly, love mercy, and walk humbly with my God.

The Measuring Stick

With what will you replace the unwanted aspects of your actions, thought patterns, and motives? Having been created in God's image, we will be most at peace, most satisfied, and most successful when we are accurately reflecting God's image. Let's look at Micah 6:8 again: "To act justly and to love mercy and to walk humbly with your God."

Justice is the protection of the rights of people to live as God-image bearers and upholding those rights when they are challenged. Pursuit of justice is woven into the fabric of our society; at least superficially, politics, government, and community are all impelled by the pursuit of justice. Of interest, however, is our relative apathy for justice at a personal level. The administration of justice begins in the heart, not the legislature. It requires that we acknowledge others' rights not to be robbed of their personhood. Yet we rob others piece by piece of their personhood by shifting responsibility away from ourselves and onto them. We demand that their personhood become subordinate to our needs and we cripple the development of their God-given potential by insisting that their primary purpose is to fulfill our needs and desires. Yes, boundary violations are an injustice.

We will no doubt be much more mindful of maintaining healthy and appropriate boundaries with others if we respect their rights to live free of unreasonable expectations to put aside their own humanity for our gratification. Pursuit of justice will also propel us to protect those who are being misused or abused by others, not only within the grand scale of politics and social movements, but also in our own homes. Our esteem will flourish, not by elevating our self-image at the expense of others, but from protecting the rightful God-image of others who are weaker.

As we saw in chapter 3, mercy is the complement of justice. And, as with justice, we are more likely to offer mercy as a society than as individuals. *Mercy* costs something. At a societal level, the cost is distributed across the group and becomes depersonalized. At an individual level, the cost is intimately personal. God requires that we love mercy. Notice that Micah does not say, "to act justly and mercifully," or "to love justice and mercy." This is significant. He does not advise that we demand justice for ourselves from others. To not demand justice for ourselves takes self-discipline, strong self-esteem, and unwavering faith in God's goodness. But God does require that we love mercy–both the giving and the receiving of mercy. Giving mercy is surrender of the right to seek justice for ourselves. Accepting mercy is surrender to the awareness that our ways are unjust and we are incapable of complete restitution.

Humility is the trait that allows us to conduct ourselves with the exquisite balance of acting justly and loving mercy. Our perfect example of humility is Jesus Christ.

Your attitude should be the same as that of Christ Jesus:

> Who, being in very nature God, did not consider equality with God something to be grasped, but made himself nothing, taking the very nature of a servant, being made in human likeness. And being found in appearance as a man, he humbled himself and became obedient to death–even death on a cross!" (Phil. 2:5–8)

Christ did not deny who he was, but neither did he need to "grasp equality with God." Humility is not denial of who we are or denial of our worth, but, rather, it is appraising our worth so accurately that we have no need to prove anything, either good or bad. A humble heart knows that its worth has been confirmed by Christ's precious sacrifice and can serve because it is not focused on self-exaltation. It can act justly because it has no need to take from others to satisfy itself. It can accept mercy because it has an accurate understanding of itself. And it can give mercy because it is does not rely on retribution to sustain its worth.

Having examined the inaccuracies of our self-concept, how we violate others' boundaries and the areas of need that we try to meet in destructive ways, we can release to God our unwanted behavior, thoughts, and motives and instead embrace God's pattern for living: acting justly, loving mercy, and walking humbly with God. Humility, justice, and mercy are completely and inextricably intertwined. Pursuit of these principles is our highest calling as adopted children of God and the normative measure of our character as individuals and as ministers. Every fruit of the Spirit, every exhortation to holy living, every commandment, and every faith-work derives from the exercise of these principles.

The Measure of God's Grace

Although the work of self-examination may be tedious, it benefits pastors in several ways. First, by knowing themselves better, pastors can reduce the likelihood that they will inappropriately use others to their own advantage, abuse their position as spiritual leaders, or become depleted and burned out. Second, accurate self-knowledge helps ministers discern their areas of expertise, interest, and giftedness. They can then focus on work for which they are most qualified and engage others to assume responsibility in other areas. They will have a clearer understanding of their part in the local bodies of Christ.

Salvation and redemption are only theological abstractions, and our preaching is lame and feeble unless we personally know what it means to be liberated from shame and free to live as beloved children—pursuing justice, loving mercy, and walking in humility with our heavenly Father. The woman who washed Jesus' feet with her tears and anointed his feet with perfume (Lk. 7:36–47) understood the magnitude of Jesus' love for her and knew of no better way to express the depth of her gratitude. But of him who "has been forgiven little," Jesus says, he will love little (v. 47). As ministers we can preach grace and we can live out grace. The first option is effective on Sunday morning; the second option extends our ministry of reconciliation into every arena of our lives. "Preach the gospel at all times. If necessary, use words."[5]

Time to Reflect

1. What patterns have you discovered by completing the exercises in this chapter?
2. Do you experience fear (or worry, concern) in particular areas that regularly motivate behavior? For instance, do you worry about losing your job, are you concerned about unity in your congregation, are you fearful that the congregation's expectations of you will consume you?
3. What are your dominant areas of need? Possibilities are order, control, significance, security, belonging, acceptance, validation, affirmation, excitement, competence, challenge, harmony, connection, and pre-dictability. Try to list at least four or five fundamental needs that drive your behavior patterns.
4. How are you meeting those needs right now? Are your methods healthy? Are you taking something away from someone else in your pursuit of your needs?
5. Are you turning to the right people for your needs? Which needs are best met through your relationship with God?
6. Write a paragraph describing what you want to be known for when you die. How closely aligned are your values and goals with God's desire for justice, mercy, and humility?
7. How well do your actions reflect what you value? Can others identify what you value based on your actions?

III.

BOUNDARY APPLICATIONS IN MINISTRY

CHAPTER 8

Straight Talk on Power

"Power tends to corrupt, and absolute power corrupts absolutely."

JOHN EMERICH EDWARD DALBERG ACTON

"They are dogs with mighty appetites; they never have enough.
They are shepherds who lack understanding; they all turn to their
own way, each seeks his own gain."

ISAIAH 56:11

Meaning, purpose, and significance are woven into the fabric of our self-concept and are needed for psychological and spiritual well-being. People naturally search for meaning, purpose, and significance through relationship. Our relational nature allows us to experience a sense of wholeness and fulfillment as our inner experience is enriched by external relationships and by participation in a collective purpose greater than ourselves. It allows us to exist in community and to connect intimately with God and others.

Parishioners come into our churches looking for answers and guidance. People are attracted to the message of grace and hope that we preach. Identification with a congregation of believers provides parishioners with an environment that allows them to develop their self-concept, formulate meaning for their lives, creatively express their purpose, and receive affirmation of their significance. Pastors have the privilege and responsibility of facilitating their parishioners' search for purpose and meaning; the most effective tools for this endeavor are presence and relationship. As we carry out this responsibility, we want to conduct ourselves with mercy, justice, and humility. We strive to develop characteristics of integrity, authenticity, and empathy in our personal and professional lives. Ideally, we pursue our vocation of ministry not primarily for personal gain, but in response to a holy calling. Our focus is on serving with honorable and uncompromising ethical and moral standards.

So why is it that clergy are by all accounts the most likely to be reported for misconduct and moral failure by the news media? Even taking into account the media's insatiable appetite for sensationalism, it is sobering that–in a profession that advocates in principle for morality, holy living, and service to others–the frequency of moral failure, misconduct, and abuse is noteworthy, if not astounding. And for every report that becomes public fodder, there are many, many more instances of misconduct that are not scandalous enough for the evening news. These instances remain private, hushed, or quietly "managed."

Worse yet, the only breaches of ethical behavior that typically come to public awareness are those of sexual misconduct, child abuse, and financial misappropriation. The general public is largely unaware of the less egregious boundary violations (which may ultimately lead to more appalling breaches) that result in personal harm, hurt, and loss to parishioners and pastors alike, and compromise parishioners' spiritual and psychological growth.

Clergy are human too, with human needs, human souls, and human brokenness.[1] Pastors experience the same challenges as their parishioners to balance personal needs with the needs of others, to find significance in their own lives and to maintain healthy boundaries. But the challenge that pastors face is intensified: pastors must prevent their *position* from becoming an opportunity to violate boundaries in order to fulfill their personal needs.

Power and Responsibility

Motivating the spiritual growth of others is a weighty responsibility because with responsibility comes accountability (Heb. 13:17). It is also a heady responsibility, for it intimates a special emissary relationship with the Almighty[2] and fosters the perception of the spiritual leader as a mediator and facilitator who is worthy of reverence and deference (cf. 1 Tim. 5). Fundamental to the position of pastor is *power* and with power comes an increased opportunity and susceptibility for misuse of the position. As with anything that is intended for good, the position of spiritual leadership can also be used in the wrong ways and for the wrong motives.

Power presupposes a relative difference in the ability of two people to influence one another. In chapter 2, we saw that a person who has greater sphere of influence–denoted by the larger circle–will have a proportionately greater impact on another person with a relatively smaller sphere of influence (*i.e.*, less power). Also to be considered are the influence of both *real* power and *perceived* power. The extent of real power will vary between congregations and denominations, and depends on polity, congregational history, and the minister's level of accountability to a governing board.

Figure 1. The Disproportionate Influence of the Minister on Parishioners

Perceived power is the level of deference or acquiescence to the pastor by the parishioners. Centuries of church history have led to a widespread notion that a "good" Christian is characterized by submission to church leaders. As with any guideline taken to the extreme, indiscriminate and absolute submission is not healthy and can lead to trouble. Although it is the responsibility of the pastor to not misuse the power intrinsic to the position of spiritual leader, indiscriminate submission is possibly the biggest contribution by parishioners to creating opportunities for the misuse of power.

Ann (A Parishioner Tells Her Story) exhibited indiscriminate submission to the authority of her pastor, Brad, presumably because she had not developed adequate self-concept and autonomy. Any time she felt slightly awkward with his demands, she attributed it to her defectiveness and deficiencies, rather than to his disregard for her boundaries, and so conceded on the basis of his position of power. Congregations that encourage or demand absolute and unquestioning submission to the pastor or other designated spiritual leaders will have to mop up the messes left behind by the inevitable misuse of power to violate boundaries. Therefore, power without accountability tends to corrupt, and "absolute power corrupts absolutely."

Inherent in ministry are a number of forces that contribute to the power differential between pastor and parishioners, whether or not the pastor welcomes the increased power. These forces are tightly linked. Some of these forces are

- embodiment of hope
- implicit trust
- idealization
- intimacy
- ministry of prayer
- spiritual authority
- preaching
- administrative function

The Hope That Is in Us

Christian believers have something of value—hope. In a world filled with grief, existential angst, tragedy, and pain, the Christian message is one of hope and peace. If our hope is for real, it will show. People will notice. If our lives are permeated with peace, people who live in confusion will want to know the secret. "Always be prepared to give an answer to everyone who asks you to give the reason for the hope that you have" (1 Pet. 3:15b). The first priority of ministry is to be a light or beacon that beckons with its inviting glow to those who are suffering in darkness and hopeless confusion. We want our hope to overflow so that it is unmistakable and contagious (Rom. 15:13). People will take note and recognize the power of

God's transforming love: "Neither do people light a lamp and put it under a bowl. Instead they put it on its stand, and it gives light to everyone in the house. In the same way, let your light shine before men, that they may see your good deeds and praise your Father in heaven" (Mt. 5:15–16).

The embodiment of hope is a characteristic, not an action. So, how does incarnating hope create a position of power? When others connect with us in search of hope, they are asking for help. We are in a position of influence and this creates a power differential. Our power can be used to invite others to embrace the same hope. In this case, we acknowledge that while we can explain the hope that is in us, it is not our business to coerce acceptance. We recognize that if we attempt to coerce acceptance, we will be taking on the responsibility of the Holy Spirit (Jn. 16:8) and challenging the boundary between God and us.

Our power also can be used more insidiously to encourage others' dependence on us, to gain admiration, to build a following of "wannabes." Sometimes people are attracted to a personality trait and attempt to assimilate that trait by imitation or association rather than by integration and personal ownership. They place their hope and salvation in their pastor, not God. In their minds the pastor becomes their redeemer. We can use our power of attraction to encourage a misplaced faith, in order to fill a personal need for feeling desirable, important, or significant. In Maryann's story (The Power of Prayer), we see a parishioner, Betsy, who was placing her hope in her pastor. Maryann sensed the inappropriateness of this dynamic and was looking for a way to address Betsy's misplaced hope.

Under the right conditions, this dynamic can occur with anyone. But it happens more often with clergy. People naturally tend to look for connections with those that they perceive as having higher status, as powerful, and as highly respected to enhance their self-esteem. Because our culture holds in high esteem those in religious vocations and the minister is generally the most conspicuous member of a congregation, it is no surprise that new visitors will try to meet the pastor personally (less so in very large churches), establish a connection, and gain the pastor's attention with a word of appreciation or engaging comment.

Implicit Trust

Trust is the belief that a person is reliable, will meet expectations (often unspoken expectations), will conduct him- or herself according to a presumed code of standards common to the position, and will not harm another who is vulnerable or weaker. In many relationships, trust is earned over the course of time. However, certain relationships, such as that of doctor-patient, banker-investor, and clergy-parishioner, warrant an implicit trust based on the position and under the assumption that the character of the person in the position of power has been "certified" or endorsed by a governing body.

Implicit trust is closely associated with incarnated hope. Until recently, our culture has not only encouraged high respect for clergy, but also reinforced the idea that clergy persons merit implicit trust by virtue of their positions. Now, with the increasing media attention on moral failure, child sexual abuse, and incidents of glaring misconduct, implicit trust may not be quite as freely given, but it is still very much a force in vocational ministry. Consider how many people come to you and, in spite of limited relational history, pour out their troubles, speak their minds, and blurt out their histories. That is trust indeed!

Trust—especially implicit trust—endows pastors with power because it presumes that they will act in the best interests of their parishioners and reduces the likelihood that the pastors' actions or motives will be questioned. Most people want to give others the benefit of the doubt. This is even more pronounced when it comes to parishioners' relationships with their pastor. In the story of Joe (Special Friends), not even his wife appeared to question his whereabouts, seemingly because she assumed (trusted) he was working hard in his ministry.

Idealization

It is not uncommon for parishioners to place their pastor on a pedestal. People respect the position of spiritual leadership and feel the need to acknowledge the minister's position; hence the titles used when addressing clergy: reverend, pastor, brother, father. Layering on top of this is the natural tendency for people to want their leader to be "perfect" (or close to perfect), solid, strong, unerring, and benevolent. If the leader is perfect, strong, and benevolent, the subjects can feel safe, secure, and cared for. People also gain significance and self-esteem for themselves by associating with someone perceived as powerful and "perfect."

Pastors typically try to connect at least nominally with as many parishioners as possible. Parishioners feel esteemed by the pastor's efforts to connect and relate, and when the pastor is idealized the parishioners' increase in esteem is even greater. In essence, the greatness of the idealized person reflects back greatness on the person who is idealizing. Idealization creates a power differential because people naturally want to please someone they admire and believe to be a role model. They hope to garner notice, affirmation, and validation by the object of their admiration. In seeking to please, parishioners relinquish autonomy in exchange for feeling significant because of their connection with the powerful and "perfect" pastor: the greater the idealization, the greater the power differential and the greater the parishioners' increase in esteem.

The dynamics of idealization are, for the most part, unconscious. This further contributes to the power differential: the less aware people are that they are idealizing the pastor, the less able they are to act autonomously and thoughtfully. They are less likely to recognize boundary problems when they do occur and less likely to enforce their own boundaries in the event that the pastor begins to encroach.

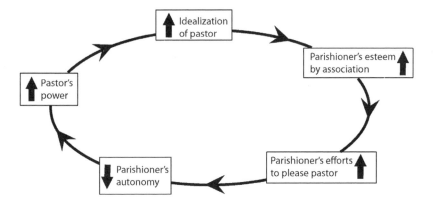

Figure 2. The Cycle of Idealization, Loss of Autonomy and Power

The increase in parishioners' esteem is, of course, achieved by association, and is therefore not a real and durable esteem. Needless to say, if the pastor should do anything that even remotely resembles imperfection, the parishioners who idealize him or her will be dismayed and incensed. Their reaction is often exhibited as an offense to their moral sensibilities, but the greater offense is to their esteem, which was being bolstered by their association with someone they perceived as being "perfect." Their idealization quickly turns to criticism and judgment when it has been determined that the pastor no longer meets the qualifications for idealization—he or she is no longer a fitting occupant for the alabaster pedestal. When Robert (The Ornament) could not meet the expectations of his parishioner, Sarah, she transformed her image of him from being the only one who could care enough for her to being uncaring, cold, and calloused.

Intimacy

In the course of ministry, pastors are often invited into the most private, intimate parts of their parishioners' lives. Parishioner concerns that have been shared with no one else are the topic of many pastoral counseling sessions. Intimacy is created first by the sharing of private concerns, troubles, and fears, then reinforced as the pastor provides guidance, support, and affirmation for the parishioner. When the parishioner's concerns are resolved or reduced, he will feel increasing intimacy with the pastor, along with admiration and appreciation.

The act of sharing emotionally laden rites of passage such as births, weddings, baptisms, deaths, and funerals; serious and life-threatening illness; tragic losses; and family celebrations also reinforces intimacy. Parishioners will often feel a special family-like connection with the pastor who participates or joins them in their significant life events.

While the pastor does not need to restrict personal information to the extent that most professional counselors and psychologists do, it is not wise to disclose excessive personal information that could impair effectiveness in ministry. Therefore, vulnerability with a pastor is asymmetrical–the parishioner offers up more private and deeply personal information than the pastor does. Intimacy contributes to the power differential when the parishioner perceives an increased level of vulnerability to the pastor because of the profound level of sharing. Parishioners that feel highly vulnerable will also be less able to assert themselves and act autonomously if or when their boundaries are being threatened.

Prayer

One of the privileges of ministry is that of praying for and with parishioners. Aside from the evident benefits of praying (Jas. 5:15–16), prayer is a profoundly spiritual act. Spirituality and spiritual acts are often mistaken for emotional intimacy, and, indeed, may generate strong feelings of emotional intimacy. Consider a common comment: "Being with him was a spiritual experience for me." Intimacy can feel spiritual, and spiritual experiences can feel intimate. As noted above, spiritual activity that is mistaken for intimacy will lead to a parishioner's sense of vulnerability and hence an increase in the power differential between pastor and parishioner.

The pastor's power is further increased by the perceived value that the parishioner places on the pastor's prayer–that because the pastor is in the position of spiritual leadership, his or her prayer is more effective. This perception should be managed by emphasizing that prayer is a mutual activity and by redirecting the parishioner's appreciation to God who hears our prayers, rather than to the intercessor who merely spoke the petitions on the parishioner's behalf.

In the story of Maryann (The Power of Prayer), she was struggling with how to prevent her parishioner, Betsy, from idolizing her. Betsy was almost throwing herself at Maryann's feet in her desperate need of a stabilizing force. The intimate emotional connection made it difficult for Maryann to pray on behalf of Betsy and Alex without encouraging the dependency. Maryann also realized that the more hospital calls she made, the more Betsy believed that it was Maryann's prayers, rather than God's grace, that sustained Alex's life and Betsy's strength to persevere. The power differential here was large because of Betsy's emotionally vulnerable state. Ironically, Betsy also had substantial power because Maryann had not found a way to extricate herself from the increasingly dependent and emotionally intimate relationship that Betsy was forging with her.

If a parishioner mistakes spiritual sharing for emotional intimacy, it is the responsibility of the pastor to ensure that the pastor-parishioner boundaries remain intact. In the above case, Maryann had not found an effective way to communicate with Betsy her need to develop an independent and intimate relationship with God, rather than depending on Maryann to fulfill that need.

Spiritual Authority

A multitude of scripture passages exhort and direct people in the body of Christ to submit to spiritual leadership. The position of pastor carries with it the expectation that parishioners respect—even submit—to the pastor by virtue of the position (*e.g.,* Heb. 13:17), but the position of pastor is also one of servanthood (*e.g.,* Jer. 23:1-4; 1 Cor. 9:22; 2 Cor. 11:27-28). In this context, the pastor is in the position of spiritual leadership in order to serve by example, looking after the interests of the flock:

> To the elders among you, I appeal as a fellow elder, a witness of Christ's sufferings and one who also will share in the glory to be revealed: Be shepherds of God's flock that is under your care, serving as overseers—not because you must, but because you are willing, as God wants you to be; not greedy for money, but eager to serve; not lording it over those entrusted to you, but being examples to the flock. (1 Pet. 5:1-3)

Unfortunately, too often the emphasis is placed on unquestioning submission to the pastor's leadership while ignoring the counterbalance of the pastor's servanthood. The position of pastor confers power because the pastor is in leadership *over* his flock. But the power differential is also reinforced and increased by the dynamic of a congregation that submits indiscriminately and a pastor who expects (or demands) submission with no regard for the personhood and right to autonomy of those in his care.[3]

The position of pastor also bears the implication that the leader represents God on earth. The issue here is not how theologically correct this is, but rather how the congregation perceives the position. Pastors do represent God to their parishioners when they provide spiritual and theological counseling, when they pray for their parishioners, and when they preach. Some parishioners tend to associate the pastor with God; the pastor's authority—and related power—are also associated with God. Parishioners who want to give honor and deference to God may transfer that submissive attitude over to the pastor as well.

Here is an obvious solution to preventing the power of the position from corrupting a pastor's character and empowering the pastor to violate boundaries: do not seek submission from parishioners. Submission is an act that is given, not taken. In that way, a pastor will be "shepherding from behind,"[4] leading by example and guiding by modeling.

Pastors who wield their power recklessly or selfishly cause great harm. Pastors must constantly test their motives when operating from their position of power. If at anytime pastors use their power to feel good about themselves, build their self-esteem, get their way, exercise their power, win, or even advance their agenda, they walk on thin ice and will inevitably violate boundaries with their congregations. Sam (Loose Lips Sink Ships) may have been feeling vulnerable to Ronald's active campaigning against contemporary music in worship services, but he was actually using his position of spiritual authority to reprimand and discredit Ronald.

Preaching

Closely associated with the power derived from the position of spiritual leader is the power that can be exerted over parishioners from the pulpit. As with the pastor's position, preaching carries with it an implied "special" connection with God. Preaching is, after all, proclaiming the word of God to the church and expounding on scripture for application in daily life. Many parishioners hear the pastor's preaching as God's Word for them. Some may test the message against their understanding of the entirety of scripture, but many others are very willing to accept whatever the preacher says as "gospel truth." They are less likely to question the trustworthiness of the sermons than the messages of social pundits, politicians, teachers, and activists.

Most of the time, the pulpit is used to interpret the truths of the Bible without ulterior motive. Unfortunately, occasionally a pastor will use the pulpit for his own purposes: to publicly denounce problem behavior among parishioners inasmuch as it threatens the pastor's position, to discipline parishioners that do not align with the pastor's agenda, or to publicly vindicate himself of accusations. This can be one of the most destructive actions a pastor can take when trying to protect his reputation, position, or image. Human agendas have no place in the pulpit and are an abject abuse of the pastor's power.

Even if the general congregation is unaware of the intended audience, the parishioners for whom the castigation is intended will feel the sting and humiliation of being singled out from the pulpit. This boundary violation will have immediate consequences: loss of trust in the pastor, loss of respect for the position of elder/pastor, feelings of shame, and—depending on the spiritual maturity of the parishioner—unwarranted fear of God (since the pastor is ostensibly representing God).

If a pastor has concerns for the spiritual welfare of a parishioner or group of parishioners, she is directed to take up those concerns directly with the parishioner(s), without using her position of power to manipulate compliance (Mt. 18:15–17). This is a situation that requires earnest self-knowledge so that the pastor can discern her motives for addressing what she considers offensive behavior. Self-preservation or self-advancement must never be motive for addressing an issue from the pulpit. This is true even if the pastor is also concerned more altruistically for the parishioners' spiritual well-being.

Administrative Role

In some churches, the pastor serves as the supervisor for various employees and staff. Parishioners commonly fill these staff positions (administrative assistant, janitorial, maintenance, subordinate pastoral functions, musicians, and so on). In this situation, the pastor fills two roles: supervisor and spiritual leader. Aside from the potential issues arising from dual role conflicts (addressed in chapter 11), the pastor also has increased power over these individuals as employees. Performance reviews and evaluations, corrective action in cases of inadequate performance, and the mere act of specifying job expectations create a power differential between pastor and employee-parishioner.

The existence of dual roles opens the possibility that the power associated with the supervisory capacity be contaminated by the power associated with spiritual leadership and vice versa. Employee-parishioners who want to gain approval from their supervisor are vulnerable to acquiescing to spiritual direction, even if they do not agree with the pastor's guidance. If attempting to gain approval with respect to spiritual growth or maturity, employee-parishioners may also be vulnerable to excessive stress in performing job duties, all in the attempt to demonstrate to the pastor that they can be both "spiritual" and good employees.

A Weighty Responsibility

Pastors (and others who function in a role of spiritual care and counsel) impact the spiritual growth of their parishioners. With that privilege comes an equally great responsibility to use the power of their position to point parishioners to God, enhance their appreciation for God's lavish love and grace toward them, and encourage an ever-deepening faith. No pastor escapes, however, the temptation to use that same privilege of power for self-serving purposes. And it is safe to say that every pastor who has fallen because of injudicious or inappropriate conduct has been able to do so by abusing his or her position of power.

Take a moment to assess your reactions to the extreme responsibility to use your power wisely, cautiously, and for Godly purposes. The list of potential forces that shape the power differential should be enough to alarm you and arouse a renewed appreciation of the need for extraordinary care in your conduct and performance of ministerial duties. No matter how long a pastor has served in ministry, it is still appropriate to be reminded of the inexorable duty to guard one's position of power against misuse and self-serving purposes. The power of the pastor is indeed a weighty responsibility, never to be taken lightly or dismissed.

Traits That Become Distorted by Power

A majority of individuals who are drawn toward vocational ministry possess strengths that can become the very foundation for failure later on. Every desirable character trait or ability will become distorted by the convergence of unmet personal needs, unchecked power, and a sinful nature (our inclination to violate the intrinsic boundary between us and God). Transient circumstances then serve as the ignition point to complete the transformation. Consider the sample list below of strengths and possible related distortions. You will probably think of other traits and distortions as well.

STRENGTH:	WHEN DISTORTED BECOMES:
Assertiveness	Bullying; intimidation
Self-confidence	Pride
Self-esteem	Narcissism, grandiosity
Truth-telling	Browbeating, lack of consideration for others
Organization	Compulsiveness, obsessiveness
Being articulate	Verbosity, overbearance
Love	Enablement
Humility	Self-effacement, dependency
Restraint	Withdrawal
Consensus-building	Lack of personal conviction
Personal conviction	Inflexibility, narrow-mindedness
Balance	Indecisiveness
Decisiveness	Impulsiveness, thoughtlessness
Desire to serve	Need to please, rescuing, codependence
Discretion	Cowardice, inaction
Bravery	Foolhardiness, irresponsibility

In conducting research with regard to qualities that lead to failure among leaders, Gary McIntosh and Sam Rima state, "[I]t became clear that a paradox of sorts existed in the lives of most of the leaders who had experienced significant failures: The personal insecurities, feelings of inferiority, and need for parental approval (among other dysfunctions) that compelled these people to become successful leaders were very often the same issues that precipitated their failure."[5] So, not only can our strengths become our weaknesses, but the dysfunctions that inform our desire to serve may also become our downfall when coupled with inordinate power.

Spiritual leaders who have fallen prey to the temptation of boundary violations often say that they never dreamed it could happen to them. It is precisely this obliviousness—or better, ignorance—to the corrupting nature of power that is their ultimate undoing. I urge you to consider: if you are not once again sobered by the weighty responsibility you carry to manage spiritual power carefully or by your vulnerability to misusing it for personal gain, your abuse of power is an eventuality. It will happen. You are not immune.

A Note on Predatory Behavior

Thus far I have addressed the issues related to boundary violations and the prevention of these breaches due to inadequate knowledge, psychological, and spiritual deficits and minimization of the risks of ministry. Another reason that spiritual leaders may violate boundaries in ministry is predatory behavior, which is the willful and conscienceless use of others for personal gratification. It is the predominant pattern of the psychopathic (also called antisocial) personality. Psychopathic personalities use and abuse others for no other reason than that they can.

Level of conscience spans the spectrum, from well-developed conscience to complete lack of conscience. We all sit somewhere on that spectrum. Marie Fortune, in her description of sexual abuse by clergy, differentiates between "wandering" and "predatory."[6] Some abuse results from lack of meticulous attention to boundaries. Moving toward the other end of the spectrum, abuse can be the result of intentional use/abuse of vulnerable others, to the extreme where the perpetrator does not recognize anything is wrong with this behavior.

It is likely that readers of this book have a well-developed conscience—conscienceless predators see no need of protecting others. You probably would not have picked up this book if you cared nothing for the welfare of your parishioners. However, because strength of conscience lays on a continuum, all of us exhibit lapses of conscience at various times. These conscience deficits may take the form of rationalizations: for instance, "Well, she had it coming," or, "All's fair in love and war." Or, "It's something I couldn't get anywhere else." Joe (Special Friends) exhibited characteristics of a significant conscience deficit. Without more detailed information on his psychological makeup, we cannot ascertain the extent of his lack of conscience. However, he apparently felt little remorse or pangs of guilt for his behavior. Instead, he rationalized his behavior: he wouldn't be half the pastor he was without Kat.

Note that people with conscience deficits (*i.e.,* psychopaths) are not necessarily flagrant about their conquests. They may very well hide their behavior—not in order to avoid shame, as do those *with* conscience—but because being found out is inconvenient; it will hamper their pursuit of gratification.

If you are aware of abuse of power by another minister, take action *now* to stop the abuse. Abuse must be reported to the appropriate authorities[7]—legal, denominational, and congregational—depending on the nature of the abuse. In addition, it may be possible to appeal to the abuser's conscience. If the abuser is not predatory, confrontation may result in the abuser agreeing to get help and taking responsibility for the boundary violation. However, damage that has already been done will not be mitigated or rectified by perpetuating the secrecy. While reporting the abuse to the authorities may seem cold and cruel, healing for both the perpetrator and victim cannot begin until the abuse stops and the grip of secrecy is broken. This is seen nowhere more clearly than in the case of Ann (A Parishioner Tells Her Story). Because her relationship with her pastor was never found out, she spent twenty years without any spiritual or mental health care to deal with the abuse. Instead, her mental health deteriorated as she continued to hide.

If, having read this section, you are concerned about the fitness of your conscience, make arrangements now to speak with a spiritual mentor or psychotherapist.

Protecting Your Boundaries

Three essential ingredients protect you from the corrupting influences of power:

1. Accurate self-knowledge
2. Adequate self-care
3. Appropriate guardrails

Achievement of accurate self-knowledge was discussed in detail in chapters 5 and 6. Adequate self-care stems from accurate self-knowledge and the resulting actions taken to meet personal needs in healthy and appropriate ways (chapter 7). Appropriate guardrails to protect the pastor's boundaries are the topic of chapters 9 through 11, but here I present specific recommendations for erecting protective curbs that will help prevent abuse of pastoral power.

"Guardrail" is the term I use for the precautions that a pastor can put in place to prevent the unintentional or unwitting approach or violation of an actual boundary. Imagine a stretch of winding two-lane road, carved along a mountainside. On one side of the road looms the rock wall that remains after blasting the mountainside away, and, on the other side, the mountainside drops precipitously a few feet from the road's narrow shoulder. Guardrails have been placed on this side of the road. They serve as markers to demarcate the edge of the road and to protect inattentive travelers who run into them from a worse fate of running off the cliff or smashing into the rock wall. The guardrails are not the actual boundary. The cliff is. The guardrails are precautionary and serve to warn travelers of the proximity of a hazard. So it is with professional guardrails: they demarcate an approaching hazard and serve as a safety net in case of loss of control. In addition to the "guardrails," signs are also posted to warn of approaching hazards; these are the "Bewares!"

Beware!

First, beware the *messiah mentality*. Many pastors have a strong bent toward narcissistic tendencies, such as grandiosity, omnipotence, and entitlement. These narcissistic tendencies can be redeemed and reformed to provide ministers with the self-confidence they need to endure weekly performance evaluations by an entire congregation; to tend to the chaotic demands of desperate parishioners; and to enjoy public speaking, being in the spotlight, and shepherding unruly sheep. But behind every desirable trait there is a shadow that requires subjugation. A messiah mentality arises from self-confidence gone dark: "I can handle this. In fact, I'm so good, I can save this situation single-handedly! With one hand tied behind my back!" Joe (Special Friends) exhibited behavior patterns consistent with a messiah mentality. Ultimately, the same overconfidence that fueled his super-pastor frenzy probably also allowed him to rationalize his misconduct with Kat.

Second, *beware the ego boost* that comes from being trusted with intimate details of parishioners' struggles. The level of trust placed in a pastor is strongly related to the position, not just the person, of the pastor. Beware the exhilaration that comes from being sought out by parishioners. Pastors are sometimes drawn to ministry in search of significance and in need of reassurance of their worth. Feeling needed, attractive, and wanted by parishioners feeds this reassurance, but will become a hazard when the pastor's need for significance or sense of importance trumps the parishioner's need for spiritual or psychological growth. Beware the satisfaction of being highly esteemed or even idealized. We may recognize that a person is idealizing us, but that does not necessarily prevent us from enjoying the elevation, even if temporary. Robert (The Ornament) was aware of the affirmation he received from Sarah's ministrations. Feeling significant and useful probably made it difficult for him to set and enforce his boundaries with Sarah and it most likely prevented him from recognizing that her idealization of him was the beginning of his fall off the pedestal. Don't allow the need for personal social relationships to be filled by ministerial relationships and church socialization.

Third, *beware the smug satisfaction of being considered a spiritual authority figure*. Parishioners may use the term "reverend"; however, God calls us to be servants. Beware the privilege of the pulpit. The pulpit is for speaking the *word of God,* not the word of the preacher. Never use the pulpit to vindicate yourself, your reputation, your authority, or your actions. Even if you believe your statements are justified and have merit, even if they fit neatly into the topic of a sermon, the risk of abusing the power of the pulpit and inflicting harm on others is too great. There are other avenues for explaining your personal positions and your side in relational disagreements and conflicts. If you act as both supervisor and pastor for certain church staff, beware the confusion of "managing" their spiritual development and "spiritualizing" their job performance. Katrina's story (Supervisor or Pastor?) could have ended much differently if she had been unable to demarcate her supervisory and pastoral roles with Jonathan. Note that she did not spiritualize Jonathan's work performance deficits by advising him to "work…with all your heart, as working for the Lord" (Col. 3:23). Neither did she attempt to manage Jonathan's family crisis.

Fourth, *beware the sense of cozy connection to those with whom you pray.* Don't replace your need for personal intimacy with the sense of connection that arises from ministering, counseling, and offering spiritual direction. Maryann (The Power of Prayer) would have some important work to do with Betsy, to help Betsy move from depending solely on her relationship with her pastor for support to identifying her primary source of strength as her faith in God. Because Maryann's ministry of prayer engendered such a strong, intimate sense of connection for Betsy, Maryann could otherwise easily encourage Betsy's idealization and overtures for friendship.

Fifth, and most importantly, *beware the ability to overstep your bounds of power precisely because of the power differential.* Power provides a cloak of protection from scrutiny of many ministerial activities, both because of the sensitive and confidential nature of much pastoral work and because increased power correlates with decreased accountability. One of the best tests for determining the appropriateness of behavior that cannot otherwise be monitored by others is to ask: "How would I feel if what I am doing hit the front page of the newspaper?" and, "Could my behavior be easily misconstrued for something inappropriate?"

Guardrails

The two types of guardrails that can prevent a free-fall over the edge of power abuse are personal accountability and organizational accountability. Personal accountability entails preestablishing expectations with carefully selected people from among professional and personal relationships. Organizational accountability is achieved through communication with lay leadership, establishing expectations, and reviewing performance. Consider some of the following possible guardrail components:

• If you are married, provide an agenda of each day to your spouse. The level of detail should be predetermined and then followed closely.

- Give your administrative assistant, office receptionist, or other routinely available staff member a detailed agenda for each day, including who you will be meeting with and where.
- Install windows in every office door in the church office. Tall and narrow window panes allow discrete visibility while protecting privacy.
- When meeting with a parishioner, predetermine the length of the meeting and then stick to it. If additional time is needed, schedule a follow-up meeting.
- If possible, make it a policy that you will not meet with a parishioner in the office when no one else is in the church office or nearby in the building.
- If you work in the office alone for part of the day, keep your office door open or, at a minimum ajar, when meeting with parishioners.
- If you perceive that a parishioner is becoming increasingly dependent on your ministerial care, solicit the involvement of a lay leader, elder/deacon, or other pastoral staff member in the parishioner's support. A parishioner's resistance to involvement by other spiritual caregivers signals potential problems. It needs to be addressed with the parishioner and increases the importance of a team approach to care.
- Establish guidelines and expectations with your church leadership board and/or denominational oversight with respect to your availability for counseling, discipleship, and pastoral care. Have discussions focused on your level of competence in various areas of need, your comfort with short- and longer-term counseling, the leadership's expectations for the depth of care you are to provide, and developing a system for managing potentially difficult cases.
- Spread out your greeting time on Sundays across as many parishioners as possible and encourage parishioners who need additional pastoral attention to make appointments for follow-up by phone or in person during the week. It is difficult but important to keep a balance between visiting with a few who have a lot to say, and touching base with many who are happy to have an occasional acknowledgment of their existence.
- Do not address from the pulpit any conflicts or concerns you may be experiencing with an individual parishioner, a small contingent, or larger faction. If you believe you must, review what you want to say with at least one other leadership member or pastoral staff member ahead of time. Never use the pulpit to "preach against" someone, whether parishioner, community member, or widely recognized social figure.
- Request regular "performance mini-reviews" with the congregational lay leadership and denominational authorities above you. The reviews may be informal and spread throughout the year. Solicit feedback and

listen for signs of potential issues, concerns, or misunderstandings that could be brewing. Regardless of the respectability of your intentions, others' perceptions matter and must be heeded in order for you to remain effective in ministry and prevent power from corrupting you. Accept feedback with humility and gratitude. Defensiveness is unproductive.

- Regularly review the list of strengths and their related distorted characteristics in the preceding pages. Add others that you think of. Ask yourself, "Are any of my strengths becoming distorted or unbalanced? Am I majoring in one strength to the exclusion of another?" For instance, are you focusing on truth telling but forgetting compassion? Is your ministry so full of mercy that you are losing control of your schedule?

- If you must provide pastoral counseling or guidance (beyond brief interchanges) to a church employee, transfer either job supervision or pastoral care to someone else if at all possible. It is generally not prudent to try to function in both roles at the same time.

- Find a way to account for your time to someone else who can vouch for you. For instance, you might be accountable to your spouse for your personal time and to the administrative assistant for ministerial time. Encourage the two of them to compare notes.

Finally, clothe yourself with humility every morning. Integrating this attitude into your daily life is the most effective guardrail you can erect. Act justly and love mercy. If you believe you are right, remember that Truth is bigger than you, and that "Truth as you have come to understand it" is subject to error. Your position of power does not exempt you from fallibility. Learn to say "I'm sorry" without excuses.

Power and Vulnerability

As we saw above, the term "power" presupposes a difference in the amount of influence that the two sides of a relationship have over each other. The result in such a relationship is that one party—the party with less power—is *vulnerable* to the other. The vulnerable person in a relationship has fewer resources and less strength in the relationship and therefore less ability to protect him- or herself from boundary violations. Thus, vulnerability is the potential for injury or damage by virtue of comparatively less strength and resources.

Vulnerability to injury exists not only because of the potential misuse of power by virtue of the position, but also by virtue of greater resources of the person with greater power. Pastors often are unaware of the relative extent of their resources in the pastoral function in comparison to those they serve: education, spiritual health, physical health, age, economic and financial benefit, social and psychological resources, and so on. Each parishioner will have unique vulnerabilities to the pastor's misuse of power based on disparate levels of resources. Some parishioners will be younger—such as children and youth—and are vulnerable on the basis of age. Some parishioners will be less educated and less experienced. They are vulnerable on the basis of information and understanding of the context of their life situation. Gender may also be a source of power if the church's theological and historical framework supports the headship or leadership of males. In this case, female parishioners will be more vulnerable to exploitation and injury.

Sexualization of the pastor-parishioner relationship is one of the most common points of vulnerability. At times, parishioners may sexualize the relationship, often as an interpretation of feelings of intimacy that develop during the course of ministry. Depending on the parishioners' level of life experience, they may even be *unaware* of the sexualization, its basis and its nature. All these factors place parishioners in a position of vulnerability to injury or damage, to being misused by the object of their sexualization. Pastors are *equally* susceptible to the phenomenon of sexualization. However, the pivotal difference between the parishioner who sexualizes the relationship and the pastor who sexualizes the relationship is that the pastor is in the position of power and therefore is responsible for maintaining the appropriate boundary, not taking advantage of the parishioner's vulnerability, and not acting on the pastor's own sexualized fantasies to fulfill personal interests or needs.

One component of Ann's (A Parishioner Tells Her Story) recovery was understanding that she was in no way responsible for her pastor's behavior and that the responsibility for the boundary violation lay with him, not Ann. As she reviewed in counseling her vulnerabilities to his manipulation, she saw that she had much less power to protect herself from his abuse than she originally thought. She believed that adultery was wrong. She also believed that parishioners are subject to the spiritual authority of their pastors. Being caught in this double bind left her paralyzed and unable to protect herself against his incremental advances on her boundaries.

Regardless of the nature of the vulnerability, the pastor is *always* responsible for maintaining appropriate boundaries, whether the parishioner or the pastor initiates the potential breach of boundaries. Parishioners who are uninformed of the nature of appropriate boundaries or who have not developed healthy boundary systems for themselves may attempt to fashion a relationship with the pastor that disregards the necessary boundaries for effective ministry. A parishioner may make overtures toward a pastor for a relationship that is inconsistent with the pastor's primary role of ministry (*e.g.*, friendship, sexual intimacy). Even in these circumstances, the pastor remains responsible for maintaining appropriate boundaries, because of a pastor's position of power.

This responsibility is indeed weighty. The pastor is responsible for not misusing power to fulfill personal needs and, at the same time, is responsible for not allowing parishioners to misconstrue the relationship to fulfill their personal needs inappropriately. "She initiated the sexual overtures," and, "He was the one who wanted me to be his friend," are not reasons for a pastor to violate the boundaries of ministry.

When Parishioners Attempt to Renegotiate the Relationship

When a pastor becomes aware of a parishioner's advances to modify the standard boundaries, the pastor may feel uneasy and anxious. The anxiety that the pastor experiences is often misinterpreted as vulnerability. Regardless of how vulnerable the pastor feels to the advances, the pastor is still in the position of power and is still responsible for addressing the behavior and maintaining healthy boundaries. A boundary cannot be crossed without the pastor's consent, and if the boundary is not crossed, the pastor has not acceded power or incurred vulnerability to the parishioner. This is not to say that a pastor may not feel vulnerable to a manipulative parishioner who makes overtures or threatens (usually implicitly) the reputation of the pastor if the pastor does not concede to the parishioner's demands for a renegotiation of the relationship.

There are two effective measures for addressing parishioner-initiated attempts at relational renegotiation. It is best to apply these measures concurrently. The first is to involve another trusted leader in the church, either lay or staff. Discussing the pastor's concern in confidence with another leader provides two benefits: the other person serves as a consultant who can offer perspective and guidance, and the pastor will feel more supported to not acquiesce to the parishioner's attempts to renegotiate the boundaries. At times, consultation with a clinical psychologist or other mental health professional will also provide valuable insight and direction when dealing with particularly challenging parishioner concerns. Discussing the potential problem keeps the pastor honest. Should the parishioner escalate, the pastor has already established an accountability relationship to help in resolving the ethical challenge.

The second measure is to immediately address with the parishioner the efforts toward boundary renegotiation. This must be done with the utmost tact, compassion, and forthrightness. The pastor may decide to address a perceived bid for boundary changes with a parishioner only to find that the parishioner denies any intent at all. Whether or not the parishioner confirms intent, the pastor will have clarified the boundary expectations and possibly improved the parishioner's awareness of how this behavior is interpreted. Early and ongoing clarification of boundaries is paramount to a redemptive outcome.

When Sarah (The Ornament) first visited with Robert, he did not initially clarify what he could offer Sarah and what she was hoping to gain from their time together. Instead, he allowed her to set the agenda for the initial and subsequent sessions. He attempted to manage the content of the sessions once he became aware that the sessions were unproductive, but he was unable to maintain appropriate pastoral boundaries, largely because both Robert's and Sarah's expectations of the counseling relationship were not made explicit initially and because Robert was unaware of his personal need to feel trusted and appreciated by a "VIP" parishioner.

Time to Reflect

1. Compared to other churches, how highly does your congregation esteem the position of pastor, based on its history and theology?
2. Take note of the behavior of newcomers and visitors in your church. What behaviors do they exhibit that indicate their desire to connect with you because of your position as pastor? What proportion of newcomers share a personal "tidbit" at their first introduction? What impression does that leave on you?
3. Think about some of the recent news stories about pastors and other spiritual leaders who have been accused of misconduct. How did abuse of power contribute to their moral failures? What aspect(s) of their power was being misused to abet their misconduct? How did lack of accountability contribute to the perpetuation of the misconduct?
4. What is the hierarchy of accountability in your congregation and denomination? Do you feel confident that there is adequate accountability in all areas of your life to prevent you from succumbing to the temptation to misuse your position of power? What guardrails need to be reinforced? What step can you take immediately to reinforce your accountability in one area?

CHAPTER 9

When Boundaries Seem Blurry

"If any of you lacks wisdom, he should ask God, who gives generously to all without finding fault, and it will be given to him."

JAMES 1:5

"'Everything is permissible'—but not everything is beneficial. 'Everything is permissible'—but not everything is constructive."

1 CORINTHIANS 10:23

Admittedly, boundaries aren't easy. They are not quantitative. Scientific formulas cannot be applied to arrive at the precise amount of boundary to be applied to a particular type of relationship, for each unique situation, or for any given personality type. Complicating the determination of appropriate boundaries is the added dimension of the roles we plays in our daily lives. Sometimes we luck out and a particular relationship fits neatly into a single role. For instance, a casual acquaintance at the supermarket fits into our role of societal member. However, one of the greatest challenges for ministers is that the role of pastor does not stay at the church. A pastor at the office is still a pastor at home, at the park, and at the neighborhood watch meeting. To quote Ziggy: "Wherever I go, there I am!"[1]

Consider the story of Beth (Good Neighbors). Beth enjoyed the freedom of her relatively well-separated roles as pastor and community member. In her case, friendship with the neighbors came first, but her role as pastor was soon activated as she became involved with her neighbors' spiritual inquires and their interest in her faith and ministry work.[2] Notably, Beth was oblivious to the subtle shift in her relationship with Cassie from one of friendship to that of pastor. Beth's story exemplifies the ubiquity of dual roles in pastoral ministry and the difficulty of balancing these roles. However disconcerting, this shift in relational nature happens frequently. Moreover, determining the appropriate response to shifts in relational nature is challenging and enigmatic. It demonstrates how easily personal and pastoral boundaries can become blurred and cause heartache for both the pastor and the congregation.

Role Confusion

Appropriate boundaries become more difficult to implement as confusion increases regarding the roles that the pastor is fulfilling. The pastor engages his personhood in the ministry of presence, and, consequently, will find himself functioning at various times in a combination of roles: administrator and mentor, preacher and coach, counselor and friend, and so on. When multiple roles are simultaneously engaged, the likelihood of role confusion increases, and along with it the likelihood of boundary confusion. There is less division of labor in smaller congregations and the pastor typically fills more roles, so there is also greater opportunity for role confusion in these settings. Furthermore, if the pastor also pursues a secondary agenda to fill personal needs through these vocational roles, it is almost impossible to discern appropriate boundaries for each context.

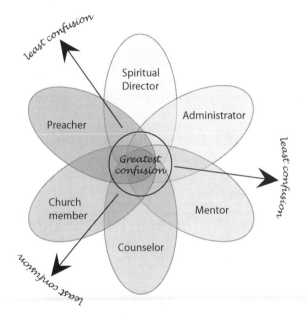

Figure 1. Confusion at the Intersection of Roles

Let's look at the classic issue of hugging. Every pastor faces dilemmas at some point in ministry regarding the advisability of hugging parishioners. There is no commandment against hugging. Our culture, while less physically demonstrative than some other cultures, does endorse hugging as an acceptable form of connection depending on the circumstances. The initiator of a hug may want to communicate appreciation, acceptance, welcome, empathy, joy, or respect. However, the initiator may also want to communicate feelings of romance, closeness, emotional intimacy, sexual desire, or invitation to deeper connection. Adding to the complexity of the communication is how the receiver interprets the hug. The initiator may intend to communicate empathy; the receiver interprets the hug as an overture for greater intimacy. The same hug, when extended to another individual, may be interpreted as compassionate support during a difficult time.

A hug may be appropriate and run low risk of misinterpretation if extended to a parishioner whose child is gravely ill. Assuming no extenuating circumstances, the parishioner will probably interpret the hug as supportive and caring. When the pastor then meets with the same parishioner to discuss curriculum planning for Sunday school, a hug is not necessary and could lead to confusion, misinterpretation, and misuse by either the pastor or the parishioner. But because the pastor gave the parishioner a hug while providing emotional support, both the pastor and parishioner may be somewhat confused as to whether a hug is now appropriate in this new context.

Given the temptations for misinterpretation and misuse, is it better to create a boundary of "no hugs"? This solution would swiftly and efficiently resolve the question of whether to hug or not to hug. It would also prevent the pastor from ministering sensitively within our cultural context and would dilute the pastor's effectiveness in meeting parishioners' needs for compassion and unconditional acceptance. Clearly this is not the best answer.

Bound(aries) by the Law?

The apostle Paul noted: "'Everything is permissible'—but not everything is beneficial. 'Everything is permissible'—but not everything is constructive. Nobody should seek his own good, but the good of others" (1 Cor. 10:23). In other words, while my behavior may be permissible, it is not necessarily advisable nor in the best interest of others. Boundaries may seem blurry when behaviors are permissible, but, depending on the context, may not be advisable or constructive. So it is with many choices we face. One piece of cake tastes good, two pieces are a little over the top but won't kill me, eating three pieces suggests loss of control but still tastes good, and four pieces make me violently sick to my stomach. Where was the boundary between healthy and unhealthy? At what point did I exchange the abundant life for gluttony?

The answer lies within the context. If I am diabetic, one piece of cake is unhealthy. If I am a relatively healthy individual, one piece of cake will not harm me. Then again, if I know that it is difficult for me to eat only one piece, then even that one piece will increase the temptation for overindulgence and ultimately lead to loss of control. The further I go down the slope, the greater the risk that I will hurt myself. I risk hurting others as well, who are looking to me to model healthy food choices. In certain contexts, eating even one piece of cake, although not against the law, may be ill-advised, either because of the temptation for me to indulge in excess (not constructive), or because my behavior tempts someone else to indulge beyond what is healthy for that individual (not in another's best interest).

Boundaries are not exactly equivalent to Law in the biblical sense. However, Paul's counsel on permissibility and prudence provides a framework for determining where boundaries should be placed. Some boundaries are guardrails of protection and precaution, placed back from the foul line, to prevent the pastor from inadvertently running over the edge into dangerous territory of harming self or another person. Other boundaries are firm, clear, and nonnegotiable. We do have clear biblical guidance on these boundaries. They *are* the foul line.

In chapter 8 we looked at some possible guardrails–prudent boundaries to protect the pastor from overstepping the bounds of power that her position affords her. Each congregation and pastor should know and agree on what guardrail expectations are indicated within the context of that local church body. Each pastor, having conducted a fearless self-examination, will develop a sense of what guardrails are best suited for her particular vulnerabilities and temptations.

Flexible Boundaries *vs.* Blurry Boundaries

Yet even when guardrails and foul lines are explicit, pastors will still face challenges in enforcing those boundaries. That is because boundaries cannot be unyielding, lest they choke the relationships they are intended to protect. Beth would not have wanted to refuse friendship with her neighbor on the off chance that her role with Cassie might change at a later date. The best boundaries have some flexibility and permeability. Flexibility is the quality of being able to move the boundary depending on the relationship and on the circumstances. In contrast, rigid boundaries permit no growth, no development of relationships. I do not let you in now and I do not let you in later. I do not share any part of myself now, nor at a later time.

A boundary that is too flexible is like a fence that is made of cardboard; it will fall over with the first stiff wind. It provides a false sense of security; it is there in name only. On the other hand, an inflexible boundary will prevent adaptation to new experiences and relationships, even if they are beneficial. A boundary that is too permeable is like a fence that is made of slats spaced so far apart that even the bears get through. The fence line is visible, but, like the fence made of cardboard, it also has no substance. Conversely, an impermeable boundary is the equivalent of a very high and thick brick wall. It prevents all contact with others and blocks out the sunlight. I become a captive to my impermeable boundary.

For instance, my boundary for sharing personal information with parishioners is generally, "Keep it brief and nonspecific." I have developed deeper relationships with a few people; with these people, I am comfortable being more specific about the difficulties I have experienced with caring for my aging mother-in-law. I allow those people to move in closer toward me. Also, the affinity for gossip of a few people has alarmed me in the past; with these folk, I make no mention of my caregiving challenges at all. I set the boundary further out with them.

Likewise, boundaries need to be permeable, able to let through relational exchanges that are exceptions to the boundary but are beneficial to both parties in the relationship. I may not normally ask for help from parishioners with home maintenance projects, but the morning after a storm blows a hole in my roof, I decide to call the church's resident roofer for guidance on making repairs. My parishioner roofer is affirmed for his expertise and willingness to help; I am able to make repairs quickly and inexpensively.

At times, the most difficult aspect of a boundary is knowing *when* to allow for flexibility. We hear competing and divergent advice from well-meaning peers: "Trust your gut," "Be true to yourself," "Your heart can be deceptive," "Talk to a spiritual mentor," "This is between you and God." We also hear the voices of our hearts and minds, playing tug-of-war with our consciences: "This is strictly my business," "It's not an issue unless someone makes a stink about it," "I need to pray about this," "How do I know if this is what God wants for me?" "I would ask for advice, but I don't think others will understand my situation," "God wouldn't allow this unless God meant for it to happen."

Without a reasoned approach to determining where boundaries should be placed and when flexibility is appropriate, the boundaries become blurred and the rationale behind them even blurrier. Our decisions on where to place our boundaries are transformed from *reasonable* to *rationalized.* Rationalization is the mechanism by which we kid ourselves into thinking that the current circumstances warrant a modification of our boundaries in spite of otherwise formidable evidence to the contrary. Rationalization is progressive, and, like the one, two, three, four pieces of cake, transforms our choices one step at a time from reasonable to foolish.

How to Prevent Slipping Off the Slope

The most basic boundary between pastor and parishioners is: "Parishioners are not there to satisfy the pastor's personal needs." It is based on the mission of the Church: to make disciples. As ministers, our calling is to nurture our parishioners' spiritual growth and freedom to serve Christ. But if our focus is on using the pastor-parishioner relationship to fulfill our personal needs, we are in effect robbing our parishioners of the freedom to live for God. Instead they exist for our benefit. While this principle may sound straightforward, the application is not. After all, pastors respond to their call to ministry at least partially to put to use their God-given talents, to find personal fulfillment and self-actualization,[3] and to (unconsciously) fill unmet personal needs for affirmation and self-worth.[4] How do we discern what is a healthy boundary, when to allow flexibility, and when to assert the existing boundary? Can we trust our gut? When? Here are several guidelines for examining the expediency of allowing a boundary to flex.

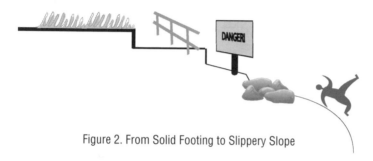

Figure 2. From Solid Footing to Slippery Slope

Test your motives. This is where accurate self-knowledge can save you and your ministry. Ask yourself what you want to achieve by allowing this boundary to flex. Is your primary purpose to satisfy a personal need, and, if so, will this be at the other person's expense or will the other person also benefit? In the case of soliciting the help of the church's resident roofer, I was definitely satisfying a personal need. The roofer may take delight in being helpful. But what if the roofer was already inundated by repair requests from others in the community who also experienced storm damage?

Assess the power differential. People have varying degrees of autonomy in their relationships with the pastor, depending on their level of individuation and sense of vulnerability to the pastor's power. For instance, do I believe that the roofer will feel at liberty to turn down my request? Is the roofer a strong enough individual to have a free choice in this matter? Are there circumstances that may cause the other person to feel obligated? If there is a possibility that the other person may feel obligated due to your position, your previous acts of service to that person, or because of previously shared confidences (among other possibilities), flexing the boundary is *not wise.* It does not matter if you believe your parishioner is unobligated; what matters is how your parishioner perceives it.

Pray. Ask for wisdom, discernment, and clear guidance (Jas. 1:5). The temptation is to approach God with our dilemma, primarily expecting the divine stamp of approval for our preferred path. This closes our hearts off to sensing the promptings of the Holy Spirit and prevents us from listening for direction that may not coincide with our ideas. Be open to twinges of conscience that whisper "be careful!" Be willing to hear from God in the voice of others as well.

Wait. If in doubt, hold off. Sometimes our dilemmas resolve themselves, or, with a bit more time, additional information surfaces that will clarify the decision-making process. Remember that relatively few situations require immediate action. If you are feeling pressure from others to make a decision, beware taking action just to relieve the pressure.

Seek guidance from trusted advisors. This step serves three purposes. First, having to speak with someone about your decision will slow down your mind and attenuate any sense of urgency. Second, seeking others' feedback is a double-check of your motives, self-honesty, and intent to act "above board": "For lack of guidance a nation falls, but many advisors make victory sure" (Prov. 11:14). If the choice we are contemplating is not one that we think will go over well with others, it's probably not a sound choice. And third, the wise counsel of others will add other perspective in our decision-making and the potential implications of our actions.

Try to anticipate the implications of your choice. Ask yourself, "What might happen if I flex this boundary?" Excessive speculation is unproductive, but a little foresight can prevent the "unforeseen"! Consider whether flexing your boundary now may progress to careless disregard of the boundary in the future or at least reduce your inhibitions to crossing other boundaries later. Does the action you are considering compare to taking a step closer to the edge, or is it analogous to climbing over the guardrail? The individuals on the other side of the boundary may also come to expect future flexibility, even when not appropriate. For example, if I invite a parishioner of the same gender to lunch, will a parishioner of the opposite gender expect I will extend a similar invitation? If I take a parishioner of the opposite gender to lunch, is it possible that it could be become routine and eventually transform into dinner dates?

Imagine how others could interpret your choice. Avoid the appearance of evil. We do not want to live our lives fearful of what others may think, waffling just because someone thinks differently than we do about an issue. But there is a difference between losing our ability to minister effectively due to fear of others' perceptions and blatantly disregarding the impact our behaviors have on others. Ask yourself, "How would it appear if what I am doing hit the front page of the newspaper?"

Consider alternatives for achieving the same goal. Ask yourself what you are trying to achieve with your choice and whether there are other ways to accomplish the same thing. For example, a single male parishioner invites me for dinner at his home to discuss how best to help his alcoholic sister. I want to provide spiritual support, compassion, and guidance. Do I visit with the parishioner in his home? Can I offer care in another setting? If he wants to offer me hospitality, can that goal be achieved if I come with my husband?

The Ubiquitous Pastor

What roles do you play? Friend, parent, aunt, caregiver for elderly parent, grandparent, homeroom parent, scout leader, neighbor, spouse, volunteer, acquaintance, minister…on goes the list. Take a few moments to jot down your specific roles. Now review your list and consider: in which roles does your position as pastor play a part? Have you sensed particular expectations from others based on your vocation, regardless of the relationship you have with them? Like it or not, people expect a minister to exemplify their preconceived attributes for a clergy person, even if the minister is doing something as secular and mundane as grocery shopping. Unlike with many other vocations, a pastor cannot shed his vocational identity when functioning in other roles. Both the community and congregation tend to judge a pastor's behavior without the benefit of an understanding of the context. As a rule of thumb, the higher the position of power and esteem held by a leader, the more our society feels justified in judging the leader's behavior. It is a fact of life and ministry. And it requires a heightened awareness and observance of appropriate boundaries. David's (Golf Buddies) friendship with Will worked well, but David was prudent, carefully maintaining appropriate boundaries that allowed the friendship to remain healthy. Will apparently also had good boundaries and did not use the privilege of his friendship with his pastor to judge, gossip, or flaunt a special status with David.

As we saw above, the pastor must be aware of the parishioners' expectations. Spoken or unspoken, congregational expectations of their pastor are not necessarily reasonable and are often inconsistent with standards parishioners have for themselves. The unspoken expectations are the most challenging; neither the pastor nor the congregation as a whole is clearly aware of them, and they only become explicit when the pastor fails to meet them. In Beth's case (Good Neighbors), parishioners expected their pastor and husband to have a constantly harmonious marriage, but the expectation did not surface until her neighbors interpreted an argument as "serious marriage problems." Furthermore, while Beth was being held to an impossibly high and unrealistic standard of complete harmony in her marriage, parishioners were not being held to the biblical standards of desisting from gossip and of not giving false testimony against a neighbor.

When unrealistic congregational expectations exist for pastors, the tendency is for the pastors to present to the church a sanitized version of themselves. Then, because the role of pastor follows them everywhere, discrepancies eventually surface between the sanitized and real selves. To combat these unrealistic expectations and prevent losing their real selves, pastors often feel compelled to display too much transparency. This results in yet another challenging boundary.

The Temptation of Too Much Transparency

You have probably experienced the internal conflict that comes from a sense that, while parishioners want to get to know you, you are trying to maintain some semblance of privacy. Parishioners want to establish a point of connection with you; you want your personal space. Parishioners want to build friendships with your family; you want to protect your family from congregational scrutiny. Parishioners want you to have answers; you know you don't have answers to life's tough questions.

So pastors must deal with the issue of how much of the pastor as person is exposed to the congregation and general public. Pastors walk a fine line between wanting to be real–authentic–with those they minister to and not revealing so much reality that there is no longer any private space and the reality is "too much information," distracting from the work of ministry. There are no fast rules of how to establish this boundary, but the following observations may be useful in finding a good balance between too much and too little self-disclosure.

Authenticity is the characteristic of being consistent in behavior and principles in all areas of life, but it does not require relinquishing all personal privacy. An individual's transparency–his willingness to let others observe details of his behavior–will substantiate his authenticity. But we do not need to know everything about another individual to have some sense of whether or not that individual "practices what he preaches." Allowing some degree of transparency to others allows them to connect with us and to appreciate our humanity. It underscores our need to be accepted as human beings with limitations and faults, no different than those whom we serve. Transparency is essentially an invitation for the congregation to form realistic expectations for us and to not idealize us. Transparency and self-disclosure can also be useful in establishing trust with parishioners to enhance the effectiveness of pastoral care.

However, too much transparency is at best unnecessary, and at worst detracts from the work of ministry. Excessive self-disclosure refocuses parishioners' energy away from the work of their own spiritual growth and onto the idiosyncrasies of the pastor's humanity. It exposes the pastor to the potential for distortions and gossip. And it can create a dynamic in the congregation in which individuals interpret the pastor's self-disclosure as validation of their position of specialness and closeness to the pastor. Perceptions of favoritism will quickly diminish the pastor's ability to work effectively with the entire congregation and inevitably leads to contention, strife, and bids for power within the congregation.

Clearly, negotiating a sane and healthy level of transparency is challenging. It requires prudence, prayerfulness, self-awareness, and a clear sense of purpose in the pastor's use of self in ministry. The advisability of self-disclosure can be assessed with the following questions:

1. In what way will this personal information help my parishioner(s) grow spiritually? (*e.g.*, My parishioner will understand that other people also deal with angry adolescent children.)
2. Is there a risk that this information may be distorted and misused by the parishioner? (*e.g.*, My parishioner could interpret my disclosure as an indication that I have a special level of trust in her.)

3. Is there a risk that this information will detract from the parishioner's own spiritual growth? (*e.g.,* My parishioner may begin to focus on my parenting style, rather than on her responsibility for how she interacts with her adolescent.)
4. Am I putting anyone else's reputation at risk of being damaged? (*e.g.,* My parishioner may conclude that my son is rebellious and out of control.)
5. Am I filling a personal need with this disclosure? (*e.g.,* I carry guilt for how I handled a situation and want to unload the guilt by confessing to someone; I want a sense of camaraderie with this parishioner.)

Self-disclosure can be used effectively in preaching. An illustration may help to personalize the application of the message and convey to the congregation that the message is equally salient for the pastor and the congregation. Even if the disclosure is offered to the congregation as a whole, its advisability is best assessed carefully, working through the above questions.

The trouble with transparency is that it is tempting to use it in order to establish greater personal intimacy with parishioners and fill personal needs of validation, acceptance, sympathy, and friendship. Excessive transparency is the foundation of many a boundary blunder. For this reason, accurate self-knowledge and good personal self-care are the greatest defenses against using transparency for personal gain.

Moving from Blurry Boundaries to Balanced Boundaries

You may have concluded already that practicing healthy boundaries is a matter of balance–keeping priorities straight, maintaining balance between vocational and personal goals, capitalizing on strengths without getting carried away, weighing the advice of others against our responsibility for our own actions, and so on. When we feel that our boundaries, either in ministry or in our personal lives, are blurry, when we are confused about how to proceed or feeling uncomfortable with the trajectory we are on, the most likely culprit is a loss of balance. Some aspect of our lives is out of kilter. Some areas that may need attention are

1. *Self-care:* physical, psychological or spiritual health, recreation, self-fulfillment
2. *Personal relationships:* friendships, family, marriage
3. *Relationship with the Lord:* personal and intimate spiritual relationship not related to vocational activities
4. *Personal life management:* finances, home maintenance, enrichment opportunities, time management
5. *Vocational ministry:* people skills, leadership skills, continuing education, clarified goals, performance feedback, synergy with lay and/or denominational leadership

Another reason that boundaries can get blurry is that other people will attempt to place expectations and demands on us. When the pressure to conform to the expectations of others prevails over our confidence to act autonomously, we second-guess ourselves or acquiesce to the demands in hopes of relieving the pressure. Allowing others to penetrate our boundaries is just as unhealthy as crossing those boundaries ourselves. But it happens frequently, primarily because we are afraid of others' reactions to our refusal. We want them to like us and accept us; we fear losing their support; we fear their criticism, accusations, or active attacks on our reputation.

Consider the story of Robert (The Ornament) again. His parishioner, Sarah, was making demands of him that were beyond his role as pastor. She wanted a shoulder to cry on, with the times to be determined by her at a moment's notice. She wanted pity, not empathy. By giving him personalized gifts, she was asking for his personalized attention. She wanted him to validate her belief that her pain was unusually dreadful and she was helpless without him. Because he was insufficiently aware of his personal needs for appreciation and significance, and possibly because he feared her wrath should he not comply with her demands, he surrendered the enforcement of his boundaries and allowed her to trample them. He chose to relieve the pressure she was exerting on him rather than assert his belief that she was capable of helping herself. It was a process that propelled him down the slippery slope without his full awareness until it was too late.

If you are experiencing confusion with respect to your boundaries and roles, try to identify potential areas of your life that have become unbalanced—either by losing the priority they deserve, or by becoming too important and consuming too much of your energy. Take time to regain balance and perspective. Tend to the areas that have become unbalanced. It may be helpful to review the ideas in chapter 6.

Time to Reflect

1. What roles do you fill, both in vocational ministry and in your personal life? How do some of these roles intersect and overlap?
2. Think about a time that your actions impacted future expectations by the congregation. Did you anticipate the implications? How did you deal with the expectations? In hindsight, would you have handled the situation differently?
3. Are there areas of your life where boundaries are difficult to establish and maintain?
4. How has imbalance in your life affected your ability to establish and maintain boundaries
5. What have you done to regain balance? How did you correct the boundary enforcement?

CHAPTER 10

Sexual Misconduct and the Not-So-Blurry Boundary

"You shall not commit adultery."

EXODUS 20:14

"But I tell you that anyone who looks at a woman lustfully has already committed adultery with her in his heart."

MATTHEW 5:28

We have seen that the topic of boundaries encompasses much more than the issue of sexual behavior. Yet sexual misconduct is usually what first comes to mind when we think about boundaries. Many boundaries require some flexibility and adaptability in order to be effective. In the area of sexual boundaries, the progression from "safe" to "sorry" is precipitous, and there is very little leeway for flexibility. Clergy sexual abuse is widespread. It affects children and adults. The proliferation of sexual misconduct and increased media attention has rocked our nation and the world. The burgeoning of Web-based communications has made it possible for more people to connect with others who have been affected by clergy sexual abuse, and people are more willing to tell their stories from the relative safety of their computers. A recent search of Web pages addressing clergy sexual abuse yielded literally hundreds of thousands of hits.[1] Sexual abuse is difficult to monitor, and even more difficult to recover from, both for the perpetrator and the victim. "Abuse" carries a much more onerous connotation than "misconduct," but, at the end of the day, abuse is abuse is abuse, whether the misconduct was perpetrated on a child or adult, male or female, of the same gender or opposite gender. Abuse is any behavior that uses another person for personal gain while causing damage to such person. All sexual misconduct is abusive; no one escapes unharmed.

The Prevalence of Clergy Sexual Misconduct

The percentage of people who engage in affairs is high. Estimates vary, depending on the survey source, sampling of the population, definition of infidelity, and the researchers' goals. It is not necessary to have a hard estimate to know that sexual impurity runs rampant in our culture. Pastors are not immune. Again, while estimates vary, infidelity and sexual misconduct among pastors exists and is disturbing, whatever the percentages.[2] To help you personalize this issue, think about the churches you have had some association with in your adult years. How many of them have dealt with, or are now dealing with, the fallout from accusations of a staff pastor's sexual misconduct? Do you personally know of any pastors that have crossed boundaries of appropriate sexual behavior? Do you know parishioners who live with the repercussions of clergy misconduct? The likelihood is that you do. Of seven churches with which I have been associated or loosely connected, five have had to address issues of inappropriate sexual behavior by a staff pastor, either during my time of association or since then. Statistics aside, clergy sexual misconduct has personally touched most of us.

One recent study was conducted of a stratified random sample of the overall U.S. population. This study found that 3.1 percent of women who attended religious services at least once a month had experienced at some time during their adult life the sexual advances of a clergy person or other religious leader from their own congregation. For more than half of those, a religious leader who was married at the time made the sexual advances.[3] In layman's terms, this means that if you know one hundred women who attend church fairly regularly, three of them have experienced sexual advances by a pastor at some time during their adult years.

Currently, two states have criminal laws prohibiting clergy sexual behavior with an adult.[4] This, however, does not preclude the action of civil suits being brought against offenders even in states that have no criminal code in place as of yet. I believe that we will witness of proliferation of criminal and civil cases as public sensitivity increases to the damage inflicted by clergy sexual misconduct.

Child Sexual Abuse

Child sexual abuse by clergy is also of grave concern. Any statistical frequency of occurrence would be staggering. But what is most heartbreaking is the lifelong damage that is inflicted on the victims. Child sexual abuse, along with physical and emotional abuse, is the equivalent of committing soul murder. Many child victims of abuse do eventually commit suicide as a direct result of the abuse that they have endured.[5] And those who manage to survive the statistical odds of committing suicide nonetheless live with the crippling effects of the abuse for the rest of their lives. Their ability to function as whole human beings is seriously compromised. These victims will spend their lives trying to recover spiritually, physically, and psychologically. Whether or not they literally die as a direct result of their abuse, they have been robbed of the life that God gave them.

Child sexual abuse is particularly heinous because of the significantly heightened level of authority, power and influence that the perpetrator has over the child victim. Clearly some perpetrators are predators who use their position of authority, power, and influence to wantonly satisfy their appetites for sexual and psychological satisfaction at the expense of their victims. But sadly, others slide precariously from good intentions to abuse, from wandering to predation. They disregard incremental boundary protections, common sense, and prudence, in exchange for filling a personal need. These pastors are not predators, at least not initially. However, when they indulge their fantasies, their judgment becomes clouded and they rationalize each step toward the precipitous cliff of sexual abuse, taking advantage of the opportunities afforded by their position and power. They eventually arrange carefully orchestrated situations that allow them to perpetrate sexual abuse on a child. Their actions become predatory.

I will not specifically address here the prevention of and response to child sexual abuse by clergy. The issues related to child sexual abuse are complex; its implications are momentous and profound. Response to such abuse requires the expertise of professionals whose primary work is with victims of child sexual abuse and the careful, compassionate, and thorough case management by the legal entities, religious governing boards, and mental health professionals.

However, if you have become tangled in a web of inappropriate conduct with a minor child, have viewed or possessed child pornography, have entertained or currently entertain fantasies of sexual behavior with a minor child, or find yourself in any way sexually attracted to a child or children, *take immediate action!* The life of a child is on the line. No amount of self-gratification will ever justify committing murder—soul murder or otherwise. Do the following:

- *Call a leader* of your denominational governing board and let him know that you need help. Let him know the nature of your concerns. You may feel vulnerable, scared, and ashamed, but this will not compare to the pain and shame you will experience if others discover your abusive fantasies or behavior later.
- *Step away* from your routine ministerial obligations immediately. Have an assistant or other church leader arrange for coverage. Someone else can preach Sunday's sermon. There are no commitments on your calendar that are as important as your commitment to stopping your precipitous slide toward the robbing of a child's life.
- *Make an appointment* to speak with a mental health professional who is trained to work with sexual boundary issues. With the help of this

professional, identify a plan of action that will insure the safety of others and strengthen your prognosis for recovery and healing.

- *Arrange for a leave of absence.* Depending on the extent to which you have acted on any fantasies, the church leadership will need to determine the most appropriate plan for response, both for you and the (potential) victim. Discuss with your denominational board or church lay leadership your plan of action and arrange for follow-up accountability.

These steps may seem drastic. You may wonder if such radical steps are in order. Ask yourself: "Am I willing to put the life of another human being at risk for the sake of protecting my image? Am I a murderer?" Jesus warned, "Whoever causes one of these little ones who believe in Me to stumble, it would be better for him to have a heavy millstone hung around his neck, and to be drowned in the depth of the sea" (Mt. 18:6, NASB). Without intervention, you may find yourself drowning in the depths of the sea with a millstone of guilt, shame, disrepute, and responsibility wrapped around your neck.

You may think, "These are only fantasies; I would never act on them." But consider that Jesus said, "Anyone who looks at a woman lustfully has already committed adultery with her in his heart" (Mt. 5:28). He knew that that it is human nature to act on our thoughts. If you entertain the fantasy, you have the capacity to act on it. You may think, "These are unwanted thoughts. I would never want to hurt a child." That is a good thing; then you are not a predator and there is hope for healing. Get the help you need to rid yourself of the unwanted thoughts and prevent yourself from doing what you don't want to do. You may think, "I want to take care of this by myself; I can control this." Have you been able to control your fantasies and prevent them from surfacing in your mind? If your thoughts and urges are unwelcome, then you don't have control over them and you *cannot* save yourself without the help of others.

Boundaries here are not optional. Every church needs to have clear guidelines for screening volunteers and staff members who work with children and for accountability among staff. I have included a number of resources for developing appropriate abuse prevention guidelines noted here.[6] If the church you are currently serving has not put into place adequate safeguards, make this a priority. Congregations that do not perceive the need for safeguards need to be educated.

If you suspect that another staff member, lay leader, or parishioner is sexually abusing a child, take action. Before doing anything else, tell a trusted colleague who can help you determine an appropriate plan of action that is adequately responsive but not overly aggressive. Then begin to look for sustainable evidence, monitor the suspect's behavior, and document your observations. If you conclude that your concerns are well founded and a child is being abused, you will need to contact the appropriate legal authorities as mandated by your state's laws. Do not be remiss to confront potential child abuse; do not allow your fears or misgivings to prevent you from protecting the children in your congregation.

Defining Clergy Sexual Misconduct

The boundaries of appropriate sexual conduct have little flexibility, and yet, confusion exists in congregations about what is appropriate and what is not. One of the most significant challenges that arises in preventing clergy sexual misconduct (CSM) is the mistaken belief that sexually inappropriate behavior with an adult parishioner implies a consensual relationship between two adults and therefore a mutual responsibility by both adults. Chapter 8 (Straight Talk on Power) demonstrates, however, that the pastor is in a position of greater power and influence than the parishioners. Parishioners are therefore vulnerable to manipulation, special attention, grooming, cognitive dismissal of reasonable concerns, confusion in recognizing and understanding the exploitative advances of their pastor, expectations for submission to authority, a desire to comply with the spiritual direction of the pastor, and subsequently sexual misconduct.

At times, a parishioner may indeed be the initiator of a sexually inappropriate relationship with the pastor. We noted in chapter 4 that parishioners often come into churches with their pain, crippling histories, dysfunction, and confusion, searching for hope and healing. So, we cannot expect that every parishioner will have healthy relational boundaries. However, the parishioner's deficits are never an excuse for taking advantage of what the parishioner is attempting to initiate. Even if a parishioner "comes on" to a pastor, the pastor must maintain clear and wholesome sexual boundaries. Sexual misconduct between a pastor and parishioner is not "just an affair." Responsibility for sexual boundary violations *always* lies with pastors, by virtue of the position of power and of pastors' free agency to regulate their own behavior.

But, many times, parishioners do not initiate the mutation of spiritual care into sexual misconduct. In these situations, a series of factors lay the foundation for a breach of sexual boundaries:[7]

1. The pastor is unaware of, or is negligent in tending to, his personal needs.
2. The pastor either consciously or unconsciously identifies a parishioner who welcomes his care and attention.
3. The pastor identifies to the parishioner her needs and then proposes to meet those needs, often in ways that strike the parishioner as unusual but nonetheless defy the parishioner's ability to label them as inappropriate.
4. The parishioner responds favorably to the pastor's subtle overtures, confirms her tacit acquiescence, and begins to accept some degree of responsibility for meeting his personal needs.[8]

These steps are the set-up for sexual misconduct. Victims of clergy sexual misconduct often report that, in hindsight, their sexual involvement with the pastor was virtually assured once the set-up was established. Some of the factors that increase parishioners' vulnerability to CSM are: conflicted marriage, loneliness, recent grief or loss, history of abuse, excessively compliant nature, spiritual confusion or conflict, low self-esteem, strong concern for others' feelings (especially not hurting others' feelings), and low sense of self-determination or agency in their own lives. Of the factors listed above, almost all of them contributed to Ann's (A Parishioner Tells Her Story) vulnerabilities to abuse.

Sexual misconduct is *any* behavior that violates appropriate sexual boundaries. Its scope is broader than engaging in oral sex or sexual intercourse. Behaviors such as kissing, hugging, patting, touching, stroking, and holding hands also constitute sexual misconduct, if the offender's intent is to communicate sexual interest within a pastor-parishioner relationship, or if those behaviors are perceived by the recipient to be of a sexual nature. All of the following also constitute sexual misconduct:

- telling crude jokes of a sexual nature
- discussing personal sexual concerns with parishioners
- giving parishioners printed material to read that contains sexual content
- telling parishioners about the pastor's sexual fantasies (which may or may not include the parishioner)
- asking the parishioner to watch a movie together that contains sexually explicit material or scenes
- making jokes about a parishioner's sexuality, sexual identity, sexual behavior, or sexual relationship with her spouse
- asking a parishioner in a joking manner to participate in sexual behavior with the pastor such that the parishioner feels confused about the seriousness of the pastor's overture
- encouraging a parishioner to participate in ambiguous behaviors with spiritual associations, such as holding hands while praying, that confuse the parishioner and reduce her inhibitions to decline more openly sexual advances in the future

All the behaviors described above may seem obviously inappropriate to the reader. However, both pastors and parishioners who have crossed appropriate sexual boundaries report that, at the time, even if they were cognizant that the actual sexual involvement was wrong, they were not alarmed or concerned over some of the set-up behaviors. Why is that? Let's look at how pastors lose clarity in the maintenance of healthy sexual boundaries with parishioners.

How the Fog Moves In

Ann's story (A Parishioner Tells Her Story) tells how clergy sexual misconduct affected one parishioner. Think about how her pastor, Brad, might present his side of this story. Although we can't know what he was thinking and all the issues in his life that led to his ultimate perpetration of abuse, it may be assumed that he was not originally a predator. In order to examine how a pastor's boundaries become obscured and eventually violated, let's assume that he had no history of sexual boundary violations and that his ministry was generally solid except for the typical bumps and challenges. If he had been asked before his involvement with Ann if he thought he was capable of sexual misconduct, he probably would have vehemently denied it.

Here is the first phase in the blurring of boundaries: *the pastor thinks he is incapable of the boundary violation.* Thinking himself immune, the pastor disregards the need for vigilance of his boundaries, disregards what would otherwise be warning signs to an onlooker, and disregards the importance of careful tending of his own personal needs. "So, if you think you are standing firm, be careful that you don't fall!" (1 Cor. 10:12). Perhaps Brad considered himself "a good man," of strong conviction and virtuous. The apostle Paul warns us: "For by the grace given me I say to every one of you: Do not think of yourself more highly than you ought, but rather think of yourself with sober judgment, in accordance with the measure of faith God has given you" (Rom. 12:3). *Sober judgment* is key. Paul does not call on us to berate ourselves, to degrade our desires and spirits for the temptations we face, or to live with false humility. What we do need is a realistic perspective of ourselves that acknowledges both our virtues and our weaknesses. We need to know our strengths and our vulnerabilities. We need to *know ourselves.*

Vulnerability is normal in human nature. It is the hunger of an unmet need, and it leads to thoughts of how we will fill the need. When we think of inappropriate, sinful ways to meet the need, we face temptation. People often confuse temptation with sin. Temptation is not sin; it is a thought. Its only consequence is in what we do with it. Do we entertain the temptation, or do we turn away from it? Unfortunately, I believe that many people think of temptation as sin itself, and so try to ignore, disown, or repress the temptations in order to preserve a self-image of righteousness. This is "thinking more highly of ourselves than we ought." Accurate self-knowledge entails owning our temptations and using them to our benefit—as warning and motivation to take care of our needs before we become so hungry that we "could eat a horse."

Continuing to evaluate how Brad went from minister to abuser, we can also assume that he was blind to the effects of brewing relational difficulties he was experiencing with his wife and the congregation's leadership board. Perhaps he was experiencing a mild sense of estrangement from the leadership board and his wife and this was causing low-level depressive symptoms. He was losing his sense of agency[9] to be an effective spiritual leader and an adequate mate to his spouse. Since he was not aware of his own depression, he could not address it. However, Ann's depression and loneliness resonated with him and he unconsciously he began to focus on Ann's sadness as a way to vicariously ease his own pain. Perhaps he subconsciously felt that he could restore his significance and agency in his own life by making a difference in a parishioner's life.

This illustrates the second phase of boundary blurring: *the pastor is unaware of his own vulnerabilities and needs.* The third phase follows closely behind: *the pastor confuses his needs with the parishioner's needs.*

When Brad began counseling Ann, his need to feel significant was being nurtured by the counseling relationship. In other words, although he overtly offered the counseling for her benefit, he was filling a personal need to feel appreciated and important to someone. When Ann stopped making appointments, he took steps to reinitiate the relationship. His personal need for the counseling relationship became his priority. This is phase four: *the pastor's needs take precedence over those of the parishioner.* Knowing that Ann was lonely, Brad began to insure the durability of his relationship with her by offering her affection that he knew she would accept and creating a connection with her that she would not easily reject. The initial demonstrations of affection were hardly "sexual"; had Ann raised concerns, he could have easily assured her that his motives were entirely innocent and he did not intend to convey any inappropriate expectations. This is phase five: *the pastor engages in "innocuous" behaviors that invite deeper connection and feel good to the parishioner but can easily be explained away should they be questioned.*

By this point, Brad began testing her level of vulnerability by asking her to do things that would normally be interpreted as inappropriate. Ann's reticence to comply was interpreted back to her as a symptom of the very problem he had convinced her was the source of her unhappiness. And he used her need for acceptability to manipulate her compliance. By agreeing to sit in his lap, she could prove to him and God that she was learning to trust, that she was willing to take spiritual direction from authority, and that he still had a reason to be proud of her. This is phase six: *The pastor engages in progressively questionable behaviors that confuse the parishioner and the pastor interprets the parishioner's acquiescence as confirmation of the acceptability of the behaviors.*

When Ann acquiesced to the progressively questionable behaviors, Brad was able to complete the transformation of the relationship. We don't know why Brad began sharing his personal concerns with Ann, but we might surmise that he wanted a sympathetic ear and he knew that in doing so, he would be able to keep her engaged and feeling "special." The relationship shifted from pastor-parishioner to peer-peer. Brad began calling Ann his "heaven-sent sister." Sometimes a pastor will attempt to continue to assert his pastoral position in the relationship, possibly to continue his image as a man of God, to maintain his perceived authority over his parishioner, or to assuage his muffled guilt over relinquishing his pastoral responsibilities. Were the betrayal of pastoral trust not enough, the role confusion increases the toxicity of the relationship and thrusts the parishioner into a web of bewilderment. Ann's role with Brad swung between parishioner, friend, confidante, sister, and lover. Because these roles were evoked simultaneously, Ann would have no way of discriminating the appropriate boundaries. The bewilderment serves to disarm the parishioner's alarm systems. The parishioner can no longer discern which alarms to believe. This is phase seven: *The pastor induces a shift in roles such that it is no longer possible to identify the appropriate boundaries.*

To summarize, the classic progression of clergy sexual misconduct is:

1. The pastor thinks he is incapable of the boundary violation.
2. The pastor is unaware of his own vulnerabilities and needs.
3. The pastor confuses his needs with the parishioner's needs.
4. The pastor's needs take precedence over those of the parishioner.
5. The pastor engages in "innocuous" behaviors that feel good to the parishioner to invite greater intimacy but can easily be explained away should they be challenged.
6. The pastor engages in progressively questionable behaviors that confuse the parishioner and then interprets the parishioner's acquiescence as confirmation of the acceptability of the behaviors.
7. The pastor induces a shift in roles such that it is no longer possible to identify the appropriate boundaries.

We have conducted an autopsy of the process by which Brad became sexually involved with Ann. The actual sexual involvement did not occur immediately. There was a protracted period of grooming before the relationship became conspicuously sexual. Review the story again and consider: At what point did the relationship become inappropriate? When did it become sexual? When did it qualify as sexual misconduct? When did it become abuse?

From Blurry Boundaries to Over the Edge

In Ann's story we notice that there were numerous occasions when Ann had misgivings about the developing relationship between her and Brad. It is easy to wonder why, if she sensed the alarms, she did not stop the progression. Why did Brad ignore the boundaries and proceed into sexual misconduct? He presumably knew right from wrong. Some pastors stop upon recognizing their flirtations with boundary violations. So why didn't Brad stop?

Aside from the simplistic answer, "He didn't want to stop," there are reasons why pastors continue on the road to sexual misconduct, disregarding all warnings of conscience and others. For every temptation, there is a point of no return, but that point is not so obvious, neither in foresight nor in hindsight. If I am tempted by Little Debbie cupcakes and could eat ten of them in as many minutes, especially if no one is around, I know that the line is somewhere between being alone or with other people, between going to the grocery store or sending my husband, between walking down the snack aisle or bypassing it, between buying Ding-Dongs or buying my favorite fruit. I also know that the line is somewhere between rewarding myself with a cup of tea or with the sweet little treats, between thinking of Little Debbies as an energy boost or taking a walk to wake up my circulation. If only someone would tell me exactly how close I can get to the line without actually succumbing to the draw of the cupcakes.

We go over the edge when we flirt with danger in spite of the warnings. Remember the graphic in Chapter 9: "From Solid Footing to Slippery Slope"? There were mechanisms to keep our ill-fated fellow safe, starting with staying on the grass. Then there was a step down, then a fence, next a big "Danger!" sign and then a pile of boulders. For some reason, the guardrails bewitched our foolish fellow, as if they were a daring invitation to cheat fate. The question is not, How close can I get? The question is, *How far away can I stay?* Our boundaries will not get confused and we cannot go over the edge if we do not try to see how close we can get without getting hurt or being guilty of sin.

To extend this concept, let's think again about Brad. When did his behavior become misconduct? (That is, how close could he get without being guilty?) Maybe the answer is, when he hugged Ann the first time, when the shoulder hugs turned into full frontal hugs, when he kissed her cheek, when he asked her to sit in his lap, when he told her about his sexual problems with his wife, when he suggested they meet at a motel. Maybe. But the relevant question is, "When did he cross the line?" (That is, How far away was he when he started to move toward the cliff?)

Brad stepped over the line when he asked Ann to participate in counseling with him, because he was pursuing the fulfillment of a personal need. Then he stepped over another line when he hugged her across the shoulders because he used the reward of acceptance and "brotherly" affection to entice her to stay in counseling. And then he stepped over the line when he took away her autonomy to think for herself and told her what she needed. The more lines he crossed, the more assured was his fall. In essence, he started going over the cliff when he solicited Ann to fulfill his needs by inviting her into counseling.

Paul's words here are excellent guidance: "But among you there must not be even a *hint* of sexual immorality, or of any kind of impurity, or of greed, because these are improper for God's holy people" (Eph. 5:3, author's emphasis). Don't do anything that even *hints* at impropriety. That's how far Paul says we should stay away from the edge. We can do several things to maintain clarity in our boundaries and not let our hunger drive us to the edge or over the edge.

First, *look for ways to stay away from the edge.* If you are wondering if it would be appropriate to kiss someone on the cheek, reframe the question: Is there a way I can communicate my affection without challenging that boundary? Sometimes we get a charge out of testing boundaries; it's human nature. Children do it all the time. But boundaries around inappropriate sexual behavior are best left unchallenged.

Second, *don't confuse intimacy with sexual behavior.* Everyone longs for intimacy—the warmth that comes from being known and accepted—not only in a marital relationship, but with friends and family as well. Pastors are at high risk for isolation, loneliness, and lack of healthy intimate relationships. The marital relationship sometimes suffers due to the demands of ministry. It is often difficult to develop friendships because so much time and energy is spent within the social network of the church, while friendships are best cultivated outside the congregation. When a pastor is craving intimacy, he is vulnerable to the temptation of engaging in a sexual relationship to quell the hunger pangs, even if the real hunger is for emotional intimacy. Joe (Special Friends) was too busy to heed his hunger for intimacy and even as he was oblivious to his need, he fell over the edge. He disregarded the "bewares!" and the guardrails. When Kat was satisfying his need, his rationalizations prevented him from recognizing that he had gone over the cliff.

Third, get in the habit of asking yourself, *"Am I flirting?"* Flirting is another behavior common to human nature. It is a game of doing or saying one thing and hinting at another, usually of a more sexualized nature. Flirting has no place in pastoral ministry since it uses parishioners to satisfy a desire for sexual frolicking. Another way to ask this question: "Is my behavior hinting at something more?" This is similar to the ideas in chapter 9 of assessing whether the behavior could be misinterpreted and testing your motives. But, especially with sexual boundaries, there are behaviors that, while not blatantly sexual themselves, hint at the possibility of something more. These behaviors are flirtatious. They could be misinterpreted, but more likely they do indeed hint at the invitation to a more intimate sexual expression. Kissing, "knowing" winks, hugging, patting, stroking, sexual jokes, innuendos, and hand-holding can all be used to hint at a desire for a deeper expression of affection and physical intimacy.

Fourth, get in the habit of asking yourself, "Would I act this way in a public setting?" In most cases, pastors who become sexually involved with a parishioner are able to because of the privacy and limited accountability their position affords them. A pastor's use of privacy to protect a parishioner's confidentiality should never be used as a cloak to rob that same parishioner of her dignity. If your behavior does not like the light, your behavior is over the line: "Everyone who does evil hates the light, and will not come into the light for fear that his deeds will be exposed. But whoever lives by the truth comes into the light, so that it may be seen plainly that what he has done has been done through God" (Jn. 3:20–21).

Victims of clergy sexual misconduct sometimes describe how a clergy member gave them unusual physical or sexualized attention in public, such as complimenting their looks, brushing their hair off their shoulder, hugging them tightly, holding their hands longer than usual, or whispering something personal to them during a religious ceremony such as communion. This confused the parishioners by suggesting that the behavior was perfectly legitimate, since it was done in the public eye and no one raised any concerns. So while public scrutiny can be a helpful test of the appropriateness of sexual boundaries, it is not a fail-safe guardrail by itself.

Fifth, *pay attention to your physical sensations.* Physical, emotional, or sexual attraction to another person is natural. Sometimes it sneaks up on us. Pastors are often uncomfortable with the thought that they could be attracted to someone other than their mates. If the pastor experiences the spontaneous attraction as uncomfortable, he will also likely pretend it isn't happening, thereby ignoring the bodily sensations that accompany the titillation. Adrenaline rushes, flushing, increased heart rate, giddiness, tingling, increased energy, hyper-awareness of the other individual, and butterflies in the stomach can all be the result of chemical changes that our bodies experience when we feel an attraction to someone else, when there is "chemistry" between two people. Don't disregard the signals. Like temptation, a chemical reaction is not sin; it's a feeling. We need to be aware of it, and decide how we should respond in an appropriate way.

Last of all, *put into place the guardrails* that were described in chapter 8. When we are set on getting what we want, our hearts are tricksters, with great capacity for convincing our minds that our thoughts and behaviors are acceptable. Rationalization and intellectualization are some of human nature's most deceiving mental processes. Internal checks (the first five recommendations in this section) are necessary but not sufficient. We need external checks as well. [10]

Emotional Affairs: "At Least I Never Crossed the Line!"

An emotional affair may sound less objectionable than a sexual, physical affair. It may be tempting to think that because no physical acts are involved, the relationship is still within bounds. But the term "emotional affair" betrays the undeniable fact that the relationship is nonetheless an affair. It is still misconduct, and it is still damaging to the victim. *It still crosses the line!* There is a distinction between emotional affairs and friendship; we will discuss boundaries of friendship in the next chapter. For now, let us consider two distinctions that characterize an emotional affair.

First, the relationship, while not overtly sexual, is sexually or romantically charged. One or both involved persons experience a sense of sexual "chemistry." Emotional affairs often involve sharing of sexual thoughts, sexual joking and jesting, flirtatious behavior, and an implied "I would if I could" overtone. Either one or both of the involved parties experience sexualized or romantic fantasies about the relationship and the other person.

Second, the relationship involves mutual emotional intimacy that is not appropriate to the pastor-parishioner relationship. A parishioner rightfully believes that sharing intimate information (within reason) with her pastor is acceptable, for the purposes of seeking guidance and counsel. However, intimate information shared by the pastor with the parishioner is over the line; that intimacy should be sought in another venue, either with a mate or spouse, close friend (not parishioner), family member, or accountability partner. Ann's (A Parishioner Tells Her Story) sharing of intimate information was theoretically appropriate (assuming that Brad observed the boundaries of pastoral counseling), but Brad's sharing was highly inappropriate. He abjectly used the counseling relationship for self-serving purposes.

While sexual affairs are occasionally initiated on the basis of pure sexual attraction, they most often start as emotional affairs, where emotional intimacy eventually gives rise to physical intimacy. Emotional intimacy is one of those lines that, once crossed, almost guarantees that the pastor will go over the edge of sexual boundaries. Pastors who are not married do not have the responsibility of honoring the marital relationship. They may believe that intimate sharing with another person is therefore appropriate. But the problem remains: parishioners should never be in a position of having to shoulder the pastor's secret or private emotional life. The pastor cannot function in his other responsibilities to the parishioner if the parishioner is functioning as a repository of the pastor's personal emotional baggage. The most basic boundary between pastor and parishioner is violated–the parishioner is used to provide an emotionally intimate outlet for the pastor.

Beyond the dangers that emotional intimacy creates for sexual misconduct, emotional affairs are in their own right destructive and victimizing. I noted earlier that communications of a sexual nature *are* sexual misconduct. These behaviors place the parishioner in a difficult and uncomfortable position; for example, she may be unable to harmonize the pastor's position with his behavior or words, she may be left wondering about his intentions, she may interpret the communication as sexual harassment.

Movements toward establishing emotional intimacy confuse the parishioner. The parishioner will be unclear about her role with the pastor. Is she now a confidante, a friend, a soul mate, a pastor to the pastor, or still a parishioner? The parishioner usually does not have much control over what the pastor shares and so is left holding a bundle of intimate information with no idea of how to handle it. She may feel conflicting emotions—on the one hand, affirmed by her pastor's trust in her, and on the other hand, uneasy with the level of intimacy. She genuinely cares about her pastor and wants to be supportive, but is ill-equipped to deal with the information presented to her. She does not want to hurt his feelings or tell him to stop when he clearly needs someone to talk to.

Emotional intimacy with a parishioner almost invariably causes confusion, pain, damage, and a violation of trust. The parishioner eventually senses that the relationship is off-balance and becoming increasingly convoluted. She may try to put some distance between herself and her pastor, but then misses the closeness that the emotional intimacy provided for her as well. The pastor, feeling vulnerable because of the intimate nature of his disclosures, may desperately attempt to re-engage the parishioner to protect his secrets. Alternatively, the parishioner who tries to extricate herself from the relationship may experience retaliation by the pastor. He may black-list the parishioner or publicly challenge her reputation in a preemptive maneuver to discredit her in case she discloses information about him to others. For the parishioner, the turmoil can be chaotic, consuming, and traumatic.

If the pastor recognizes eventually that the emotional affair is unhealthy or out of bounds and tries to end it, he will likely lose countless hours of sleep wondering what will come of his intimate disclosures, wasting precious energy doing damage control and attempting to mollify the hurt emotions of the parishioner who now feels disenfranchised and confused about the termination of the relationship. When the pastor distances himself from the parishioner, she may feel "dumped" and assume responsibility for the loss of the relationship, believing that something is inherently wrong with her as a trustworthy friend or intimate companion. Ultimately, no good comes from emotional affairs, and the likelihood that the affair will end in pain and destruction is overwhelming.

If you believe that you may have already crossed the line of emotional intimacy with a parishioner, take steps to end it and rectify the breach of boundaries. Because of the risk of hurt and confusion, it is best to discuss the situation with a trusted colleague and a mental health professional before taking action. Develop a plan of action. Your primary goal here is not to mitigate the risks you face of embarrassment or the parishioner's disclosure of your personal information, but to help the parishioner understand the nature of the breach and the fact that you alone are responsible for that breach. This may require intervention by a well-qualified third person, counseling support (not by you) for the parishioner and reassignment of the parishioner for future spiritual care to another pastoral staff member. Handled with care, compassion, and wisdom, the damage caused by an emotional affair may be mitigated. The single most important factor in a good prognosis is the pastor's willingness to accept full responsibility for the breach, the hurt to the parishioner, and his delinquency to provide safe pastoral care to the parishioner.

Pornography: Clergy Sexual Abuse with a Nameless Victim

As with clergy sexual misconduct, there has been a proliferation of pornography use by pastors in the last couple decades. Privacy in the office, always-on Internet access, and ready availability of pornography have all contributed to this pandemic. Corporations and other organizations in the public sector are faced with the pandemic as well. Pastors are not immune to the temptations of pornography, and its use is as damaging to them as to anyone else. But because of the demands and challenges pastors face, the lure of pornography is particularly tantalizing, and, because of the pastor's position, its destructiveness is amplified.

As noted previously, lack of intimacy is a particular problem for pastors. The lack of intimacy, when not addressed in healthy ways, increases the pastor's temptation to substitute intimacy for a false sense of connection and sexual acting out. Pornography offers a "quick fix." The viewer, for the moment, feels intimately connected with the provocative image on the screen and provides a venue for sexual acting out (either by fantasizing or masturbating) that is relatively safe and private.

At some point in every pastor's career, he will experience a sense of boredom in his work. The church membership is the same as two years ago, the parishioners have the same problems, the programs are the same, the sick calls are the same, and even the sermon preparation becomes monotonous and uninspiring. In spite of the position of power that pastors hold, challenges of ministry can leave a pastor feeling powerless, ineffectual, and unappreciated. Trying unsuccessfully to ignite passion in a lukewarm congregation, getting and keeping enough volunteers for the children's ministry, achieving consensus with the leadership board on priorities for building improvements, and such can drain the confidence and energy out of even the most well-grounded pastor.

The human brain is wired to seek novelty, variety, and stimulation. Pornography offers an escape from the mundane, from the drudgery of daily ministry. Perhaps the most powerful lure of pornography is the promise that the viewer will experience an enhanced feeling of desirability and control. The seduction of pornography lies in the viewer's perception that the images are there for him, that an anonymous somebody actually *wants* to provide the viewer with pleasure. The viewer equates the desirability of the image with his own desirability. And, unlike with human relationships, the viewer thinks he has complete control over the demands the pornographic "relationships" place on him.

Pornography use inevitably becomes an addiction; the viewer ends up having no control over the pornographic relationship. Like drug use, pornography use alters the chemistry of the brain, creating endorphin rushes that the brain begins to crave. Very few people can say that they viewed pornography only once (unless by accident) and never went back to it. Perhaps as many as 70 percent of men have used pornography regularly at some point in their lives. Women, while less vulnerable to the appeal of pornography, can also become addicted.

On the surface, it may seem that viewing pornography does not hurt anyone (except the pastor), but the truth is pornography use by pastors is clergy sexual abuse. The pastor is using someone, who remains nameless, for personal gratification. Just because the victim is nameless does not reduce the severity of the abuse. Pornography use is sometimes rationalized by the assertion that those who elect to publish sexual images of themselves do so out of their own free will. However, they would not do so if there were no market. No demand, no market. The pastor that views pornography is increasing the demand and therefore tempting others to devalue themselves.

Why is pornography use by pastors so destructive? Consider these factors:

- Because pastors are expected to meet very high standards of morality,[11] when the pastor's addiction is found out, the congregation's and pastor's pain and shame are amplified: the higher the pedestal, the further the fall.
- Pastors, rightfully or not, are perceived as representatives of God. The discovery of a pastor's addiction to pornography can catapult parishioners into a full-blown faith crisis from which they may not recover.
- Pastors who are using pornography cannot effectively guide and counsel other parishioners who are in its grip.
- Pornography induces the viewer to objectify people, not only the people whose images he is viewing, but also those in his pastoral care. Other people are subtly and unconsciously transformed from human beings into objects to be used for self-gratification. The pastor puts parishioners at risk of being inappropriately used.
- Pornography use is a progressive addiction and slavemaster that demands ever-greater novelty and stimulation. It eventually leads to sexual acting out. Pastors who engage the services of prostitutes; are sexually promiscuous with others; or have been arrested for voyeurism, exhibitionism, fetishism, and other forms of sexual acting out almost always started down their path with pornography.

The destructive effects of a pastor's pornography use are profound. It threatens to nullify every ounce of a pastor's effectiveness as a person and a minister. If you find yourself tempted by pornography, or you are already trapped and unable to control your behavior, ask for help. As with other addictions, it is not something you will conquer by yourself. Speak with a mental health professional who has experience treating addictions, preferably sexual addictions.

Protection from the Seduction of Pornography

Many organizations recognize the liabilities incurred by employee access to pornographic Web sites: the loss of employee productivity and the repercussions to the entire organization due to increased risk of sexual harassment claims, potential for access and trafficking in child pornography, and loss of morale by those who must compensate for the decreased productivity. These organizations have also put technological mechanisms in place to monitor employee Internet use and block undesirable websites. Most organizations have employment termination policies in place regarding access to pornographic Web sites. But churches generally have less ability and technical expertise to monitor Internet use. The pastoral function requires relative autonomy and privacy. The majority of churches have limited staff, only one pastor, and thus minimal accountability. Written employment policies, church-endorsed codes of conduct, and explicit disciplinary protocols are absent from many churches. All of these factors increase a pastor's susceptibility to becoming entangled by an addiction to pornography.

If your church is not already monitoring Internet use on church computers, have it set up. Have the lay leadership or denominational governing body identify several people whose responsibility it is to monitor Internet access logs.[12] Knowing that Internet use is monitored is probably the most effective means of eliminating temptation to use pornography. If you have a home computer, have Internet access on that computer monitored as well.

Set up spam filters on the church e-mail server. The preponderance of spam is pornographic in nature, often containing embedded files with pornographic images. A passing curiosity sparked by spam can easily develop into an addiction.

Educate your congregation on the destructive effects of pornography. The more aware your parishioners are of its pervasiveness, allure, and detrimental effects, the more strength you will have to oppose its enticement in your own life and your parishioners will benefit from the education as well.

Limit the amount of time you spend surfing the Internet. Use your computer to do your work, then get off. Like television, the computer can induce a semi-hypnotic state that dulls our cognitive abilities and immobilizes our bodies. It is much harder to close a pop-up window with sexual content when we feel stupefied and sluggish.

Our sexuality is an inherent part of our being; it is a gift from God and intrinsically good. However, governing our sexual nature, channeling it toward wholesome outlets, and preventing its exuberance from distorting our relationships requires knowing the truth about ourselves, diligence, commitment, and accountability. May God grants us wisdom and grace to redeem all that God created us to be!

Time to Reflect

1. Think back on a time when you experienced a palpable "chemistry" between yourself and a parishioner. How did you recognize the feeling? What were your bodily sensations?
2. How did you react cognitively to this situation? What allowed you to step back and decide against allowing the chemistry to blossom?
3. Have you experienced an attraction to a parishioner that you then entertained in your fantasies for a period of time? In what ways did your fantasizing thoughts make it more difficult to interact with the parishioner?
4. What specific circumstances or life stressors make you more susceptible to sexualizing your parishioner relationships? How can you address those stressors or situations without compromising your boundaries with the congregation?
5. Do you personally know a pastoral colleague who has engaged in clergy sexual misconduct? What do you know about the story, how the relationship became unhealthy, what the circumstances were that caused that pastor to be susceptible? What can you learn from that situation?
6. How do you currently insure healthy sexual and intimate relationships in your own life? Is there an area that needs work? If you see that the strain of ministry has had a toll on an important personal relationship, what can you do to rectify that?
7. How do you currently protect yourself from the temptations of pornography, sexually inappropriate relationships, and emotional affairs? What guardrails are missing or inadequate? Do you need to put up additional safeguards?

CHAPTER 11

Real-Life Boundaries in
Real-Life Ministry

*"Man is not born to solve the problem of the universe, but to find
out what he has to do;
and to restrain himself within the limits of his comprehension."*

JOHANN WOLFGANG VON GOETHE (1749–1832)

*"Purchase not friends by gifts; when thou ceasest to give, such will
cease to love."*

THOMAS FULLER (1608–1661)

The church body serves many purposes. One of its compelling functions is to teach us how to get along. It is one of the best places to practice boundaries, to learn how to function as a unit–the body of Christ–while maintaining our individuality. As with all organizations, secular or otherwise, the local congregation develops a corporate identity and personality over time. No two congregations are alike; how well each congregation functions is largely determined by its generational history,[1] the health of the existing relationships, and the resourcefulness of its leadership. We reviewed the operation of boundaries in the body of Christ in chapter 4. Now we move toward actively applying the principles of boundaries to ministry in the congregation.

In a myriad of capacities pastors are in a unique position to poignantly model healthy boundaries with the congregation. Over the span of a congregation's history, the healthier the modeling of boundaries by its pastors and other leadership, the healthier the system-wide functioning by all individuals and in all roles. This phenomenon holds true even when the identity of the individual parishioners changes over time. Thus, a pastor's modeling of boundaries has the ability to affect the psychological health of the congregation not only during that pastor's tenure, but in future generations of leadership as well.

In chapter 2 we examined how the boundary between self and mommy develops. From birth, every child places demands on its environment and the people within its sphere of awareness. A child learns that expectations are unrealistic when demands are not met as anticipated, but also learns that mommy does not exist solely for the sake of the child and that the child is able to meet some needs independently of mommy. The child who is well cared for but does not receive the fulfillment of every demand made experiences what has been termed "optimal frustration,"[2] a primary motivator toward growth and autonomy. The mommy that attempts to meet every demand will produce an enmeshed, symbiotic relationship with her child that obstructs the child's development of sense of self, agency, and individuation. Note that enmeshment—*i.e.,* unhealthy boundaries—is the result of inhibiting the child's discovery of what it is capable of on its own, *not* the result of unrealistic expectations placed by the child on its mother.

The same principle holds true throughout life. Excessive and unrealistic expectations are a given. They are problematic, not because they exist, but because we try to meet those expectations even when doing so is depleting to ourselves and growth-inhibiting for those whose expectations we are meeting. To the extent that meeting excessive expectations depletes us or prevents others from being responsible for themselves, we develop unhealthy relational styles. Pastors who are overwhelmed by the demands of ministry are not the victims of unrealistic expectations; they are the victims of their own inadequate boundaries. As such, effective boundaries with the congregation serve to protect the pastor from depletion and encourage parishioners to take responsibility for themselves to the greatest extent possible. Pastors can implement effective boundaries with congregations in a manner that nurtures relational maturity in the entire congregation, curtails organizational conflict, and reduces the likelihood of burn-out for the pastor.

Personal and Physical Boundaries

In the press to perform ministry duties, we may forget some of our most obvious and basic boundaries. The following is a reminder that we are created beings with physical limits and an existence circumscribed by our thoughts, emotions, and actions.

- *Body.* Our beings are physical. We have souls that are spiritual but we are nonetheless constrained to our bodily "homes." If our bodies do not function as designed, our lives are correspondingly restricted. Good physical health enables us to function well in the physical world; boundaries that protect our bodies are central to effective ministry.
- *Soul.* God created us with souls, the very breath of God. Each soul is special, unique, and the intricate handiwork of God. My soul belongs

to me. The soul is the seat of personal responsibility. We may attempt it, but we cannot transfer responsibility for ourselves to others.

- *Geography.* Just as our souls are constrained by our bodies, our bodies are constrained by geography. Geography makes the boundary of space possible. Space is sometimes the boundary we need to protect ourselves from expectations that we cannot or should not meet. It's also obvious that we cannot be in two places at once. How ironic that occasionally we still try to do that!
- *Time.* There are twenty-four hours in a day, seven days in a week. I cannot add hours to my day, days to my life. Boundaries of time constrain our existence to the present. No matter how much I ruminate on the past or worry about the future, I exist in the present. The present is the best place to be because it is only in the present moment that I can impact the direction of my own life and my surroundings.
- *Thoughts and ideas.* One facet of my existence is my thought production. My thoughts are unique and my ideas are a form of expression of the creativity that God instilled in me. There is a boundary between my thoughts and Truth. There is also a boundary between my thoughts and the thoughts of others. If I adopt the thoughts of others indiscriminately, I disregard the separation between others and me, losing autonomy.
- *Emotions and feelings.* Another facet of my existence is emotion. No one feels exactly the same way I do. In order to exist as an autonomous human being, I must acknowledge that another's feelings do not belong to me and neither can I blame my emotional experiences on others.
- *Things.* While I may own possessions, they are *not part of me.* I can enjoy them and use them to bless or hurt others, but they are not my identity, nor do they enhance or detract from my sense of self and self-worth.

Disregarding these personal boundaries leads to all kinds of dysfunctional behavior. Possibilities include

- thinking we can read the minds of others and presume to know their thoughts
- physically crowding another person with no regard to that person's needs for personal space
- committing to accomplishing tasks that will realistically take twice as long as we are able to allow for
- insisting that our ideas are correct (Truth)
- allowing the feelings of someone else to influence our emotional state
- expecting to be just as beautiful, strong, thin, agile as someone else
- trying to "undo" our past

- blaming others for our conduct
- subsuming someone else's conflict as our own

On the other hand, solid awareness of and respect for these same boundaries enables us to experience autonomy, productivity, and joy. Respect for these boundaries does not guarantee a conflict-free life filled with happiness. It does mean that we will not intentionally bring unnecessary suffering on ourselves or rob others of their autonomy and personal freedom.

Relational Boundaries

Our skill to implement relational boundaries is directly related to our awareness and respect for our personal boundaries. Effective relational boundaries require a clear understanding of which aspects of relational transactions belong to us, which correlates directly to where our beings start and end.

Here are some examples of relational boundaries:

- Others have the duty to be responsible for themselves. I do not try to take over their lives from them.
- Others are free to think differently from me. I do not feel threatened if they see things differently, have different priorities and goals, have different opinions.
- Others have the right to decide how they want to spend their time and other resources, and how they will act. I do not impose my priorities and goals on them.
- Others are called to develop themselves to their highest potential. I do not insist that I know better what they need or how they should grow.
- Others are free to express creativity in their own ways. I do not mandate how they should express themselves creatively.
- Others have the right to experience feelings and emotions freely. I do not demand they feel a particular way; I do not try to absorb their emotions for them.
- Others have the right to dignity and respect; they have a right to be treated fairly. I do not demean, shame, or embarrass them. I do not inflict injustice on them. I do not take advantage of them for my own personal gain.
- Others are free to love, enjoy life, and pursue personal goals. I do not attempt to control their choices.

Relational boundaries perform two functions: they prevent others from running us over and they prevent us from running others over. Pastors are subject to a profusion of expectations from parishioners and the congregation as a whole, which can easily result in pastors being run over. And because of the pastor's position of power, character traits, and personal relational style, pastors can also easily run over their parishioners. Let's examine several areas of ministry that commonly create boundary challenges.

Priorities

Priorities are the guidelines by which we determine how we will spend our resources. Your ministry should also be guided by your priorities. Start with your job description. If your church has not developed one for your position, request that it be developed. Otherwise, you cannot know what the congregation expects from you. Regularly review the priorities within your job description with the church's leadership board. If the resources required to fulfill your responsibilities exceed the resources available to you, discuss this with the board. If the job description legitimately requires sixty hours a week of your time, tell the board how much time you have available and what you believe you can realistically accomplish in that amount of time. It is the responsibility of the church leadership or governing board to determine how to distribute responsibilities among staff and lay leadership within the constraints of available resources.

Our human boundaries of time, resources, and health preclude us from doing everything. It is tempting to feel guilty for what we are not able to accomplish, but since we are exhorted to not think more highly of ourselves than we ought (Rom. 12:3), there is no legitimate shame in acknowledging our human limitations. Unfortunately, some churches abuse their pastors. Their expectations for ministerial service are unreasonable and the congregation is unconcerned for the limitations of their pastor. Pastors may fear that they will be dismissed from their positions if they do not meet the church's performance standards and this fear is sometimes well founded. So in an effort to preserve their employment, they overextend themselves to their own demise. Infrequent requests for extra effort may be feasible, if allowance is made for replenishing the depleted resources at a later time (*e.g.*, taking time off, transferring responsibility for another task to someone else). Attempting to fulfill ongoing unreasonable demands communicates to the congregation that you do not respect yourself, that it is acceptable for the congregation to abuse its pastor in this way, and it abets the congregation's abusive treatment of their pastor.

If you find yourself in such a situation, think carefully about how far you want to extend yourself and deplete your finite resources. It is possible that the problems can be addressed by modeling healthy boundaries, educating the church board about the demands of your job, and working together to identify priorities and establish realistic goals. However, if you find that you are repeatedly unable to satisfy the expectations of the governing board, it may be better to find another ministry position. Under these circumstances, it is better not to wait until you have burned out and are experiencing ill health physically, emotionally, and spiritually.

Even in a church with realistic goals and priorities, the pastor will find competing interests that must be reconciled. For example, one parishioner may believe that a food pantry ministry is needed while another may want a mid-week children's program developed. The pastor, with the congregation, will have to determine which programs are staffed, funded, and implemented, given the resources available within the church. The effective pastor remembers that the church is the ministry of the entire congregation, not just an avenue for the pastor to implement his own visions. Neither does he need to take on full responsibility for identifying which programs should be implemented and maintained. He is responsible for facilitating the congregation's determination of their future, not making their future for them. Sam (Loose Lips Sink Ships) found out the hard way that he could not write his congregation's future–they would need to work through that trajectory themselves.

This boundary may be expressed in another way. When parishioners come to you with ideas for ministry, listen attentively and then solicit their recommendations about how their ideas might be implemented. Rather than taking on their ideas as an additional demand on your time, facilitate a conversation on how they might be able to put wings to their ideas. Get your parishioners used to coming to you not just with complaints and visions but also possible solutions. This communicates that you respect their opinions and think highly of their ability to act for themselves. It also protects you from becoming the focal point for interpersonal conflicts and competing interests within the congregation.

Time Management

We want to get to all the meetings, counsel and provide spiritual direction to as many people as possible, visit everyone who is sick, write killer sermons, officiate at a funeral, and still have a personal life. Ministers generally have more difficulty than other professionals leaving their work at work, so the delineation between work and personal time is easily erased without careful time management. If you do not have a planner, start one now.

- Set aside time for personal pursuits and family. Block out the time in your planner. This is time that is spoken for. Do not reallocate this time for ministry-related activities except under exigent circumstances or if the personal time can be made up elsewhere.
- If a ministry-related request for your time arises, don't commit without checking your planner. Tell people you will have to get back to them. Resist pressure to respond immediately.
- Before you commit, make sure you are not overbooking yourself. Your calendar should have empty blocks of time. Allow for margin in your days.
- If you have trouble setting aside time to do routine work, block it out; it's a date with your own to-do list.
- If your time limitations prevent you from doing what someone is requesting, you don't need to apologize. Just explain that your time

is already committed. You might suggest alternative ways for them to satisfy their request or the possibility that you meet their need at a later date.

- Good time management models healthy boundaries to parishioners. If a parishioner is unhappy with how you are allocating your time, remember that unrealistic expectations are part of normal human development and you can play a part in creating the "optimal frustration" that encourages your parishioner to grow psychologically and spiritually.

- Respect your own time boundaries. If Monday is your day off and you don't honor it, why should anyone else? How you manage your time influences what your congregation expects from you.

Personal Life

Pastors are people too, with personal needs no different from those of their parishioners. Personal activities, relationships, spiritual and intellectual development, creativity, and recreation are vital to the pastor's maintenance of sense of self, identity, esteem, and self-care. The more a pastor's identity is dependent on his ministerial position, the less grounded he will be. Pastors whose identity is predominantly defined by their ministry will be incapable of setting healthy boundaries with the congregation with respect to time, responsibility, and self-worth.

In the example of Sam (Loose Lips Sink Ships), Sam's identity was highly dependent on the successful revitalization of the church. As a result, he perceived Ronald's objections as personal threats to his self-esteem and retaliated with abrasive, offensive words. Perhaps if Sam had invested in other areas of his life that supported his sense of self, he would not have felt so vulnerable to loss of self-esteem. He may have been more patient, spoken more graciously, and not viewed Ronald as a threat instead of a parishioner struggling to reconcile his past with the future of the church.

The personal sphere of your life is the place to develop friendships. You need an outlet for relationships that do not place ministerial demands on you, where you are free to be you without scrutiny, where your personal challenges and struggles can be expressed without fear of misinterpretation or congregational disillusionment. You may be able to develop a friendship with a parishioner who is mature and has healthy boundaries, but the church should not be your primary source of friendships. We will discuss friendship within the congregation later in this chapter. It is important to spread out the pillars of support into other areas of your life so that your affiliation with the church does not meet all your needs for affirmation, significance, and relationship. The individual whose sense of self is anchored by multiple support systems is less likely to topple than the individual who invests himself entirely in one area. Don't put all your eggs in one basket!

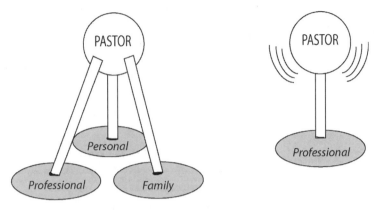

Figure 1. Are you firmly planted or wobbling on one leg?

Take time for personal development; self-care of your emotional, spiritual, and physical needs; rest; recreation and play; and hobbies. Make space and time for these activities in your daily life. No amount of ministerial busyness can replace good sleep, healthy diet, spiritual nurture, and other personal care to sustain a balanced life.

In the story of Joe (Special Friends) we see how one pastor was overly invested in his ministry as the primary source of affirmation and significance. His entire world revolved around his pastoral activities and apparently successful ministry. He was blind to his personal need for intimacy, supportive friendships, and time away from his vocational duties. He apparently also had a rather grandiose, but false, image of himself as "the pastor who could do it all," and thus ignored the needs of Joe, the person.

You may find parishioners in your congregation who are interested and willing to participate with you in recreational or other personal activities. If you can separate your roles of pastor and friend in this association and exercise the liberty to not function as pastor, this arrangement may be beneficial. However, remember that it is always easier to increase the permeability of your boundaries if warranted than to have to close them up after discovering the boundaries are inadequate. Set expectations early; err on the side of caution. It is easier to commit to a six-week exercise class with a parishioner that does not promise an ongoing and progressively deepening relationship than to discover that the parishioner you have been jogging with is having trouble keeping the roles straight and you have to try to explain that your shared jogging routine just isn't working out for you.

In David's case (Golf Buddies), his recreational association with Will served him well and provided the companionship he needed to support his pursuit of a personally fulfilling activity. The relationship worked because both David and Will understood the relationship to be primarily recreational, and as their friendship grew, David maintained strong boundaries around church-related matters. David allowed the relationship to develop over time, rather than fully investing himself immediately. Will had healthy personal boundaries as well, so that when David needed to refer Will for professional help beyond David's capabilities and in light of their personal friendship, Will did not perceive the referral as a failure on David's part to provide support and empathy.

Family

The space for family can easily be encroached upon by pastoral activity and by the congregation. Because of the pastor's position, her family often experiences the strain of the congregation's expectations and demands. She has a responsibility to protect her family from unreasonable expectations of the congregation. A pastor's family members need the same freedom as other parishioners to grow and live without having unrealistic expectations for behavior and spiritual maturity imposed on them. The pastor may need to reinforce the stipulation that her spouse and children are not part of a "package deal" (unless the pastor's spouse was specifically hired by the congregation).

Beth (Good Neighbors) thought that good boundaries had been established between her family and the congregation. But after her neighbor friend Cassie began to attend her church, she discovered differently. She was unaware of the incongruence between the congregation's stated expectations for her family and how the congregation actually interpreted Beth's and her husband's marital disagreements and her family's attendance at another church. Initially, Beth was dumbfounded when the chairman of the board of elders declared that she would be taking a leave of absence. Let's hope that after she regained her composure, she was able to discuss openly with the board their true expectations and possibly educate them as well about the pastor's humanity. Beth learned the hard way: Keep private conversations private because others do not have the benefit of the context in which to judge the pastor's behavior.

The pastor must also fulfill the responsibilities of his role within the family unit. Being a pastor is not an excuse for ignoring family responsibilities. Joe (Special Friends) took advantage of his wife's tacit acceptance of his emotional absence, leaving her to raise the boys, care for their home, and manage the household. He was so preoccupied with his pursuit of success that he did not fulfill his home responsibilities, eventually forsaking his marital responsibilities as well. There may be seasons when pastoral responsibilities require greater attention than family responsibilities. The reverse may also occur. However, an imbalance of priorities that persistently neglects the family is unhealthy for both the pastor and his family, dishonors his marital commitment, and does not model appropriate boundaries in family relationships to his congregation.

Pastors must face the same relational challenges of family that parishioners do. There is no place like home to spur on spiritual and psychological growth. The valuable lessons learned in the privacy and intimacy of the family—lessons in respect and honor, consensus building, limits of responsibility and control, servant leadership, patience, and kindness—will all be applicable in the congregational setting as well.

Another boundary that must be negotiated with the family is that of parishioner confidentiality. On one hand, the pastor does not want to keep "secrets" from his spouse. On the other hand, too much detail about parishioners' private matters and relational issues with congregation and lay leadership can hinder a spouse's comfort at church and dishonor the pastoral commitment to parishioners' confidentiality. There are several helpful questions to ask yourself if you are considering sharing a confidence with a spouse:

1. Will this information affect my spouse's ability to function freely in the congregation as a part of the body of Christ? Will it affect my spouse's relationship with particular parishioners?
2. Why do I want to tell my spouse? For accountability and insight? ("I don't quite trust my judgment in this situation.") To vent? ("I am soooo frustrated...") Because my spouse wants me to? ("OK, but you have to keep this confidential.") To gossip? ("You won't believe what so-and-so told me...")
3. How will talking with my spouse enhance my ministry?

If talking with your spouse has the potential for impeding ministry, restricting your spouse's participation in the life of the church, or denigrating the reputation of a parishioner, don't do it. You may be needing insight and perspective, but if speaking with your spouse has the potential to hurt either your spouse, parishioner, or ministry, approach another professional colleague who is capable of maintaining good boundaries and keeping confidence.

Dual Roles with Parishioners

Because pastors function in multiple roles within their position of leadership, dual roles are inevitable. And it can be challenging, although not impossible, to maintain healthy boundaries between pastor and parishioner and between roles. In chapter 8 (Straight Talk on Power) we discussed the potential problems that may develop in the pastor-employer dual relationship. Chapter 9 illustrated role confusion. Pastors will at various times find themselves in other roles as well: counselor, spiritual director, teacher, preacher, program administrator, volunteer coordinator, minister of mercy, or organizational administrator. Harmonizing these roles is necessary, especially in small churches where the pastor does not have the luxury of divesting responsibility from some of them.

Maintaining healthy boundaries in dual (or multiple) roles is not impossible. Most of the time it is not even difficult. But, occasionally, the boundaries of one role will collide with the boundaries of another role. A counselee may be unclear about the appropriate times and venues to discuss personal and private details of the counselee's life. Without adequate awareness of boundaries necessary to perform his various functions, a pastor may find himself listening to a counselee's private matters in a public area of the church building. This was Robert's experience (The Ornament). His parishioner, Sarah, was unclear about her pastor's various roles. She did not distinguish between his role of counselor, in the privacy of his office, and his role as congregational leader, when greeting his parishioners after the service. Robert sensed the inappropriateness of her attempts to engage him immediately after the worship service and attempted to redirect her expectations of him by agreeing to meet with her in his office after the service to provide counseling. He did not, however, clearly explain his boundaries with her, what he could and could not do for her, his need to tend to other responsibilities and the distinction between his role as pastor to many and his role of pastoral counselor to her.

A pastor may function as volunteer coordinator, canvassing for workers to staff Sunday school. He may also function as pastoral counselor, working with a parishioner to accept her limitations and her need to say "no" occasionally to others' requests for her time. Does the pastor solicit this parishioner to teach the toddler Sunday school? The responsibilities of his two roles collide. The resolution need not be difficult if the pastor's primary focus is on the well-being of his parishioners: his parishioner needs no encouragement to take on yet another responsibility. However, if the pastor's priority is to appear competent in mobilizing volunteers, he may cross the boundary of using the counselee to fulfill a personal need.

In the case of pastor/employer dual roles, a pastor's priorities are based on the interest of having the parishioner/employee perform his job adequately for the benefit of the entire church, and of encouraging the parishioner's spiritual growth. If the pastor needs to address performance deficiencies with the parishioner, will this detract from the pastor's ability to provide spiritual direction and pastoral care? The goals of solid job performance and increased spiritual maturity need not be incongruent, if job performance issues are dealt with early on and if the parishioner has adequate ego development to tolerate supervision. However, if the parishioner exhibits resistance to supervision and direction, the pastor's ability to function in her pastoral role may be compromised. A parishioner who is at odds with his supervisor will likely be unable to accept spiritual guidance and pastoral care from the same person.

Katrina (Supervisor or Pastor?) started out by rationalizing and excusing Jonathan's performance deficiencies. She may have thought that she was giving him the benefit of the doubt, trying not to nit-pick, or was being long-suffering. Usually, however, postponing the need for supervisory feedback increases the likelihood that the dual roles will conflict. By addressing the tension of her dual roles with Jonathan, Katrina was able to maintain good boundaries, reclaim her supervisory role, and, most significantly, act as a pastor who could facilitate Jonathan's growth and maturity around a crisis of which she had been previously unaware.

Thus, reconciliation of the expectations from dual or multiple roles is best achieved by answering: What is best for the parishioner? Do my interests threaten to supersede the best interests of my parishioners? Have I clarified to my parishioner my responsibilities in each role and how I intend to fulfill those?

Boundaries in Communication

Communications in any system, be it church, family, or work, can get messy. And no matter how careful a pastor is to monitor his communication style, what happens with the communication at the receiving end is beyond his control. The pastor's responsibility is to insure that his delivery of communication is clear, direct, and gracious, and that it does not solicit others to carry out the pastor's purposes. These guidelines will improve the clarity of a pastor's communication style and reduce the risk of toxic verbal interactions.

1. Do not triangulate. As the term implies, triangulation involves three people: A, B, and C. When A tells B something about C, in hopes that B will effect some behavioral response in C, that is triangulation. This dynamic places B in a position of power over the relationship between A and C. At times, parishioners will approach their pastor to discuss an issue between the parishioner and someone else. If the purpose of the conversation is to seek guidance on addressing the issue with the third person, pastors can provide direction and insight to their parishioners. But a parishioner who discusses his issue with the pastor in hopes that the pastor will address the parishioner's issue with the third person places the pastor in a triangle that will not end well. In these cases, help your parishioners to determine the best approach to addressing their issues directly with the persons the issues relate to. Insist on direct communication.

2. Avoid pass-through communications. Pass-through communications involve three people as well, but there is no intent for B to effect a response in C. Pass-through communication goes something like, "B, would you let C know that I won't be able to help her with kitchen duty?" There are times when there is no alternative but to ask someone to communicate a message on your behalf. But when the message-giving is intended to avoid dealing with conflict, pass-through communication is detrimental to the overall health of the

organization; it provides no opportunity for A and C to address the potential conflict.

3. Squash gossip. Don't start it, and stop others who may try to start it. This boundary is fairly straightforward. In practice, it can become a little more difficult to maintain, since the purpose of a person's communication regarding someone else may be unclear at the outset. A pastor can help parishioners monitor their penchant for gossip by asking them why they are telling the pastor this information. If nothing else, this sends a message that parishioners are expected to monitor their motives.

Sam's (Loose Lips Sink Ships) comments to the church council about Ronald failed on all three of these guidelines. He spoke of Ronald to the council presumably so they would exert pressure on Ronald to stop his campaigning against contemporary music. He addressed Ronald's behavior to the council in a way he had not done with Ronald directly, and he engaged in gossip by suggesting that Ronald's behavior was associated with evil.

The counseling role is particularly susceptible to dynamics of triangulation when dealing with spouses. A wife may come to her pastor reporting that her husband treats her disrespectfully and with increasing anger outbursts. The pastor who then confronts the husband is engaging in triangulation. Aside from the possibility of putting the wife at risk of escalating abusive behavior from her husband, the pastor is also likely to hear an opposing view from the husband in his own defense. What does the pastor believe? It is far better for the pastor to explore with the wife how she might address with her husband his behavior, carefully planning for a safe and productive discussion.

There is no room for triangulation, message passing, or gossip in pastoral ministry. Speaking words seasoned with grace (Col. 4:6), speaking truth in love (Eph. 4:15), addressing conflict directly (Mt. 18:15), and speaking in kindness (1 Tim. 5:1–2) are God's guidelines for communication in the body of Christ. The pastor's boundaries for healthy communication will protect the health of the pastor and of the congregation, educating and encouraging the congregation toward healthy communication. Once again, we have an opportunity to profoundly impact the health of the entire congregation.

Affection in the Body of Christ

Who among us does not appreciate a gentle touch, warm hug, or knowing smile? Humankind was created to need and seek out affection from others. Without physical demonstrations of acceptance, love, and nurturing, we wither. The church is a family—a spiritual family—bound together by our shared adoption into God's family. Affection for those we live with in the context of the church is natural. Philippians 1:8 describes Paul's affection and longing for his spiritual family.

Affection, done right, blesses and encourages. Affection, gone wrong, wreaks damage and destruction. Boundaries around affection are some of the most difficult to establish; they are notoriously shifty. Is hugging OK? *It depends.* Is a shoulder rub acceptable? *It depends.* It depends on the cultural and circumstantial contexts, the nature of the relationships of those sharing affection, the comfort level of the people, and so on. A pastor may kiss his wife on the lips in the privacy of his office; no one becomes uncomfortable with his demonstration of affection. A passionate smooch in the narthex feels awkward to bystanders. A father may hug his adult daughter in a full-body embrace. When he hugs his daughter's friend the same way, both she and her friend feel uneasy.

How do we keep our affection holy and healthy? How do we model and encourage healthy affection among our parishioners? First, let's review the foundation of healthy affection. Healthy affection

1. is offered, not imposed and not taken
2. respects the comfort level of the person receiving the affection
3. is genuine and sincere and does not communicate anything other than its explicit intent
4. neither expects something in return nor seeks to gain from it

We will exercise good boundaries around affection by learning to read the body language of those we approach. Are they moving toward us, or stepping back? If we reach out our arm, do they extend theirs, or constrict their personal space? Do they make eye contact or look to the side or down? Do they respond with the same energy, less or more?

Check your attitudes about affection. Do you think in terms of "giving" a hug? "Offering" a hug? "Getting" a hug? If you want a hug, do you ask, "Can I have a hug?" or do you move in and take it? The quality of our affectionate behaviors is determined by our attitudes. People on the receiving end usually will sense our attitudes and intentions, unless their boundaries have been seriously or persistently violated in the past and they have a poor reference point of healthy *vs.* unhealthy affection and touch.

Healthy affection does not include "slips." An inappropriate kiss on the mouth is not excused with, "Oh, I'm sorry. I meant to kiss you on the cheek!" Right affection in the church is nonsexual. Regardless of whether the act is welcomed, if the recipient interprets the affection as sexual, it is not healthy affection. It is sexual behavior, no matter the apparent intent of the initiator.

Healthy affection is unconditional. If the recipient is uncomfortable, the initiator must be accepting and understanding, not imposing her affectionate behaviors. The one offering an act of affection is not scouting for the possibility of more intense, more frequent, or more sexualized behavior.

First, the pastor's own boundaries around affection need to be well established and healthy. Then he can address the boundary challenges of parishioners who are overly enthusiastic with their affection, overbearing or insensitive to the comfort level of recipients. Pastors are primary targets of people whose level of affection is excessive. This yields an opportunity for the pastor to educate parishioners and model more effective and appropriate boundaries. Pastors can greet their parishioners with an outstretched hand, indicating that they are open to a handshake. Parishioners that persist in soliciting a hug can be offered an arm across the shoulder; it is difficult for a person to engage in a full-body embrace when being gently restrained to the side. Kisses on the cheek are best left unreturned. A possible exception might be a younger male pastor being kissed by an elderly lady who wants to convey maternal affection. If a parishioner, especially of the opposite gender, persists in kissing the pastor, the pastor may be able to discourage the behavior by turning the head away from the parishioner, or holding the head several inches away from the parishioner's face.

Hopefully, body language eventually dampens the parishioner's zeal. But when these efforts do not yield the desired results, it is time to speak with the parishioner directly. Generally, parishioners who overstep the boundaries of socially acceptable affection within the church are not doing so intentionally. They may not know what the pastor is comfortable with, may not have had healthy modeling of affection at home, or may lack intuitive ability to read body language. They may be clueless how others interpret their behavior in the congregation. Direct, compassionate, and nonshaming admonition is essential. The pastor cannot control the parishioner's reactions and so will need to be clear in his own mind that even if the parishioner is upset, the pastor's responsibility is to protect his own boundaries, protect the welfare of other parishioners, and educate the parishioner regarding the offensive nature of the behavior.

Pastors do well to apprise themselves of the historical patterns for affectionate behavior in the congregation when they first are installed. One would hope that the normal level of affection in the congregation is healthy. If, however, parishioners are very "touchy-feely," the pastor may need to establish a new set of expectations with her congregation, beginning by modeling. However, if modeling does not sufficiently correct the norms of the congregation, conversations and education may be in order. "Touchy-feely" of itself is not necessarily unhealthy. But those with histories of boundary violations (abuse victims, codependents, etc.) and those whose personal boundaries are not sufficiently developed (children and developmentally disabled persons) are at risk for boundary breaches or abuse, because they are inadequately equipped to protect their own boundaries. It is the responsibility of the pastor, as the shepherd of the congregation, to insure the health and safety of her sheep. She will need to help guard them from misuse by others whose affection is overbearing or inappropriate.

Friendship, Favors, and Gifts

Parishioners rightly should appreciate their pastors (1 Tim. 5:17). Appreciation may come in the form of words, gifts, favors, and friendship. A majority of parishioners who extend acts of appreciation to their pastors do so without expectation of reciprocity. Their acts are truly gifts, offered unconditionally, no strings attached. Those acts of appreciation are sometimes the only affirmation a pastor receives during difficult and wearying times of ministry. Even overtures of friendship can be interpreted as parishioners' acknowledgement of their pastor's humanity, personal needs, and likability.

In some professional settings, acceptance of gifts is discouraged or not allowed. Psychotherapists and counselors have codes of ethics and state regulations that govern the acceptance of gifts. Gifts given to supervisors and coworkers are generally frowned upon except at socially acceptable times, such as boss's appreciation day. But the church is a less formal and structured environment. Gifts and favors are acceptable in a family, if not expected. When offered unconditionally, favors, gifts, and friendship will not pose a challenge to the recipient pastor.

However, pastors need to be aware of the potential for relational boundary problems under two circumstances: (1) the pastor relies too heavily on these acts of appreciation for affirmation and self-esteem and (2) the parishioner has expectations for the pastor's reciprocity. Pastors who are inadequately tending to their personal needs outside of the congregation become increasingly dependent on parishioners' affirmation and acceptance. Pastors can then become conditioned to act in certain ways that earn them appreciation, and they lose their autonomy to minister for their parishioners' sake. The acts of appreciation become currency. Accurate self-knowledge and adequate self-care are the best prevention against relying on the kindnesses of parishioners to maintain pastors' identity and esteem.

Unfortunately, parishioners may indeed offer acts of appreciation—friendship, gifts, or favors—with an expectation for the pastor's reciprocity. Sarah used gifts in an attempt to condition Robert (The Ornament) to meet her perceived needs, even when her demands were not the best thing for her, nor what Robert could provide. In these situations, acts of appreciation are given with an implicit caveat: "I'm giving you this so that when I want something, you'll be willing to give it to me." Again, the acts become a form of currency. It may be uncomfortable to think that people would actually use gifts to manipulate us. However, the reality is it happens all the time—not just in churches, but in families, business organizations and academic institutions, personal friendships and politics. The terms and conditions of the gift remain covert and unspoken, and we try to ignore the nagging feeling that our acceptance of the gift obligates us to its conditions.

Although the terms for conditional acts of appreciation are usually not verbalized initially, the giver will eventually make the conditions explicit–either when compliance with the expectations is not forthcoming, or when the giver is ready to call in the favor. Sarah's donation of funds to purchase new hymnals (Robert: The Ornament) had terms attached: to be treated as a "VIP parishioner." The terms of her donation were not initially verbalized, but when she believed that she was not being treated with the special care she thought she deserved, she withdrew her offer. A pastor's best prevention for becoming hostage to conditional giving is to confront the eventually verbalized expectations for reciprocity head-on. This can feel like an awkward conversation, but when done with tact and openness, can be very healing ("speaking the truth in love"). Hostage-holding is achieved by implied threat (*i.e.*, what *might* happen if…), and when the "threat" is brought into the light, it loses its potency.

Parishioners do not always place conditions on their gifts and acts of appreciation intentionally. They may have learned the behavior or they are accustomed to this dynamic within their own families. The church is a place for them to learn a healthier, unconditionally loving way of relating. Here is a wonderful and poignant opportunity for the pastor to model healthy self, healthy relationships, and healthy boundaries. But it requires courage, good self-knowledge, and strength of character.

When parishioners present to the church their interest in funding a special project or providing a pro bono service, the leadership also has the responsibility to assess the parishioners' intent, relational history with the church as an organization, and ability to give unconditionally. The leadership may need to work with the pastor to assess these potential areas for trouble. For instance, a parishioner who wants to donate money toward new hymnals may be attaching an unspoken condition: "I don't like the new music, and I want the church to use the hymnals that I am buying." It behooves the pastor and church leadership to explore with the parishioner his interests in funding this special project before accepting, before the conditions are not met, before the gift becomes the spark that ignites an epic struggle within the church.

Pro bono services also have the potential for developing into struggles for position, power, or special treatment. A parishioner in the asphalt paving business offers to repave the church parking lot for the cost of the asphalt only. The church agrees. Then the discussions begin; the parishioner wants the traffic flow rerouted, the leadership has a different idea. Discussion turns heated and the parishioner finally exclaims, "Look, if I'm doing this as a favor to the church, then at least I would expect to have a say in how the parking lot gets paved and marked!"

All said, *pro bono* services and gifts for special projects can be a blessing to the church, but must be managed carefully, thoughtfully, and with courage to not succumb to conditions that negatively impact the ability of the church and pastor to minister effectively. A good understanding of the ramifications of boundary development, degree of individuation, and relational style will help the pastor to assess parishioners' maturity level and ability to separate the self from the gift.[3]

Dating a Parishioner

Pastors who are single may want to date. Dating parishioners happens. But it should be undertaken with eyes wide open. Dating entails a dual relationship. The more disparate the roles, the more difficult they are to reconcile. Balancing dual roles of pastoral counseling and preaching must be handled with care. However, a dating relationship is very personal so the duality is between the professional pastoral relationship and the personal dating relationship. Balancing dual roles of pastoral care and dating requires all the more mindfulness.

Ideally, the pastor who is dating a parishioner should discuss openly with the parishioner the tensions between the pastor's responsibilities within the dual roles—as pastor and date. It is simpler to keep the boundaries straight if they have been identified and discussed. As the dating relationship progresses, the pastor may do well to step aside from pastoral counseling responsibilities with the parishioner and delegate that responsibility to someone else in leadership.

The most challenging issue related to dating a parishioner is what happens if the dating relationship ends. The relationship may end by mutual agreement; this is the least challenging of all circumstances. But if the relationship ends unilaterally, the potential for trouble is magnified. If the parishioner is left feeling rejected, the pastor may lose the ability to minister adequately to the parishioner. The pastor's preaching may lose its effectiveness; the pastor's care and guidance may be rejected, viewed with suspicion, or be misunderstood as an overture to reinitiate the dating relationship. A parishioner who is hurt by the rejection of a terminated dating relationship and does not have adequate boundaries and individuation may be tempted to start rumors, attack the pastor's credibility and reputation, and be unable to return to the original relational position of parishioner.

The other challenge related to dating within the congregation is the possibility that the pastor engages in inappropriate romantic, emotional, or sexual relationships with parishioners under the pretense of "dating." Parishioners never know if the motives for the pastor's care and counseling are strictly pastoral or an invitation to a personal dating relationship. And the challenge to distinguish between inappropriate and appropriate behavior and intentions is even greater than in an uncomplicated pastor-parishioner relationship.

For this reason, the pastor that is considering pursuit of a dating relationship should seek counsel from a ministerial colleague who can help clarify roles and responsibilities; a counselor who can help the pastor sort through personal feelings and the prudence of pursuing a dating relationship with a parishioner; and a trusted lay leader within the congregation who can advise on the potential pitfalls, watch for signs of disturbance within congregational dynamics, and monitor the appropriateness of the pastor's and parishioner's behaviors in and out of church. All three—the ministerial colleague, the counselor, and the lay leader—should also assess whether the pastor's dating interest is truly dating, or a pretense for misconduct or boundary breaches within the functions of pastoral ministry.

Dating a parishioner, if ever, should be a very infrequent occurrence. Casual dating of various parishioners within a congregation is very detrimental to the overall congregational health. This pattern breeds jealousy, power struggles, resentment, and divisiveness. Any dating requires prayerfulness, mindfulness of its impact on the parishioner and congregation, and piercing self-examination.

Boundaries in Counseling

The work of pastoral counseling is particularly disposed to boundary problems. Many moral failures, professional bungles, and relational heartaches are the direct result of mismanaged counseling activities. Ann's experience (A Parishioner Tells Her Story) demonstrates how counseling can enable the breach of boundaries with parishioners. Pastors' positions almost always require some amount of pastoral counseling, but, until recently, typical seminary training has not offered in-depth education of basic counseling and motivational interviewing skills, specific issues involved in pastoral counseling, or application of clinical interventions in the pastoral counseling function.

Adequate training and awareness of the pastor's personal and professional limitations are the best prevention for boundary violations in the pastoral counseling role. Many excellent resources address clinical issues in pastoral counseling. A selected list is provided under this note.[4] Some common contributors to boundary violations in counseling include:

- *The feelings of intimacy that may develop* because of the depth of sharing. Furthermore, prolonged counseling contact with a parishioner increases the likelihood that romantic, sexual, or intimate feelings or fantasies will develop.
- *The neediness of counselees in their times of crisis and transition, and therefore their vulnerability* to being used to satisfy a pastor's personal needs for affirmation, rescuing, intimacy, relationship, etc.
- *The pastor's insufficient awareness of his or her limitations* due to lack of education, grandiosity, lack of judgment, or a combination of these.
- *The privacy of the counseling setting,* which fuels the temptations to overstep limits and cross boundaries. In addition, "confidentiality" can be used to camouflage inappropriate behavior, excessive personal involvement by the pastor, or questionable counseling interventions.

• *The pastor's professional qualifications and availability are not clarified,* so counselees' expectations of the pastor are unrealistic.

Pastoral counseling is not a replacement for professional mental health care. The functions of pastoral and psychological care are interwoven inasmuch as they both focus on the care of the soul. Nonetheless, the pastoral counseling role within the church is generally confined to short-term, spiritually focused interventions, while professional mental health care focuses on psychological and psychiatric issues.[5] Most pastors do not possess credentials that certify them to practice psychotherapy or mental health counseling.[6] It is vital that parishioners grasp this distinction and do not expect pastoral counseling to substitute for professional mental health care.

The concept of not using parishioners to satisfy personal needs obviously extends to the function of pastoral counseling. However, counseling involves a heightened level of intensity and intimacy, which can override the pastor's judgment of potential boundary problems. For this reason, pastors should regularly assess their personal needs and vulnerabilities (self-knowledge), reevaluate their professional qualifications (education and training), refresh their understanding of the scope of the pastoral care ministry in the church, and remind themselves of the necessary relational boundaries with parishioners. The importance of accurate self-knowledge has already been discussed in chapter 5. Here we will look at some additional boundary considerations.

The following guidelines are divided into areas of professional qualifications, scope of ministry, and interactions with parishioners.

Professional qualifications

1. Do not call yourself a "counselor" or "therapist" unless you have state-sanctioned credentials that qualify you to provide mental health care.
2. Do not charge for your services. You will incur professional liability beyond that of standard pastoral services provided within the scope of ministry of your church.
3. Learn to distinguish between a life event that requires spiritual guidance and more complex mental health, behavioral, or character problems that transcend the immediate presenting problem of the parishioner.
4. Establish a professional consultative relationship with a licensed mental health professional with whom you can review cases as needed. Actively engage your professional consultative support; don't wait until a parishioner case has turned critical or unmanageable. Seek pastoral care supervision[7] if you develop feelings for a counselee that are beyond the confines of the pastoral relationship.
5. Assess for underlying medical or mental health concerns that may be impacting the parishioner's ability to function and integrate newly

learned information. If the parishioner presents with untreated medical problems, facilitate the parishioner's access to appropriate care. If presented with underlying mental health issues (*e.g.,* depression, generalized anxiety, hallucinations, suicidal thoughts or history of suicide attempts, explosive anger, history of being abused or abusing, substance use), make a referral for the appropriate care. This may include referrals to mental health counselors, psychiatrists, and community-based support groups such as AA.

6. If you determine that the parishioner is in danger (to self or someone else), seek the appropriate care immediately. Do not hesitate to contact a supportive family member or a friend for assistance; confidentiality cannot be maintained in these emergent cases. In addition, cases of child or elder abuse must be reported to appropriate authorities as mandated by your state laws.[8]

7. Educate yourself adequately regarding mental health issues so that you can accurately identify situations that require treatment outside the scope of your training and pastoral care. Refrain from diagnosing. *Know when to refer. If in doubt, refer!*

Scope of ministry

1. Determine the number of hours a week that you are available for pastoral care and counseling ministry. Stick to it, except in the most extraordinary circumstances (*e.g.,* a traumatic event in the community). Determine the maximum time allotted for sessions and stick to it. If more time is needed with a parishioner, reschedule.

2. With the church leadership, identify the goals that your church wants to pursue through pastoral care and counseling. Spiritual guidance? Discipleship? Stabilization in crisis? Resource for referrals? Short-term solution focused consultation? Grief and bereavement support? Keep these goals in mind when engaging with parishioners in pastoral care and counseling.

3. Parishioners' needs that fall outside these parameters should be referred to appropriate care. Referrals should include names, contact information, and follow-up with parishioners to encourage compliance.

Interactions with parishioners

1. Never work harder at your parishioner's problem than he is working. If you make recommendations but observe no follow-through, the parishioner may need some time to contemplate and rouse the motivation to act on the recommendations. But the parishioner remains responsible for resolving his concerns. The next topic of conversation may need to be the parishioner's resistance to implementing strategies for growth and change.

2. Do not manipulate parishioners to change or make decisions for parishioners. Again, change is the responsibility of the parishioner. Guard your parishioners' right to autonomy. Manipulative maneuvers will result in short-lived change or increased resistance; making decisions for parishioners encourages dependency rather than growth. The pastor's role is to facilitate change, not manipulate compliance; to teach problem-solving, not solve the problem.

3. Maintain confidentiality when possible. Mental health and medical care professions have very strict rules on confidentiality. While most states do not require similar protections for parishioners under pastoral care, breaches of confidentiality can result in great harm to parishioners and destroy the sacred trust placed in their pastor. There may be instances, nevertheless, in which confidentiality cannot be maintained, so don't make unconditional promises of confidentiality to parishioners.

4. Do not become sexually, emotionally, or romantically involved with parishioners you are counseling. Providing pastoral counseling to someone with whom you have developed a friendship is likewise difficult and ill-advised.

5. Assess your counselees' level of individuation and boundary development. Parishioners with insufficient autonomy, who exhibit patterns of manipulation, or who have displayed boundary problems in the past will require your heightened attention to boundary maintenance in the counseling relationship.

6. Resist the urge to draw on counseling cases for sermon illustrations. Parishioners may believe that an illustration is based on their situation, even if not. Details can be changed, but parishioners may recognize their situation in your illustration and feel betrayed or exposed.

The work of pastoral care and counseling offers tremendous opportunities for ministry and the ability to touch hurting, broken, and challenged lives. More than the spiritual guidance that we might provide, the simple acts of caring, listening, and being present offer hope and healing to our parishioners. Being mindful that our boundaries in pastoral counseling, as well as our other ministerial roles, not only protect our parishioners and us, but insure that our ministry is effective and that grace is not only taught but modeled. Our Lord's love for us extends to the deepest depths of our beings—pastors and parishioners alike.

Time to Reflect

1. Review the various areas of boundaries discussed in this chapter. What boundary areas do you find more difficult to maintain?

2. What ideas come to mind regarding the boundaries that are working and those that are not?

3. What can you do now to strengthen your boundaries in these areas?

CHAPTER 12

Beginnings and Conclusions

"When we finally learn that self-care begins and ends with ourselves, we no longer demand sustenance and happiness from others."

JENNIFER LOUDEN

"Be on your guard; stand firm in the faith; be men of courage; be strong."

1 CORINTHIANS 16:13

Boundaries Begin with You

Perhaps you are wondering, Is there anything left to say about boundaries? Yes, there is. Ultimately, the only thing that makes boundaries work is *you*. Talk is cheap; action is priceless. Healthy boundaries don't just happen; you must intentionally establish them.

Regardless of how invested you have been to this point in maintaining good boundaries, there is always room for additional work, if for no other reason than that boundaries left unattended are prone to weaken. If you believe that your boundaries need improvement, make it a priority to establish appropriate boundaries that will protect you and strengthen your ministry. This requires first identifying areas of your life that have suffered or in which you have been less effective than you would like due to inadequate boundaries. Take stock of your daily routine, family life, time spent in ministry, personal satisfaction with life, relationships, and spiritual journey. Do any of these areas experience regular commotion or chaos, damage, or demands that threaten to overwhelm you?

Common symptoms of possible boundary problems include

• strained relationships
• financial problems

183

- marital discord
- excessive work
- a resistant congregation
- recurring illness
- feelings of isolation or loneliness
- submerged anger or irritability
- diffuse but persistent sadness
- hopelessness
- loss of self-confidence
- addictive behaviors
- distractibility and inability to concentrate
- poor judgment and discernment
- neglect of routine responsibilities

Note that we may experience some of these indicators at various times when boundary problems are not the primary cause. Occasional tension with a friend does not immediately point to boundary problems, but repeated tensions with a friend, or patterns of distancing with several friends, are strong indicators that boundaries are at least the partial culprit for the relational difficulties. Look for enduring patterns in your life. Those are the areas of your life that need your immediate attention.

Next, review what you have done in the past to manage those areas and determine possible reasons those efforts have not been successful. It is often helpful to record your assessments, conclusions, and proposed changes in a journal or other written form. What changes might help you to better manage those areas? What will you need to do in order to successfully implement the changes? Will you need outside support? Who would be most helpful to you in establishing new boundaries to gain balance in those areas of your life? Try to be intentional about the process. If at first you don't succeed, try again. Change your approach, draw on additional support, ask for help from a counselor or ministerial colleague, and review some of the information and guidance presented in this and other books dealing with boundaries.

Establish, Maintain, and Monitor Your Boundaries

Establishing adequate boundaries is the beginning but boundaries do not maintain themselves. We need to maintain them. We can say, "I only have forty hours in the week to devote to my job," but our boundary is only as good as our willingness to enforce it. Maintaining that boundary requires that when our workload exceeds forty hours, we say, "Sorry, I can't do that. I'm already booked this week." If we don't enforce, or maintain, that boundary, we may as well have never put the boundary in place to begin with. Establishing appropriate boundaries is not nearly as challenging as maintaining them. Life will constantly test our boundaries. Without watchful guard, we will find our boundaries eroding before our eyes. Forty hours will turn into forty-five, then into fifty hours of work.

Ideally, we want to maintain our boundaries such that they aren't compromised at all, unless, of course, we decide that some permeability and flexibility is appropriate. Most boundary breaches occur, not because we have inadequate boundaries, but because we don't do a good job protecting them and the pressure of the moment swamps our best intentions to enforce them. We must detect the breach quickly and decide how to reset the boundary, correct the incursion, and prevent further breaches before more damage is done. The best solution here is to directly address the boundary violation with the person affected by our breach or the person who is breaching the boundary. We may need to apologize to someone, clarify to that individual our expectations of ourselves, explain our intentions for future interactions, and determine an effective means of preventing a future breach. If someone else violates our boundary, a direct conversation is still in order. We explain that this behavior disregards our boundary, why our boundary is in place, and our expectations for the parishioner's future behavior.

In Maryann's situation (The Power of Prayer), Betsy was challenging her boundaries, particularly that she could not be Betsy's sole source of support and that it was not Maryann's actions that would bring healing—healing is God's area of expertise. Maryann was uneasy about Betsy's persistent challenge of the boundaries, but she did not have the necessary conversation with Betsy to reestablish the appropriate boundaries, reset the expectations, and explain to Betsy how the boundaries were there to protect Betsy from becoming dependent on Maryann in an unhealthy way. Perhaps after Alex's most recent medical crisis subsided, Maryann would gather the courage to reestablish the boundaries with Betsy.

After establishing and maintaining our boundaries, we also need to monitor them. Are they effective? Do we feel balanced, whole, protected from unreasonable expectations? Are others comfortably aware of our boundaries, do they respect them, are they protected from our inappropriate expectations? These qualities are the signs of healthy, well-maintained boundaries. If, in spite of careful implementation and maintenance, we notice that some area of our lives continues to experience strain or imbalance, it is possible that we will need to modify the boundaries related to that area.

Perhaps Sam (Loose Lips Sink Ships) would eventually realize that his fervor for revitalizing his congregation was preventing him from speaking with grace and love, leading him to shoot barbs at parishioners and threatening to rob the congregation of their responsibility to choose their future. He would need to review his boundaries—what he was realistically responsible for—and what his role was. He would need to communicate to Ronald the nature of his boundary breach with Ronald, own his part in hurting and using Ronald, and clarify his understanding of the healthier boundaries he would then establish to prevent such breaches in the future.

Monitoring boundaries for effectiveness or possible negative impact means that we go back to Micah 6:8 and reaffirm our commitment to act justly, love mercy, and walk humbly with God and God's people. Even in our failures, we have the opportunity to model God's grace, illustrate the process of spiritual maturation, and demonstrate how God redeems our brokenness for God's name's sake. In taking responsibility for our boundary violations, their detrimental effects, and the necessary corrections, we model with poignant clarity to our parishioners the challenge of developing healthy boundaries and the growth that ensues from appropriate ownership of responsibility. Boundary failures need not shackle us with shame if we are sincere in our efforts to monitor them, protect others, and live healthy.

Joe (Special Friends) indisputably crossed the boundary of appropriate sexual conduct with parishioners. Let's assume he was eventually found out. His wife, Sarah, began to suspect, did a little investigating, and confronted him. As with many pastors who are caught in sexual misconduct, Joe was extremely embarrassed. But he was not ashamed of his failure; he was embarrassed that he got caught and of how his "special relationship" appeared to the church. His misrouted shame prevented him from genuinely taking responsibility for his behavior. Sadly, his rationalizations persisted even after his misconduct was brought to light. As a result, he gave lip service to the leadership's requirements for his healing and restoration. However, if he had been closely monitoring his boundaries long before engaging in misconduct, he might have had opportunities to correct the problems and prevent his conscience from becoming hardened by persistent disregard for the boundaries.

Healthy Pastor, Healthy Church

Being a healthy pastor will not guarantee that the congregation will be healthy. But the pastor is the church's spiritual leader, with great power to shift the dynamics of the congregation. A pastor's unhealthy habits and boundaries will quickly spill over into the entire church. The body of Christ suffers as a whole when one part does not function properly, especially if that part is vital to the body's overall well-being. So, more is at stake than the pastor's personal, emotional, and spiritual health. The pastor's health affects the entire congregation.

The interesting thing about appropriate boundaries is that they are always healthy for both sides. At times, people may resist your well-placed boundary. They may not like that you will no longer accept a certain behavior from them, because that will require change, a new way of communicating, increased personal responsibility, etc. However, just because they don't appreciate the boundary does not render it inappropriate. For example, you decide that you will no longer take responsibility for finding your spouse's repeatedly lost keys. Your spouse may be unhappy with your unwillingness to drop everything to look for the misplaced keys. But if you continue to rush to your spouse's aid or take the blame for the lost keys, your spouse will never be motivated to identify alternative methods for keeping track of the keys, taking responsibility for her own belongings.

Implementing appropriate boundaries that are inconvenient to someone else requires courage. It requires that we reconcile our potential unpopularity with doing what is best for those in our sphere of influence and ourselves. It requires unconditional love. We do not shirk our responsibilities out of fear that we will lose popularity or experience others' negative reactions. Rather, the boundaries we establish are born out of love for self and others.

Appropriate boundaries communicate to others that we have the highest regard for their ability to become all that God created them to be, for their intrinsic worth, and for their unique God-image. We should maintain that same regard for ourselves. These are the boundaries that bless and this is our highest calling as ministers: that, through healthy relationships and good modeling of justice, mercy, and humility, we spur each other on toward love and good deeds (Heb. 10:24ff).

Help! I Stepped Out of Bounds

It is impossible to walk through life without sometimes overstepping our bounds or transgressing someone else's boundaries. That is the reality of our broken nature. Boundary breaches may be damaging; how we deal with them will make the difference between mitigating or amplifying the damage. Taking corrective action can be difficult. We may feel ashamed of the violation; we may not recognize the extent or significance of the breach. Owning responsibility for a boundary violation and its subsequent damage requires confession; confession calls for repentance and a change in our ways. Yet there is no growth without trial, error, and correction.

How do we respond to our own boundary violations? To some extent, our response depends on the magnitude and severity of the violation, but, regardless of the severity, we can take these steps to correct a breach once we have identified it.

- *Assess the damage.* Who was directly hurt by the breach? Was there collateral damage? Were there secondary victims?
- *Identify how the breach occurred.* Was it because of inadequate guardrails, poor self-care, personal irresponsibility, defiance, ignorance, insufficient information, excessive flexibility, or a combination of some of these?
- *Confess the violation* to the individual who has been offended or damaged. Note that you may need to apologize to yourself!

- *Reset the boundary.* Does it need to be more stringent or lenient? Do additional guardrails need to be erected?
- *Make restitution and reparation.* Reparation is essentially a diligent effort to repair the damage. Restitution is repayment for the losses suffered.

Restitution is sometimes achieved just by being attentive to the offended individual's reactions to our breach and keeping communication open. It depends on the extent and severity of the violation. Generally, severity is related to the extent of damage. Sexual misconduct is more destructive than entertaining sexual fantasies of a parishioner. Personal verbal attacks are more damaging than unfocused general irritability. If you are concerned or believe that you have crossed a boundary with significantly damaging consequences, your response requires more than an apology and commitment to fortify the boundary.

Serious boundary violations cannot be remediated alone. Violations such as physical or verbal abuse, raging tirades, and intimidation are gross boundary violations that require immediate correction. Seek counsel. Discuss the concern with a ministerial colleague and the church's lay leadership. Develop a plan to address the violation that includes not only genuine repentance, but the utmost sensitive care for the offended party. The pastor who has violated significant boundaries with a parishioner is in no position to facilitate the parishioner's healing. Another lay leader, lay minister, or staff pastor will need to take on that duty. As the offender, your obligations will be to seek the necessary help to prevent future violations, implement appropriate guardrails to protect others from a similar offense, and actively engage in accountability with someone who will assist in your recovery and growth.

Not Just Out of Bounds: When a Pastor Goes Over the Cliff

Boundary violations dealing with sexual misconduct, inappropriate emotional or romanticized relationships, or illicit behavior with a minor child require immediate action. If you realize that you have crossed such a boundary, you are obligated by your commitment to ministry to confess the violation. You will not be able to extricate yourself or your parishioner from the entanglement. As with other serious boundary violations, you are incapable of facilitating the parishioner's recovery. Attempting to rectify the violation yourself will result in incomplete repentance and healing for yourself and inadequate care for the parishioner. There are two goals: get help for yourself and insure that the parishioner's care is delegated to someone with the expertise to address the damage.

Recognizing that you have not only stepped out of bounds but have fallen over the cliff is possibly one of the most frightening things you will ever face. Pervasive and paralyzing anxiety, guilt and shame, hopelessness, crippling fear, and an overwhelming sense of entrapment will have most likely become your bedfellows. But there is hope; it is waiting for you to reach out and take hold of it. Reaching for hope comes in the form of confession. First, confess to God, for, "If we confess our sins, he is faithful and just and will forgive us our sins and purify us from all unrighteousness" (1 Jn. 1:9).

Then, identify someone to whom you can confess, someone else who is able to walk with you through the process of repentance, recovery, and healing; someone whose faith is strong and whose commitment to you will be unwavering. Remember, you are not able to extricate yourself; you need the strong arm of a committed friend to help pull you up. This person will serve as your advocate—advocate for the Truth and advocate for your care and recovery. "Therefore confess your sins to each other and pray for each other so that you may be healed. The prayer of a righteous man is powerful and effective" (Jas. 5:16). Pray; ask your advocate to pray for you. It is at least as important *that* you pray, than *what* you pray. Prayer is your lifeline to your Heavenly Father in your time of crisis.

The congregation whose pastor has engaged in an illicit or severely inappropriate relationship with a parishioner will generally assemble a response team whose responsibility it is to oversee the recovery of the pastor, parishioner, and church.[1] It will be their determination, along with possible input from denominational leadership, what steps toward healing will be required of you. Don't rush the process. A rushed process will not avail healing, but rather more dishonesty and fabricated repentance that will lead to future failures and inadequate accountability for the damage.

Remember that "healing" is not equivalent with a return to active ministry. In some cases, your illicit behavior may have legal consequences, impeding you from ever returning to your former ministry.

It is tempting, especially if your boundary violation was brought to light by a third party, to diminish your blame and responsibility for the violation by claiming that the relationship was consensual, or by calling into question the parishioner's psychological or spiritual health, the veracity of the parishioner's side of the story or the parishioner's reactions to the violation. Remember that blame shifting is inherent in our broken nature (Gen. 3:12–13), that because of your position of power, you are solely responsible for maintaining appropriate boundaries with parishioners, and that thorough healing comes from thorough repentance. Blaming the parishioner for any portion of the violation or attempting to discredit the parishioner in any way will inflict further damage and hurt, making both of your recoveries all the more unlikely.

The Promise of God's Compassion, Healing, and Presence

Falling over the cliff is frightening. Getting caught up in a web of temptation, sin, and betrayal of your pastoral obligations may feel impossible to recover from. Or, perhaps you simply struggle to maintain balance in your life; compassionately serve your parishioners and congregation; stay within bounds of the pastoral role; keep a healthy emotional distance between yourself and your parishioners; act justly, love mercy, and walk in humility; or maintain sexual purity. Regardless of the nature of your struggles, God's love can minister to you with the same power that it has to reach our broken world. One Truth never changes:

> Praise the LORD, O my soul;
>> all my inmost being, praise his holy name.
> Praise the LORD, O my soul,
>> and forget not all his benefits–
> who forgives all your sins
>> and heals all your diseases,
> who redeems your life from the pit
>> and crowns you with love and compassion…
> The LORD is compassionate and gracious,
>> slow to anger, abounding in love.
> He will not always accuse,
>> nor will he harbor his anger forever;
> he does not treat us as our sins deserve
>> or repay us according to our iniquities.
> For as high as the heavens are above the earth,
>> so great is his love for those who fear him;
> as far as the east is from the west,
>> so far has he removed our transgressions from us.
> As a father has compassion on his children,
>> so the LORD has compassion on those who fear him;
> for he knows how we are formed,
>> he remembers that we are dust…
> But from everlasting to everlasting
>> the LORD's love is with those who fear him,
>> and his righteousness with their children's children–
> with those who keep his covenant
>> and remember to obey his precepts. (Ps. 103:1–4; 8–14; 17–18)

Time to Reflect

1. What impact do inadequate boundaries have on the physical, emotional, and spiritual aspects of your life? Do you notice yourself getting more impatient? Feeling hurt or rejected? Feeling overwhelmed, resentful? Hating an aspect of your job? Saying something like, "If only she would just…?"

2. Review the list of common signs of inadequate boundaries at the beginning of this chapter. Which ones do you most commonly

experience? What boundaries in your life are most likely responsible? Which boundaries most need your immediate attention?

3. What have you learned from experience to be the most effective measures of recovering from a boundary breach?

4. How have you personally been impacted by clergy sexual misconduct or sexual abuse (directly or indirectly)? How might your experiences help you to minister to others and protect your congregation?

5. What mechanisms have been put in place in your church to respond to gross boundary violations by leaders, staff, volunteers, and parishioners? Are these adequate? Does more need to be done, and, if so, what?

Notes

Chapter 2: A Psychological Framework for Boundaries

[1]A book written for the layperson that offers a good overview on the concept of boundaries is John Cloud and Henry Townsend, *Boundaries: When to Say Yes, How to Say No to Take Control of Your Life* (Grand Rapids, Mich.: Zondervan, 1992).

[2]Margaret S. Mahler, *On Human Symbiosis and the Vicissitudes of Individuation,* with M. Furer (New York: International Universities Press, 1968).

[3]The term "mommy" is used here in keeping with common terminology of theorists in the schools of ego psychology and object relations psychology, who focused on the most primitive and primary relationship a baby experiences–that of mother–when discussing the development of ego. In our discussion, "mommy" is a prototypical persona; the relationship with "mommy" can easily be extended to other significant figures in a child's early development.

[4]For a solid review of Object Relations theory, see Peter Buckley, ed., *Essential Papers on Object Relations (Essential Papers in Psychoanalysis)* (New York: New York University, 1986).

[5]An excellent but challenging discussion of the behavior patterns (defense mechanisms in psychological terminology) that are used to protect the self against anxiety and discomfort can be found in the text Nancy McWilliams, *Psychoanalytic Diagnosis: Understanding Personality Structure in the Clinical Process* (New York: Guilford Press, 1994).

[6]Heinz Kohut was a leader in the development of the theory of self psychology and in the application of its constructs for the effective psychological treatment of narcissistic personality disorder. An in-depth review of Kohut's seminal work can be found in Allen Siegel, *Heinz Kohut and the Psychology of the Self.* (New York: Routledge, 1996).

[7]One good example is Charles Whitfield, *Boundaries and Relationships: Knowing, Protecting and Enjoying the Self* (Deerfield Beach, Fla.: Health Communications, Inc., 1994). This is a good basic book for both the lay reader and professional, and addresses the psychological and spiritual aspects of boundary development and maintenance.

[8]A cue ball and cue stick (or just "cue") are used for playing billiards. The cue stick serves as an extension of the player's arm and is used to shoot the cue ball at a second ball. The cue ball serves no purpose other than to transfer the energy and direction of the energy from the player's arm and cue stick to the pool ball being targeted during a play. With amateurs such as myself, the cue ball endures intensified abuse because it takes me a very long time to pocket all my balls. If I am playing unusually well, the cue ball doesn't end up jumping the bumpers and landing on the floor or flying across the room!

Chapter 3: A Theological Basis for Boundaries

[1]I use the term "adequate" as acknowledgment that individuation is a process and level of individuation lays on a spectrum from complete symbiosis to ideal individuation. Therefore, while people may not individuate to the ideal, adequate or good-enough individuation enables people to experience themselves and life as satisfying and healthy.

[2]Scripture references are offered as a sample of what God has revealed about Godself to us in the Bible. They are not intended to be "proof-texts," the decisive arguments for my theses. In keeping with the premise that we need to examine a concept and synthesize it into the aggregate of our experiences, a seeker of Truth will always consider one idea within the context of which it was originally proffered and within the context of the "whole counsel of God" (Acts 20:27).

[3]To the woman he said, "I will greatly increase your pains in childbearing; / with pain you will give birth to children. / Your desire will be for your husband, / and he will rule over you." To Adam he said, "Because you listened to your wife and ate from the tree about which I commanded you, 'You must not eat of it,' "Cursed is the ground because of you; / through painful toil you will eat of it all the days of your life. / It will produce thorns and thistles for you, / and you will eat the plants of the field. / By the sweat of your brow / you will eat your food / until you return to the ground, / since from it you were taken; / for dust you are / and to dust you will return" (Gen. 3:16–19).

[4]See also Ezekiel 11:18–20: "They will return to it and remove all its vile images and detestable idols. I will give them an undivided heart and put a new spirit in them; I will remove from them their heart of stone and give them a heart of flesh. Then they will follow my decrees and be careful to keep my laws. They will be my people, and I will be their God."

[5]Justice is the application of merited consequences for boundary violations. Mercy is the withholding of those merited consequences. Merited consequences cannot be withheld if they are not first to be applied; therefore, if there is no justice, then there is no mercy. Conversely, justice without mercy extinguishes relationship, because consequences for boundary violations alienate the offender, rather than invite reconciliation and fellowship.

[6]See Henry Blackaby, Richard Blackaby, and Claude King, *Experiencing God: Knowing and Doing the Will of God* (Nashville, Tenn.: B&H Publishing, 2008). This book develops the concept that we are most fruitful in our endeavors when we identify where God is working and join with God there. Acknowledging God's sovereignty requires humility and will prevent us from overstepping our bounds in intervening in situations for which we are not responsible.

[7]The term "unconditional positive regard" was coined by humanist and psychologist Carl Rogers, who advanced the therapeutic modality of Person-Centered Counseling, also known as Rogerian psychotherapy. He promoted the idea that every individual has internally the resources to resolve his or her own problems and develop his or her full potential. Carl Rogers, *On Becoming a Person: A Therapist's View of Psychotherapy* (New York: Houghton Mifflin, 1961, 1989).

Chapter 4: Boundaries in the Body of Christ

[1]*Brokenness* as used here refers to the state of God's creation as a result of the fall (Adam's and Eve's original sin or boundary violation), and is sometimes referred to as "sin nature," "original sin," or "fallen nature." I have opted to use the word *brokenness* to connote a state, not an action or choice. The term is also intended to evoke a sense of compassion in the reader, since the brokenness of creation is truly a sad and dire state of affairs, and would lead to fatal and endless despair except for the redeeming work of Christ. See Romans 8:19–25. Theologically speaking, a fourth cause may also be considered; that is, "that the work of God might be displayed in his life" (Jn. 9:3). Jesus' disciples came across a blind man and asked Jesus, "Rabbi, who sinned, this man or his parents, that he was born blind?" (Jn. 9:2). Jesus replied that neither the man nor his parents had sinned; in other words, no one was to blame. It is human nature to think that suffering always calls for blame. This was also the case with Job (Job 8). However, while suffering is used by God to accomplish his plans, it is nonetheless the result of a fallen creation, not part of the original order of creation, and therefore a secondary cause to the brokenness of creation itself.

[2]Compare James 4:17: "Anyone, then, who knows the good he ought to do and doesn't do it, sins." So God has provided both positive and negative boundaries: do this, don't do that. Commands "to do" are equally salient in God's creation design.

[3]See Cornelius Plantinga Jr., *Not the Way It's Supposed to Be: A Breviary of Sin* (Grand Rapids, Mich.: Eerdmans Publishing Co., 1995).

[4]The following books may be of interest: C. S. Lewis, *The Problem of Pain* (New York: Harper Collins, 1996). C. S. Lewis, *A Grief Observed* (New York: Harper Collins, 1996). Henri Nouwen, *The Wounded Healer: Ministry in Contemporary Society* (Garden City, N.J.: Image, 1979). Dan Nolta, *Compassion–The Painful Privilege* (Newberg, Oreg.: Barclay Press, 2006). Peter Kreeft, *Making Sense Out of Suffering* (Ann Arbor, Mich.: Servant Books, 1986). Ajith Fernando, *The Call to Joy and Pain: Embracing Suffering in Your Ministry* (Wheaton, Ill.: Crossway Books, 2007).

[5]I am distinguishing here between maturation and sanctification: maturation is the psychological process of becoming a complete and autonomous individual, and sanctification is the spiritual process of adopting more and more the mind of Christ. There is obviously overlap in these two processes, and it might even be argued that they are the same since adopting the mind of Christ and assimilating God's plan for our lives (sanctification) would include developing a wholesome, healthy, and well-balanced sense of self (maturation) and *vice versa.*

[6]Think of a classroom of thirty eighth graders. The more disruptive, underachieving, and disrespectful one student is, the more difficult the teacher will find it to inspire the other

students to rise above this "lowest common denominator." Additionally, the energy of a social group focuses on achieving and maintaining homogeneity. Therefore it will also be difficult for a student to overcome the inertia of homeostasis and perform at his own higher level of ability.

[7]Jay Kessler, *Being Holy, Being Human* (Minneapolis, Minn.: Bethany House Publishers, 1994), 51–52.

[8]I am aware that Paul said, "To the weak I became weak, to win the weak. I have become all things to all men so that by all possible means I might save some" (1 Cor. 9:22). Here, Paul is referring to the principle of meeting people where they are at in order to minister the gospel of grace to them. This is not the same thing as doing for other people what they need to be doing for themselves, or taking over the operation of the body of Christ to the exclusion of others' participation in the life of the body.

Chapter 5: Know Yourself

[1]"Soul" is possibly yet a distinct fourth component of human existence.

[2]NASB: New American Standard Bible; NCV: New Century Version; ESV: English Standard Version.

[3]Psychologists and psychiatrists use the MMPI for diagnostics. It offers penetrating insights for those who can overcome their temerity of exposure. The MMPI must be administered and interpreted by a certified mental health practitioner.

[4]Another taxonomy, the Keirsey Temperament Sorter, is closely related to the MBTI. It was created for self-administration and is available in: David Keirsey and Marilyn Bates, *Please Understand Me: Character and Temperament Types* (Del Mar, Calif.: Prometheus Nemesis Book Company, 1984).

[5]A good summary of the common defense mechanisms can be found in chapters 5 and 6 (pages 96–144) of Nancy McWilliams, *Psychoanalytic Diagnosis: Understanding Personality Structure in the Clinical Process* (New York: Guilford Press, 1994).

[6]Classical psychoanalytic theory maintains that the term "borderline" is not a personality organization but rather a level of psychological development with respect to the integration of the reality principle (which directs the ego to defer gratification when the desire for gratification conflicts with reality). In this case, "borderline" is the term that describes those individuals whose developmental level fall between the psychotic and neurotic ranges of reality-testing. However, the *Diagnostic and Statistical Manual of Mental Disorders*, 4th edition (DSM-IV-TR), following conventional diagnostic practices, includes a classification for Borderline Personality Disorder. As such, I have opted to include Borderline Personality in this list as a discreet personality organization, because of its widespread acceptance among the general public and psychology-related professions.

[7]Kate and Dan Montgomery, Ph.D., *The Self Compass: Charting Your Personality in Christ* (Montecito, Calif.: Compass Therapy, 2007). This book provides a comprehensible and accessible theoretical framework for understanding personality from a Christian perspective. It also offers guidance for self-discovery, character growth, and spiritual development.

[8]Keirsey and Bates, *Please Understand Me*, op. cit.

Chapter 6: In Pursuit of Truth

[1]Robert S. McGee, *The Search for Significance: Seeing Your True Worth Through God's Eyes* (Nashville: Thomas Nelson, 2003). This book offers an in-depth theological and practical study on existential meaning and worth through relationship with God.

[2]The association between personal rest, worship, and God's intrinsic boundary as Creator has profound implications. Consider Leviticus 23:3, "There are six days when you may work, but the seventh day is a Sabbath of rest, a day of sacred assembly. You are not to do any work; wherever you live, it is a Sabbath to the LORD." This and other similar passages suggest that rest is *unto* the Lord–an offering as an act of worship–and to be observed *because God said so*, because the Lord created us with a need for Sabbath rest and worship.

[3]There are numerous books and resources that offer guidance on the practice of meditation within the context of Christian tradition. The following are good starting points: Thomas Merton, *Spiritual Direction & Meditation* (Collegeville, Minn.: The Order of St. Benedict, Inc., 1960); James Finley, *Christian Meditation: Experiencing the Presence of God* (New

York: Harper Collins, 2004); Mary Jo Meadow, Kevin Culligan, and Daniel Chowning, *Christian Insight Meditation* (Somerville, Mass.: Wisdom Books, 2007).

[4]Retreat should be distinguished from sabbatical. In today's society, sabbatical typically refers to a period of time devoted to a specific goal (or goals) outside the normal routine—for example, to conduct research, write a book, pursue a hobby, begin a new business venture. Sabbatical activities may include rest, relaxation and reflection, but usually within the framework of a broader goal. The ideal spiritual retreat is the pursuit of *nothing.*

[5]Harry Stack Sullivan, *The Interpersonal Theory of Psychiatry* (New York: W. W. Norton, 1997), 374. Sullivan was a pioneer in the areas of interpersonal psychology, developmental stages, social psychiatry, and the impact of dysfunctional interpersonal patterns on mental health.

[6]Codependence may be loosely defined as an addiction to controlling others' behavior in order to maintain a sense of stability, a sense of predictability, and the feedback necessary for sustaining one's self-concept. The term was originally coined to describe the behavior patterns of those in relationship with someone who is "dependent" on alcohol (or other substance), but has been since recognized as a pattern that people may exhibit in their relationships with others, regardless of the presence of chemical dependence.

[7]*Twelve Steps and Twelve Traditions* (New York, N.Y.: Alcoholics Anonymous World Services, Inc., 1981).

[8]Gary L. Harbaugh, *Pastor as Person: Maintaining Personal Integrity in the Choices and Challenges of Ministry* (Minneapolis, Minn.: Augsburg Publishing House, 1984). This is an excellent resource for examining how the person of the pastor is the primary instrument in the ministry of presence and why (w)holistic health and balance are fundamental to personal integrity.

[9]Ibid.

[10]As discussed in chapter 2, exclusive reliance on external sources of validation and affirmation result in desperate attempts to gain others' approval and prevents the development of an internal self-concept. The *balance* between external and internal sources of validation is crucial to one's health and development.

[11]Michael Todd Wilson and Brad Hoffmann, *Preventing Ministry Failure* (Downers Grove, Ill.: InterVarsity Press, 2007). In the section "Foundation Stone 1," the authors discuss in depth the importance of relationships and accountability as foundational to effective long-term ministry.

Chapter 7: The Measure of Our Character

[1]Gary L. McIntosh and Samuel D. Rima Sr., *Overcoming the Dark Side of Leadership: The Paradox of Personal Dysfunction* (Grand Rapids, Mich.: Baker Books, 1997).

[2]Another good system for self-assessment can be found in Friends in Recovery, *The Twelve Steps: A Spiritual Journey. A Working Guide for Healing Damaged Emotions,* revised edition (San Diego: RPI Publishing, Inc., 1994), 69–95.

[3]Abraham Maslow, "A Theory of Human Motivation," *Psychological Review* (50:4): 370–96.

[4]*Twelve Steps and Twelve Traditions.*

[5]This quote is attributed to St. Francis of Assisi.

Chapter 8: Straight Talk on Power

[1]There are a variety of well-written, compelling books available that deal with the unique tensions of being human and representing the Holy One. I suggest: Gary L. Harbaugh, *Pastor as Person: Maintaining Personal Integrity in the Choices and Challenges of Ministry* (Minneapolis, Minn.: Augsburg Publishing House, 1984). Gary L. McIntosh and Samuel D. Rima Sr., *Overcoming the Dark Side of Leadership: The Paradox of Personal Dysfunction* (Grand Rapids, Mich.: Baker Books, 1997). G. Lloyd Rediger, *Beyond the Scandals: A Guide to Healthy Sexuality for Clergy* (Minneapolis, Minn.: Fortress Press, 2003). Jay Kessler, *Being Holy, Being Human: Dealing with the Incredible Expectations and Pressures of Ministry* (Minneapolis, Minn.: Bethany House Publishers, 1994). This book is no longer in print, but is still one of the best books I have come across that

deals directly with the humanity and limitations of pastors and the effect of congregational expectations on pastors' health and ability to minister effectively.

[2]Paul refers to this in Hebrews 5:1, harkening back to the days of the covenant of law: "Every high priest is selected from among men and is appointed to represent them in matters related to God, to offer gifts and sacrifices for sins." Pentecost ushered in a new era that permits the common person to approach the throne of God without an earthly intermediary (Christ is our high priest), but the necessity of spiritual leadership–elders and teachers–with authority over the Church persists even in the era of grace.

[3]Psychologically speaking, the therapist must act as the guardian of the client's autonomy. In a similar fashion, the pastor is the guardian of parishioners' autonomy. Exercise of spiritual authority that disregards parishioners' right to autonomy is not just, merciful, or humble. Phyllis Greenacre, "Certain Technical Problems in the Transference Relationship," *Journal of the American Psychoanalytic Association* (7): 484–502.

[4]The similarity of spiritual leaders to shepherds is significant. Shepherds do not herd their sheep by walking ahead and expecting the sheep to follow. Shepherds walk behind the flock and move the flock by walking toward the sheep to communicate that they want the flock to move on. Using this method, the shepherd merely suggests the direction he wants the sheep to move; it is actually the sheep's choice to move.

[5]McIntosh and Rima, *Overcoming the Dark Side of Leadership*, 11–12.

[6]Jean Anton, ed., "Sexual Abuse by Religious Leaders: Looking Back 20 Years–What Has Changed? What Is Needed? An Interview with Rev. Dr. Marie M. Fortune," *Working Together: A Newsletter of FaithTrust Institute* 24:2 (Winter 2005): 1-5.

[7]Child or elder abuse *must* be reported to the appropriate legal authorities. The history of several decades has demonstrated that internally managed efforts within religious organizations to stop abuse, hold perpetrators accountable, and mitigate the damage have failed.

Chapter 9: When Boundaries Seem Blurry

[1]Created by Tom Wilson.

[2]The story of Beth also illustrates the phenomenon of attraction to ministers precisely because of their position of pastor (specifically here the embodiment of hope and the appeal of connecting with someone in a position of power).

[3]Abraham Maslow, "A Theory of Human Motivation," *Psychological Review* (50:4): 370–96.

[4]See Gary L. McIntosh and Samuel D. Rima Sr., *Overcoming the Dark Side of Leadership: The Paradox of Personal Dysfunction* (Grand Rapids, Mich.: Baker Books, 1997), chapter 4.

Chapter 10: Sexual Misconduct and the Not-So-Blurry Boundary

[1]These books share the stories of women who experienced clergy sexual abuse: Dee Ann Miller, *How Little We Knew: Collusion and Confusion With Sexual Misconduct* (Lafayette, La.: Prescott Press, 1993). Beth Van Dyke, *What About Her: A True Story of Clergy, Abuse, Survival* (Enumclaw, Wash.: Winepress Publishing, 1997).

[2]I have chosen to not present specific survey statistics here because I believe that a discussion about which statistics are most accurate will distract our attention from identifying the very real dangers and rampant problems that our churches and pastors face with regard to sexual misconduct.

[3]Mark Chaves and Diana Garland, "The Prevalence of Clergy Sexual Advances Towards Adults in Their Congregations," *Journal for the Scientific Study of Religion* (forthcoming).

[4]Texas Penal Code Title 5, Ch 22 (22.011): Defines clergy sexual assault when "the actor is a clergyman who causes the other person to submit or participate by exploiting the other person's emotional dependency on the clergyman in the clergyman's professional character as spiritual adviser."

Minnesota Criminal Code 609.344: "The actor is or purports to be a member of the clergy, the complainant is not married to the actor, and: (i) the sexual penetration occurred during the course of a meeting in which the complainant sought or received religious or spiritual advice, aid, or comfort from the actor in private; or (ii) the sexual penetration occurred during a period of time in which the complainant was meeting on an ongoing basis with the actor to seek or receive religious or spiritual advice, aid, or comfort in private. Consent by the complainant is not a defense."

[5]Candace Benyei, *Understanding Clergy Misconduct in Religious Systems: Scapegoating, Family Secrets, and the Abuse of Power.* (Binghamton, N.Y.: Haworth Press, 1998), 79.

[6]Stanley Grenz and Roy Bell, *Betrayal of Trust: Confronting and Preventing Clergy Sexual Misconduct* (Grand Rapids, MI: Baker Books, 2001). Richard Gula, *Ethics in Pastoral Ministry* (Mahwah, N.J.: The Paulist Press, 1996). Karen McClintock, *Preventing Sexual Abuse in Congregations: A Resource for Leaders.* (Herndon, Va.: The Alban Institute, 2004). Beth Ann Gaede, ed., *When a Congregation is Betrayed: Responding to Clergy Misconduct* (Herndon, Va.: The Alban Institute, 2006).

[7]For the majority of this chapter I will refer to the clergy person as "he" and the victim of clergy sexual misconduct as "she." I am well aware that female clergy are just as capable as male clergy of engaging in sexual misconduct. Furthermore, I am also sadly aware of the abuse of power by pastors who engage in homosexually oriented misconduct. Still, while acknowledging that CSM affects both genders and encompasses both heterosexually and homosexually oriented behavior, I will employ the pronoun of "he" in reference to the pastor and "she" in reference to the victim of CSM.

[8]Diana Garland and Christen Argueta, "How Clergy Sexual Misconduct Happens: A Qualitative Study of First-Hand Accounts," *Social Work & Christianity* (forthcoming).

[9]I use the term "agency" to describe an individual's power to effect change in his life. Loss of agency results in learned helplessness. Victims of abuse lose their sense of agency and do not believe they can do anything to change their situation. This loss of agency is most poignant with victims of childhood abuse, because, at the time of their abuse, they truly had no ability to change what was happening to them. The loss of agency is carried into adulthood, even after the individual gains more autonomy and power over himself. Adults who feel that their current situation or their future is in the hands of others also experience a loss of agency.

[10]These two books provide extensive information on the prevention of sexual misconduct: Nils Friberg and Mark Laaser, *Before the Fall: Preventing Pastoral Sexual Abuse* (Collegeville, Minn.: The Liturgical Press, 1998). G. Lloyd Rediger, *Beyond the Scandals: A Guide to Healthy Sexuality for Clergy* (Minneapolis, Minn.: Fortress Press, 2003.)

[11]The expectations may not be realistic, but they are real.

[12]A relatively new service for monitoring Internet use is called Covenant Eyes®. It is comprised of software that is installed on any computer and logs almost all Internet access from that computer, whether desktop or laptop. The software then submits the logs to the Covenant Eyes Web server, which rates the sites for degree of objectionable and "mature" content and sends reports to a designated accountability person. The service includes reporting on attempts to modify or tamper with the installed software, which will discourage particularly computer-savvy staff from disabling the software. Information on this service can be found at *www.covenanteyes.com.*

Chapter 11: Real-Life Boundaries in Real-Life Ministry

[1]See Edwin Friedman, *Generation to Generation: Family Process in Church and Synagogue* (New York: Guilford Press, 1985). This is a classic and excellent discourse on family dynamics both within the family units that comprise the congregation and the larger church family system.

[2]Heinz Kohut, *The Analysis of the Self* (New York, NY: International University Press, 1971).

[3]Chapter 2 offers a primer on the development of the self, boundaries, and individuation from a psychological perspective. Understanding the concepts presented in this chapter is not only important for the pastor's personal edification, but also for understanding parishioners, their reactions to life stressors, their relational style within the church family, and their degree of spiritual and psychological development.

[4]David Benner, *Strategic Pastoral Counseling: A Short-Term Structured Model* (Grand Rapids, Mich: Baker Book House, 2003). Donald Capps, *Giving Counsel: A Minister's Guidebook*

(St. Louis, Mo.: Chalice Press, 2001). Howard Clinebell, *Basic Types of Pastoral Counseling: Resources for the Ministry of Healing and Growth* (Nashville: Abingdon Press, 1984). Richard Parsons, Robert Wicks, and Donald Capps, eds., *Clinical Handbook of Pastoral Counseling, Vol. 1*, expanded edition (Mahwah, N.J.: Paulist Press, 1993). Richard Parsons and Robert Wicks, eds., *Clinical Handbook of Pastoral Counseling, Vol 2* (Mahwah, N.J.: Paulist Press, 1993). Robert Wicks, Richard Parsons, and Donald Capps, eds., *Clinical Handbook of Pastoral Counseling, Vol. 3* (Mahwah, N.J.: Paulist Press, 2003). This volume combines some of the most salient information from the previous two volumes. Howard Stone, ed., *Strategies for Brief Pastoral Counseling* (Minneapolis, Minn.: Augsburg Press, 2001). David Steere, *Spiritual Presence in Psychotherapy: A Guide for Caregivers* (New York: Brunner/Mazel, 1997).

[5]Psychological treatment focuses on the cognitive and behavioral aspects of human behavior. Psychiatric treatment focuses on the organic, biological aspects of mental health disorders. Some providers of psychiatric care also provide psychotherapy; however, the number of care providers who will address both facets of mental health care has dropped dramatically over recent decades because of the reimbursement and managed care policies of insurance companies.

[6]Credentialing generally entails completion of an advanced degree in a mental health field from an accredited school, completion of a period of formal supervision, and licensing by the state in which a person practices. Laws regulating the licensing of mental health practitioners vary, but common titles are "Licensed Professional Counselor," "Licensed Clinical Social Worker," "Licensed Psychologist," "Licensed Marriage and Family Therapist," "Licensed Mental Health Practitioner," "Certified Addictions Counselor," and so on.

[7]David Steere, ed., *The Supervision of Pastoral Care* (Louisville, Ky.: Westminster/John Knox Press, 1989). This book addresses the supervision of pastoral care from the standpoint of the supervisor. However, the information is invaluable and can be applied in both dynamics of receiving and giving supervision.

[8]It is wise to educate yourself on your state's mandated reporter laws, before you need to know. In the thick of a crisis, you need to know your responsibilities.

Chapter 12: Beginnings and Conclusions

[1]Beth Ann Gaede, ed., *When a Congregation is Betrayed: Responding to Clergy Misconduct* (Herndon, Va.: Vs.: The Alban Institute, 2006). Candace Benyei, *Understanding Clergy Misconduct in Religious Systems: Scapegoating, Family Secrets, and the Abuse of Power* (Binghamton, N.Y.: Haworth Press, 1998). Anson Shupe, William A. Stacy, and Susan E. Darnell, eds., *Bad Pastors: Clergy Misconduct in Modern America* (New York: New York University Press, 2000). Karen A. McClintock, *Preventing Sexual Abuse in Congregations: A Resource for Leaders* (Herndon, Va.: The Alban Institute, 2004). This book is geared primarily toward preventing abuse, but includes information on responding to allegations as well.